TUỆ SỸ, LÊ MẠNH THÁT & THÍCH PHƯỚC AN

Compiled and Produced
ĐẠO SINH – NGUYÊN GIÁC
& TÂM THƯỜNG ĐỊNH

ENLIGHTENED EMPEROR
TRẦN NHÂN TÔNG

GIÁC HOÀNG TRẦN NHÂN TÔNG
(1258 - 1308)
SƠ TỔ THIỀN TRÚC LÂM

LOTUS MEDIA
2020

ENLIGHTENED EMPEROR TRẦN NHÂN TÔNG
GIÁC HOÀNG TRẦN NHÂN TÔNG (1258 - 1308)
SƠ TỔ THIỀN TRÚC LÂM

Copyright © 2020 Lotus Media Inc.
xuất bản lần thứ nhất tại Hoa Kỳ.
Bìa và trình bày: Quảng Pháp và Thiên Nhạn
All rights reserved.
ISBN: 978-1-67813-863-9

TABLE OF CONTENTS / MỤC LỤC

DEDICATION

This book was an effort to honor the Enlightened Emperor (Trần Nhân Tông, who was also a famed and prestigious Zen Master and the founder of Trúc Lâm Lineage) on his 760th birthday and 710th years of his passing, as of 2019.

To all Vietnamese that see him as the national hero – a representation of our Vietnamese and Buddhist heritage.

ACKNOWLEDGMENTS

We would like to acknowledge all the authors that gave us the elements and permissions to compile and edit these works. This is a collective effort from many individuals. So, we are trying to live the Enlightened emperor and Zen Master's teachings as a way to continue him, like:

SPRING

Amidst graceful willow and fragrant blossom,
Birds sound their song.
The shadows of floating clouds
Cross my veranda.
When a visitor arrives
I don't ask about the world's affairs.
We lean against the railing only
and view the garden green.

TO LIVE IN THIS WORLD
In this world of dust
Is enjoyment of the Way attained
by following the natural path
To eat when hungry, to sleep when weary

When at home are such treasures readily available
there is no need to hunt afar for them
Treating all and everything
with a free heart
Is the essence of Zen.
(These two poems were translated by Võ Đình)

May all be safe
May all be well
May all be at ease
May all be happy.

From the publishers.

EMPEROR TRẦN NHÂN TÔNG
THE FIRST PATRIARCH
OF TRÚC LÂM YÊN TỬ (1258-1308)[*]

Born on November 11th of 1258, his real name was Kham. He was the oldest child of King Tran Thanh Tong and Queen Nguyen Thanh. Despite living in luxury, at a young age, his mind was already interested in Zen. At the age of 16, he was promoted as crowned prince. He had tried to reject it many times by promoting his brother, but his father would never accept it. He married the oldest daughter of Queen Nguyen Tu, who later became Queen Kham Tu. Living in happiness at the time, he still preferred to become a monk.

One time at midnight, he left the palace to the Yen Tu mountain. At sunrise, he arrived at the Thap temple at the Dong Cuu mountain. Being too exhausted, he rested in the temple. Noticing his unique characteristics, the abbot offered him good treats. When the King's father got the news, he urged his men to go on a search.

---

[*] Source - http://www.truclamvietzen.net/ZenFounders.htm

The King was found later on. With no other choice, he had to return to the palace.

At the age of 21 (1279), he became king. Even though he had the upmost power, he still maintained purification for his Zen practice. Each day, he practiced at Tu Phuoc temple, which was located within the city. One day, while taking a lunch nap, he saw that from his navel grew a big lotus flower with a golden Buddha's statue on the top. A man standing by pointed his hand to him and said, "Do you know this Buddha? He's the Vairocana Buddha (The Great Sun Buddha)." After waking up, the King told his father the dream. King Tran Thanh Tong was exalted by this strange incident.

King Tran Nhan Tong preferred vegetarian foods, therefore, his body was slim. His father noticed his health condition so he asked for the reason. King Nhan Tong confessed his desire for renunciation. King Thanh Tong in tears mourned, "I'm already old. I always count on you. How could you do it? How will you continue the duty of our ancestors by doing that?" King Nhan Tong listened in tears.

King Nhan Tong was quite intelligent and aggressive in learning. He had read many books and understood thoroughly all Buddhist scriptures and other public writings. In his spare time, he liked to discuss Zen with Zen Masters or practitioners, especially, High official Tue Trung. The king's discernment was at the upmost level. He respected High official Tue Trung as his teacher. When the Mongolians invaded the country, he had to put aside his religious interests to concentrate on the national defense. Because our army was united, we were able to defeat the Mongolians twice in 1285 and 1288. In his era, there were two significant conferences: 1) of all high-rank generals and officials at Binh Than; and 2) of all senior citizens at Dien Hong to discuss strategies for the national defense.

In 1293, Tran Anh Tong became king. For the following six years, he was beside his son to support him in his new role. In October of 1299, he was ordained as a monastic monk and stayed at the Yen Tu mountain. For the years that he resided in this place, he focused on ascetic virtues. Thus, his title was "Huong Van Dai Dau Da" (The Great Ascetic monk). Later, he established temples, meditation centers, and performed teachings to other monks and the public. Many of them attended his lecturings. Next, he established a lecture hall at the Pho Minh temple and performed a lecture there. Several years later, he traveled to the Bo Chanh camp. This is where the Tri Kien pagoda was built. The First Patriarch decided to stay there until 1304, he traveled around to abolish places with inappropriate worshipping and to teach them the practice of the ten precepts. In the winter of that year, King Tran Anh Tong requested him to perform a ritual for his ordainment of Bodhisattva precepts at the palace.

Later, leaning on his wand, he walked to the Sung Nghiem temple at the Linh Son mountain to propagate Zen sect. On January 1st, he assigned Master Phap Loa to the Bao An temple at Sieu Thoai province to perform a ceremony. Three months later, he came to the Vinh Nghiem temple at Luong Giang and assigned Master Phap Loa to perform a ceremony. This time, the First Patriarch exposed "Truyen Dang Luc" and requested National Advisor Dao Nhat to expose a Lotus sutra to the mass. At the end of the retreat season, he returned to Yen Tu mountain and dismissed all laymen and helpers in the temple. He only kept 12 novices, who often followed him to places. One time, on Master Phap Loa's request, he went to Tu Tieu pagoda to expound "Truyen Dang Luc." At the end, all novices were asked to leave, except Master Phap Loa. The First Patriarch then climbed on various places around hut to search for caves. Master Phap Loa curiously asked, "Master, at your old age, you're still active. If anything happens to you, who could we count on in propagating Buddhist Dharma?" The First Patriarch replied, "Time has come for me, therefore, I want to make a long-term plan."

On October 5th of that year, a servant of Thien Doan princess arrived. He notified, "Thien Doan princess is critically ill. She would like to see you once again before she passes away." The First Patriarch sadly replied, "Time has come." He left with only one novice to see the princess. Five days later, he arrived at the palace. After the event, he departed to the Sieu Thoai temple on the 15th of the month. The next morning after his arrival at the temple, he walked to a temple at the Co Chau village and wrote this verse:

People's life is on a breath
Their greed is endless
Devil fortress is like a dungeon,
While the Buddha realm is full of joy

On the 17th of that month, he stayed at the Sung Nghiem temple at Linh Son mountain. Queen Tuyen Tu invited him to a luncheon at Binh Duong pagoda. He delightedly said, " This is the last offering." Next day, he walked to the Tu Lam temple at Ky Anh Sanh mountain. Suddenly, he experienced a headache so he immediately called two bhikkhus and asked, "I would like to go up to Ngoa Van mountain, but don't have energy to do it. What can I do?" They answered, "We could help you, Master." When they reached to Ngoa Van, he dismissed the two bhikkhus, "Return to the temple and practice. Remember not to underestimate life and death."

On the 19th day, he asked novice Phap Khong to get to Tu Tieu pagoda at Yen Tu and asked novice Bao Sat to see him. On the next day, Bao Sat departed. When he passed Doanh Tuyen lake, he saw a dark cloud flew from Ngoa Van mountain to Loi Son, then dropped down to Doanh Tuyen. This caused a high water rising. In a moment, it went back to normal level. Next, he saw 2 dragons with sharp eyes popped the heads out of water for a moment, then, they submerged into the water. That night, Bao sat rested in an inn at the foot of the mountain. He had a bad dream.

On the 21st day, he arrived at Ngoa Van pagoda. Seeing him, the First Patriarch smiled, "I'm about to go. Why are you late? If you have anything unclear on Buddhist Dharma, you should ask me now."

Bao sat asked:

- When Ma Tsu was ill, the rector asked, "How were you for the past several days?" Ma Tsu replied, "The sun is the Buddha, so as the moon." What does it mean?

The First Patriarch raised his voice:

- What are the five Chinese emperors and three ancient kings

Bao Sat asked:

- What does it mean by "Flowers blossom as many as silk. Bamboos in the south are as many as those in the north?"

The First Patriarch replied:

- They blind your eyes.

Bao Sat remained silent.

Days later, the sky was dull. Birds circled above with tragic cry.

On the night of November 1st, the sky was clear with sparkling stars. The First Patriarch asked, "What time is it?" Bao Sat replied, "It is midnight, Master." He lifted the curtain to look at the sky, then said, "It's time for me to go." Bao Sat asked, "Where are you going?" He replied:

Nothing was created
Nothing was terminated
If that is understood
The Buddha will always in presence
Where should there be the coming and returning?

Bao Sat asked, "What does it mean by no birth and no termination?"

The First Patriarch slapped Bao Sat in the face and scolded:

- Stop speaking nonsense!

Then, in the posture of lion, he passed away. This was the year of 1308, when he was 51 years old.

Based on the First Patriarch's will, Master Phap Loa cremated his body and reserved his remains in an ash pot. Later, King Anh Tong and his officials brought his remains back to Duc Lang for worshipping. The king also built a pagoda next to the Van Yen temple in Yen Tu mountain. He named it "Hue Quang Kim Thap" (Hue Quang pagoda). Meanwhile, he honored the First Patriarch with the title "Dai Thanh Tran Trieu Truc Lam Dau Da Tinh Tue Giac Hoang Dieu Ngu To Phat."

The First Patriarch's writings are:

Thien Lam Thiet Chuy Ngu Luc
Dai Huong Hai An Thi Tap
Tang Gia Toai Su
Thach That Mi Ngu (revised by Master Phap Loa)

EMPEROR TRẦN NHÂN TÔNG AND THE TRÚC LÂM SCHOOL

BY PROF. **LÊ MẠNH THÁT**

According to various historical materials of Vietnam, the Emperor Nhân Tông is recognized to be the founder of the Trúc Lâm Dhyāna School, which flourished for a long time in the history of Vietnamese Buddhism. In spite of this, it has been generally assumed, at least since the latter half of the 18th century when Tính Quảng and Hải Lượng could collect enough materials for their compilation of the *True Record of the Three Patriarchs*, that this school could survive only three generations and, more particularly, that subsequent to the first three patriarchs of these generations no one could be regarded as their outstanding Dharma-successor. As a consequence, it has again and again been claimed by some historical researchers in Vietnam that a glorious period of Buddhism, which naturally includes the Trúc Lâm school, came to an end altogether at the passing away of the last of these patriarchs. In reality, after the Third Patriarch Huyền

Quang's death in 1334, Buddhism went on to develop well with many prominent figures in this Dhyāna lineage as will be discussed below. Accordingly, the question as to the Emperor Nhân Tông's relation with the Trúc Lâm school would not need dealing with in the present study. On account of some misunderstandings as just mentioned, however, a rather brief elucidation of it should be presented here.

In one of the preceding chapters we have discussed some problems of Nhân Tông's thought, particularly of what he has formulated in the "Worldly Life with Joy in the Way":

Achieved in the midst of worldly life,
That merit is increasingly admired.
Unfruitful cultivation in the mountains
Is nothing but a vain attempt.

And we have, too, considered it to be the central thought of the Trúc Lâm Dhyāna doctrine. In this connection, is it truly satisfactory to maintain that the Trúc Lâm school should be attributed to some Dhyāna Masters alone, especially the monastic ones, as has been claimed in most of the studies on the history of Vietnamese Buddhism hitherto? In effect, a history of this school was once compiled without any differentiation of its being either monastic or lay lineage, as what Ngô Thời Nhiệm advanced in an introduction to his *Trúc Lâm Tông Chỉ Nguyên Thanh* (*Fundamental Principles of Trúc Lâm Doctrine*). Unfortunately, the approach he applied in his works has not been popularly adopted, let alone the fact that it is sometimes regarded as not reflecting properly Buddhist tradition in Vietnam or even as nothing other than some distortion.

In spite of this, Thời Nhiệm's position in his study on this school should not be considered quite groundless, especially when we have evidently seen that the period in which the Emperor was leading a monastic life was not devoid of various political and military activities. That is to say, as being a Dhyāna Master, he was enthusiastically engaged in receiving a Chinese delegation, boosting the relationship between Vietnam and Champa and the extension of the country's territory in the south, and directly commanding the campaign of putting down the Laotian Army's havoc in the northwestern borderland. His monastic life, therefore, can by no means be regarded as a secluded renunciation from the world as has been generally viewed and described. On the contrary, it is a life fraught with earthly affairs intimately related to the country as well as the people. Accordingly, it is not quite unreasonable and groundless for any presentation of the "activities of the Three Patriarchs" in the direction Ngô Thời Nhiệm has set forth.

Thus it may be said that this is a precise approach even though it has not been popularly admitted and developed owing to some distorted views on the part of the Buddhist clergy as well as of the circle of historical researchers. They have usually maintained that to become a Buddhist monk is to renounce the world altogether so as to concentrate all efforts, physical and mental, on the practice of Buddhist teachings. If it were the case, how could it occur that Princess Huyền Trân was married to the Cham king and the two districts Ô and Lý were annexed to the map of Đại Việt, and that Nhân Tông could dissuade the Emperor Anh Tông from appointing so many officials and bestowing so many titles in the latter's court? Indeed, at a glimpse of Nhân Tông's life as a Dhyāna

Master, we can see straightly that he never desisted from national affairs or gave up his concern with the activities of imperial court under the leadership of the Emperor Anh Tông.

However, since those days it has been insisted in the Buddhist clergy that after he had been formally ordained a Buddhist monk, Nhân Tông "gave up the throne to enter the monastery where, as a result of his earnest devotion to the Way of Dhyāna, he could eventually penetrate into its essentials," as is remarked by Diệu Trạm in a preface to the re-edition of the *True Record of the Three Patriarchs* in Thành Thái the Ninth (1897). This remark has later been cited repeatedly in history books, according to which the Emperor is assumed to have mustered up all his efforts for the Way. Some say, "Shortly after his victory over the enemy, Nhân Tông handed over the throne to Anh Tông to seek a serene life in the practice [of Buddhism] and became the First Patriarch of the Trúc Lâm school. He breathed his last at the Ngọa Vân Temple on the quiet Yên Tử mountain when he was just fifty-one years old." Not only do they think that Nhân Tông could have renounced the world to seek a serene life, but they also say: "He wanted to get rid of daily troubles in society in order to seek after the mysterious principle that controls human life."[1]

Such immature remarks are evidently neither satisfactory nor in accord with historical facts related to the Emperor's life as recorded in the *Complete History of Đại Việt* and the *Recorded Sayings as the Lamps of the Saints*. Furthermore, if analyzing his transmitting the

---

[1] Trần Lê Sáng, Tìm hiểu văn phú thời kỳ Trần-Hồ in Tuyển Tập 40 năm tạp chí Văn Học, 1960-1999, Tập 2, Tp. Hồ Chí Minh: Nxb. Tp. Hồ Chí Minh, 1999, pp.231-232. [LMT]

patriarchal office to Pháp Loa in terms of what is recorded on the latter's memorial tablet and later cited in the *True Record of the Three Patriarchs*, we can find a startlingly remarkable incident that has never occurred in the history of Buddhism in both China and Vietnam before. The inscription tells us in the first place:

In the fifth month Điều Ngự[2] moved to a temple on the peak of Mount Ngọa Vân. On the 15th day, having told all of his students to go out of the hall after the poṣadha service, he transmitted a mind-gātha to the Master [Pháp Loa] and handed down the robe and begging bowl to him, telling him to preserve them carefully. On the first of the first month of Mậu Thân, Hưng Long the 16th (1308), the master, following his instruction, undertook the abbot's office to succeed the Dharma-lineage in the Cam Lộ Hall of the Siêu Loại temple. In order to 'open the hall' and perform the ceremony of transmission [...], the king had the preceding patriarchs' name-tablets placed [on the altar], greatly ritual music played, and incense burned. Then, he personally led the master to the patriarchal altar for prostration. After eating gruel, he ordered ritual music to be played and the Dharma-drum to be beaten while all the people began to gather in the Dharma-hall. Anh Tông then came to the temple, too. After the positions for visitors and hosts were formally divided, King Anh Tông, as a great patron of Buddhism, took the visitor's place inside the hall while the Highest Minister and other courtiers stood in the yard. Then, Điều Ngự sat down in the Dharma-seat to deliver a sermon. After the sermon, he left the seat and helped the master into it. Keeping his hands folded, palm to palm, Điều Ngự stood in front of the master and

---

[2] Skt., damya-sārathi, a guide of those who have to be restrained.

interviewed him. The master bowed to Điều Ngự, received the Dharma-robe and put it on. Điều Ngự stood aside and then sat down on the cane bed to hear the master preaching. Thereafter, he appointed the master to be the abbot of the Siêu Loại temple on Mount Yên Tử, who would thus be [the patriarch] of the second generation of the Trúc Lâm lineage. Besides, in order to encourage the study of both Buddhist and non-Buddhist literature, he transferred [to the master] 100 cases of non-Buddhist books and 20 cases of the Chinese Buddhist Canon.

From what is narrated in the inscription above, we may be aware of the following noteworthy points. First, in the fifth month of Hưng Long the 15th (1307) Pháp Loa was called to the Ngọa Vân temple on Mount Kỳ Đặc to receive the robe and begging bowl as well as a gātha. The gātha is lost today so we cannot know what it conveys. However, seven months later, that is, on the first day of the New Year Mậu Thân, Hưng Long the 16th (1308), Nhân Tông had his transmission of robe-and-bowl formalized in the Cam Lộ Hall of the Siêu Loại temple in present-day Bắc Ninh Province in the presence of the Emperor Anh Tông and the Highest Minister Trần Quốc Trấn. Secondly, after the ceremony of transmission and the discourse of Pháp Loa, Nhân Tông handed down to him 20 cases of Buddhist texts in addition to 100 cases of non-Buddhist books and exhorted him to "encourage the study of both Buddhist and non-Buddhist literature."

Based upon the act of handing down "non-Buddhist books" alone, it may be unequivocally stated that this represents an ideal Buddhist personality that Nhân Tông implies in the "Worldly Life with Joy in the Way":

Keeping mind-precepts pure, making form-precepts perfect,
That is an Adorning Bodhisattva, internally and externally.
Righteously serving one's lord, respectfully obeying one's father,
That is a Great Man of loyalty and filial piety.

In this connection it is evident that the personality of a Bodhisattva and that of a Great Man must be combined with each other to produce a Buddhist personality according to the tradition of the Trúc Lâm school. Thus, to study Buddhism does not exclude non-Buddhist knowledge of all kinds; and non-Buddhist subjects in turn embrace the studies of Buddhism. Naturally, such a concept of education has existed in the history of Vietnamese Buddhism since the old days, in the time of Mâu Tử (160-220?) and Khương Tăng Hội (?-280) at least. And even after the Emperor Nhân Tông's time, it was continuously and mightily maintained by such outstanding figures as Master Hương Chân Pháp Tính (1470-1550?), Master Minh Châu Hương Hải (1628-1715) and, particularly, Master Hải Lượng Ngô Thời Nhiệm (1746-1803), and so forth. The ideal Buddhist in the view of the Trúc Lâm school is thus quite different from that of the Ch'an school of China.

Generally considered, before being handed down the robe and begging bowl, Pháp Loa went through an interview, which is apparently likened to that of any Ch'an monks in Chinese monasteries, as recorded in the inscription on his memorial tablet and cited later in the *True Record of the Three Patriarchs*:

One day, when the master returned from the place of Tín Giác for an interview, Điều Ngự, who then was preaching [on Dhyāna], set forth the stanza "Thái Dương Ô Kê".[3] [Upon hearing it,] the Master seemed to be partly awakened. Being aware of this, Điều Ngự told him to stay with him. One night, having presented to Điều Ngự a stanza of his own, which was then crossed out on the spot with only a stroke by Điều Ngự, the Master entreated his instructions four times. After being told that he had to undertake [the quest for the truth] by himself, he retired to his room, extremely puzzled. At midnight, seeing by chance the dropping wick after burning, he got instantaneously awakened. Afterwards, he presented the view of what he was awakened at to Điều Ngự and the latter showed greatly pleased. Since then, the Master vowed to cultivate the Twelve Ascetic Practices.

The process of seeking after enlightenment carried out by the Trúc Lâm school thus appears in some aspects to be equivalent to that of a Ch'an monk in China and even of a Dhyāna monk in Vietnam prior to Nhân Tông's time. Furthermore, from his discourses at the Sùng Nghiêm temple in Hưng Long the Seventh (1299) cited in the *Recorded Sayings as the Lamps of the Saints*, and in the Kỳ Lân Hall of the same temple written down in the *True Record of the Three Patriarchs*, it may be assumed that some features of the manner of preaching on Dhyāna in Nhân Tông's time are seemingly identical with those in the monasteries of China and of Vietnam in the earlier times, which has been generally discussed above in the *Cheng-te chuan-teng-lu* (*Record of the Transmission of the Lamp in the Cheng-te Period*) or in the *Thiền Uyển Tập Anh* (*Collected Prominent Figures of Dhyāna Garden*).

However, from the ceremony of transmission held on the 1st of

---

[3] Skt., damya-sārathi, a guide of those who have to be restrained.

the 1st month of Mậu Thân (1308), we discover quite a different manner of transmitting Buddhism. The fact that Nhân Tông handed down to Pháp Loa 100 cases of non-Buddhist works as well as 20 cases of Buddhist texts copied in blood, accompanied with his exhortation for the latter "to encourage the study of both Buddhist and non-Buddhist literature" does not only reflect the educational standpoint of the Emperor and Buddhism in Vietnam. It further demonstrates the view that "the Buddha's teachings should be handed down to the world by means of Confucianist intellectuals," which was maintained by the Emperor Trần Thái Tông in a preface to his *Thiền Tông Chỉ Nam* (*A Manual of Dhyāna Teaching*). And this view was undoubtedly set forth by the Emperor Lý Thánh Tông when he gave orders for the foundation of both the Thảo Đường Dhyāna school and the first university of Đại Việt, which was represented through the building of Văn Miếu (the Temple of [Confucianist] Literature) in 1070 and then of Quốc Tử Giám (the Imperial Academy of Learning).

Such a type of ideal Buddhists must have possessed a good all-round education in which no knowledge would be viewed as absolutely foreign to Buddhist teachings. Indeed, it is quite absurd to claim that to study Confucian doctrine is to refute Buddhism or even to place oneself in opposition to Buddhism as has been groundlessly assumed hitherto. Confucianism has never had a predominant position in the Vietnamese history, much less an exclusively top position. It may be said that each Confucianist intellectual was a Buddhist aspirant even though strict criticisms, which mostly originated from those who had gone through Confucianist examinations, were at times made as to a certain form of Buddhism for several different reasons. And this incident has its own reason; that is to say, Confucianism has existed in Vietnam within the pattern of Buddhism.

When the Emperor Thái Tông stated that "the Buddha's teaching should be handed down to the world by means of Confucianist intellectuals," his statement, which did not proceed by chance from a certain monk or intellectual but from an emperor, a national leader, would undoubtedly be taken as the guiding principle of the cultural and educational policy of his government. Consequently, the imperial court's policy on Confucianism in the Trần dynasty would be to make use of Confucianism as a device for the sake of Buddhism. It is only with such a precise and comprehensive vision that one can recognize that the period under the Early Lê dynasty can by no means be regarded as of "the exclusive predominance of Confucianism." Why were there the *đình* examinations held with such a number of questions related to Buddhism, especially to the doctrine of Trúc Lâm school, as those of the 1502 examination in which the highest graduate was Lê Ích Mộc (1459-?)? Fortunately, it is thanks to the preservation of examination topics in question that we can today know something of education and examination under the Early Lê dynasty and thus reject some false ideas of the so-called "exclusive predominance of Confucianism".

The educational tradition of Vietnam has since then been that of general education. That is to say, studying Confucianism is to serve the benefits outside Confucianism, or rather, those of the people and Buddhism. This is the point usually neglected in some writings on the history of education and examination of Vietnam so far. Maybe their authors have forgotten that the establishment of the Temple of Literature in 1069-1070 was actually carried out by order of a Buddhist Emperor who was simultaneously the founder of the Thảo Đường Dhyāna school, too. This fact alone is able to show how the Emperor Lý Thánh Tông dealt with Confucianism in his time. Accordingly, despite that not any document has been preserved as to the Emperor Lý Thánh Tông's policy just mentioned, we are certainly convinced that in so doing he must have initiated what was later proclaimed by the Emperor Trần Thái Tông that "the Buddha's teaching should be handed down to the world by means of Confucianist intellectuals."

In this connection it is not surprising at all when the inscription cited above reads that "Nhân Tông handed down a large number of books, Buddhist and non-Buddhist, to Pháp Loa and exhorted him to encourage the study of both traditions." This, however, does not mean that the former would be somehow inclined to the growth of the Trúc Lâm school alone. As has been said before, he did insist that "mind-precepts" and "form-precepts" were of an "Adorning Bodhisattva". "Mind-precepts" or "nature-precepts" is a short form of the phrase "the precepts of Bodhi-mind," or rather, "the precepts of Bodhisattva," which are of a characteristic type applied to both monastic and lay Buddhist practitioners.

The stress on mind-precepts, therefore, represents the Emperor's view of non-differentiation between monastic and lay practice. Indeed, had he maintained that to live a monastic life would be to renounce the world, he might not have handed down to Pháp Loa so many books of non-Buddhist history and literature. For, what is the use of handing down books of secular history and literature if one is never concerned with worldly life where everyone is always making their greatest efforts to seek some position under the sun?

And it then would be too strange for us to understand why Pháp Loa, as being a monk, did receive them. Yet it should be kept in mind that by the time Pháp Loa received the robe and begging bowl to succeed the Trúc Lâm lineage, he was still very young, just at the age of 24.

In his young age Pháp Loa may have received a rather basic education but not acquired all the sciences of his time. Though there was then no such an "outbreak" of information as in our modern age, various branches of learning were certainly well developed and hence a rather rich amount of knowledge. As a result of the popular technique of printing in woodblocks in China and in our country several years earlier, for instance, a series of publications was publicly produced. For that reason it is quite natural for us to think that Nhân Tông's decision to transmit what has been mentioned above to Pháp Loa would be aimed at demonstrating his own ambition; that is to say, he expected Pháp Loa to have enough Buddhist and non-Buddhist knowledge to fulfill his mission as an ideal Buddhist, but not as a narrow-minded successor who would occupy himself only with nothing but *samādhi*, preaching on sūtras or some other monastic affairs.

In other words, the Emperor wished his successor not to be set off the track he had ever tread on enthusiastically and successfully. The years in which he was leading a monastic life were fraught with activities for the benefit of the country as well as Buddhism; and he hoped Pháp Loa would be able to achieve an active way of living as such. Yet, during the remaining 22 years of his life, Pháp Loa could devote his life to purely Buddhist activities only. Today, no documentary evidence is found as to his engagement in secular affairs. Is it due to his utterly one-sided activities that more than thirty years after his death the stone tablet in memory of him could be engraved and erected, i.e., in Nhâm Dần, Đại Trí the Fifth (1362)?

According to the *Recorded Sayings as the Lamps of the Saints* and the *True Record of the Three Patriarchs*, the relationship between Pháp Loa and the Emperor Anh Tông is said to have been very friendly. The *Complete History of Đại Việt*, however, says that in the last days of his life Anh Tông refused to meet Pháp Loa. Concerning the latter's death in 1330, the *Recorded Sayings as the Lamps of the Saints* tells us that when Pháp Loa was sick, the Emperor Anh Tông came and saw him; and when he died, the Emperor conferred a Dharma-title on him and wrote a funeral lament in memory of him. In addition, at the Emperor's request Huyền Quang transcribed the discourses as well as the life story of Pháp Loa for printing, to which the Emperor himself wrote the preface. This proves that Pháp Loa exercised a great influence upon Anh Tông; yet we do not know why his memorial tablet was not made until the latter's death.

Whatever happened, the Trúc Lâm school founded by the Emperor Nhân Tông eventually had its successor. Since the time when he was officially handed down the robe and begging bowl until his death in 1330, Pháp Loa concentrated all his efforts upon Buddhist affairs: instructing Buddhists, monastic and lay, to "take refuge in the Triple Gem" and "observe precepts," establishing the Quỳnh Lâm temple, the Tư Phúc temple and more than 20 other temples, and particularly conducting the task of copying and printing the Buddhist Canon. He is the author of at least nine works: *Tham Thiền Kỷ Yếu, Kim Cương Tràng Đà La Ni Kinh Khoa Chú, Niết Bàn Đại Kinh Khoa Sớ, Pháp Hoa Kinh Khoa Sớ, Lăng Già Tứ Quyển Khoa Sớ, Bát Nhã Tâm Kinh Khoa Sớ, Hưng Vương Hộ Quốc Nghi Quỹ, Pháp Sự Khoa Văn* and *Độ Môn Trợ Thành Tập*. He also occupied himself with preaching Buddhist teachings, especially the *Avatasaka-sūtra*, in many different Dharma-halls of the country.

It may be said that the last point just mentioned of Pháp Loa's activities is the most striking one with regard to the characteristics of the Trúc Lâm school. For it points out, in the first place, that this school does not maintain the transmission of Buddhism outside sūtras; nor does it consist in making use of *kung-an* or *hua-tou*. On the contrary, the study and interpretation of sūtras are centered on so as to be a pivotal factor in the process of practicing Dhyāna Buddhism. In some aspects, this is rather similar to Hui-neng's Ch'an doctrine, in which sūtra is still emphasized and interpreted in the course of Ch'an Buddhism. However, whereas Hui-neng was interested in the *Lotus Sūtra* or the *Nirvāṇa-sūtra*, it is quite different in the case of the Trúc Lâm school where its First Patriarch, the Emperor Nhân Tông, took the *Avatasaka-sūtra* to be the guiding thought. Let us read the following *gātha* of the Emperor before his death, the first four lines of which are extracted from the *Avatasaka-sūtra*:

All dharmas do not arise.
All dharmas do not pass away.
If able to understand as such,
The Buddhas are always present.
What is the use of "going" and "coming"?

Secondly, the content of the *Avatasaka* deals with the truth-seeking process of each human being, typified by the pilgrimage undertaken by young Sudhana to visit fifty-three worthies, Buddhist and secular. These visits are described to have taken place in various forms, from the most secular one of love between boys and girls to the transcendent state of perfect insight into the mutually unobstructed interpenetration of all things. Thus, it is not by chance that this sūtra became so popular by the time the Trúc Lâm school came into being in Vietnam. In reality, its popularity genuinely made possible the manifestation of the thought in the "Worldly Life with Joy in the Way" and helped develop it into a guiding thought in the activities of Vietnamese Buddhism.

It must be said that the thought of the *Avataṃsaka* spread rather popularly in the time of Master Thường Chiếu (?-1203), who maintained that Buddhism should not be separated from the world. In the *Collected Prominent Figures of Dhyāna Garden*, to answer the question "What is the meaning of 'Dharma-body is present everywhere'?" posed by a Dhyāna student, Thường Chiếu cited two passages from the Chapter "The Appearance of the Tathāgata" in the *Avatasaka* (80 volumes) translated into Chinese by Sikṣānanda.[4] It should be remembered that Thường Chiếu is the master of Thông Thiền (?-1228). And the latter, according to the*Lược Dẫn Thiền Phái Đồ* (*Chart of Dhyāna Lineage*) in the *Recorded Sayings of Thượng Sỹ*, is the founder of the Trúc Lâm lineage, which may be presented as follows:

Thông Thiền

---

[4] Lê Mạnh Thát, Nghiên cứu về Thiền Uyển Tập Anh, Nxb. Tp. Hồ Chí Minh, 1999, pp.239, 481-482. [LMT]

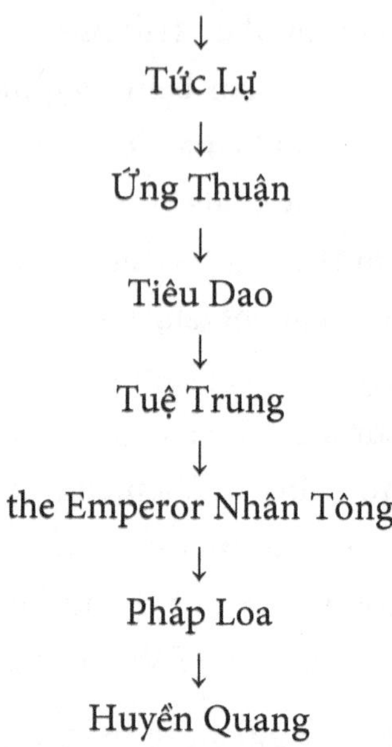

It may be said that the thought of the *Avatasaka* is of a doctrinal system, according to which a thing can exist only through its correlation with others. Otherwise stated, there may never be anything so called 'existence independent of others'. Consequently, it is natural that, under the influence of such a doctrine, Thường Chiếu could do nothing but putting all activities of his life, or rather, of Buddhism into a fixed system on the historical background of his time. It is therefore not surprising at all that Thường Chiếu set forth the view of "not being separated from the world" in his reply to the question of Thần Nghi (?-1216) "Is your way of living the same as others'?". Just in the Pháp Vân and Kiến Sơ Dhyāna lineages by the end of the Lý dynasty there appeared some lay Dhyāna masters, particularly Thông Thiền of the Kiến Sơ school. As has been cited above, according to the *Chart of Dhyāna Lineage*Thông Thiền is considered to have founded the Trúc Lâm lineage of Yên Tử. He himself was a layman. So was Ứng Thuận.

And this is obviously the result of strong impact exerted by the *Avataṃsaka*. Tuệ Trung Thượng Sỹ also referred to this sūtra in his poems. In the "Thị Chúng," for example, he dealt with the study and practice of Buddhism following Sudhana's example in the latter's encounters with his predecessors:

The world is attached to falsehood, not truth.
Yet either falsehood or truth is of worldly mind.
So as to go to the other side,
Study elaborately Sudhana's visits to his predecessors.

It is based upon the thought of the *Avatasaka* that such antithetic categories of mankind's thought as being and non-being, false and true, right and wrong, and so on, have been once for all solved. What is called being or non-being can exist only in some relation. There is truly neither absolute being nor non-being. In the light of the *Avataṃsaka*, being and non-being are merely the two sides of the same reality. They do not exclude each other. What is so called "being" may exist only in its relation with what is so called "non-being", and vice-versa. For that reason, in his preaching at the Sùng Nghiêm Temple in the 12th month of Giáp Thìn (1304) the Emperor Nhân Tông states that, because of one's ignorance of such a mutual relation between being and non-being, one can see only the finger pointing to the moon but not the moon itself, just as the one who sits under the tree to await a rabbit instead of chasing it or the one who looks for his horse on a map instead of searching its traces on the ground:

Non-being and being,
Neither is absolutely being or non-being,
Just like searching one's sword by marking on the boat;

Or searching one's horse on the map.
Being and non-being,
Neither exists apart from each other,
Just like making a hat of snow, shoes of flowers;
Or sitting under a tree to await the rabbit.
Being and non-being,
Today and in the old days alike,
If clinging to the finger so as not to see the moon,
That is to be drowned on the ground.

The *Avataṃsaka* and the thought therein thus have become not only the new source of thought for Buddhism in the times of Lý and Trần but also a popular theory for the leaders of Đại Việt in their view of their own country and society in relation with others of the time, from which they could reach their culminating point, that is, the birth of the Trúc Lâm school, in building a peaceful and prosperous Đại Việt. Today, it is generally agreed that in the history of our country there has never been any dynasty that maintains the view of "being close to the people" as the Trần dynasty, especially the Emperors Thái Tông, Thánh Tông and Nhân Tông. We can see obviously that this view truly originates from the philosophical system of the *Avataṃsaka* developed within the age-old tradition of the country. Further, it may be said that never before in the history of Vietnamese Buddhism has the *Avataṃsaka* been so fully and effectively interpreted as in the time of the Emperor Nhân Tông and later on, that is, since the Trúc Lâm school's appearance on the arena of the nation.

In 1330 Pháp Loa died. In the last moments of his life there was the presence of Huyền Quang, who was then already so old, nearly twice older than Pháp Loa. Therefore, it is obvious that the Trúc Lâm school could not be attributed to these three patriarchs alone in spite that they have been generally known as the only three patriarchs of this school, especially when Tính Quảng and Ngô Thời Nhiệm collected some fragmentary materials to compile a book on the three patriarchs of the Trúc Lâm school under the title *True Record of the Three Patriarchs*. For, besides Huyền Quang who died in 1334, i.e., only four years later than the Second Patriarch's death, there were other immediate disciples of the latter such as Cảnh Huy, Cảnh Ngung, Huệ Chúc and, most particularly, Kim Sơn.

Dhyāna Master Kim Sơn was not only considered by the Emperor Anh Tông to be the master who "possessed the 'bones and marrow' of Phổ Huệ," as in the words of the *Recorded Sayings as the Lamps of the Saints*, but further bestowed by him to be *Trúc Lâm Tam Đại Thiền Tổ* (*The Dhyāna Patriarch of the Third Generation of Trúc Lâm School*) shortly before his death in 1358. The *Recorded Sayings as the Lamps of the Saints* gives us the following account:

"When he was about to pass away, the king presented a gātha to Kim Sơn, saying: 'Whatever serious sickness I am suffering, I, your disciple, would like to send [this gātha] to Your Holiness the Dhyāna Patriarch of the Third Generation of Trúc Lâm School. I have been sick for a week, lying by night and taking medicine by day. I have not eaten a grain of rice but chewed every grain. If being asked what taste it is like, I would reply with 'no taste'. Let me present my gātha:

Taking medicine for curing illness.
Without illness, no medicine is needed.

Now is rice without grain
That is all chewed by a person without mouth.
In addition, he wrote a letter to invite Kim Sơn to the Động Tiên hall to examine him."

Accordingly, the Third Patriarch of the Trúc Lâm school was Kim Sơn and not Huyền Quang. Of the extant materials, with the exception of the *True Record of the Three Patriarchs*, none describes the latter as *The Dhyāna Patriarch of the Third Generation* but only as *Dharma-successor*, that is, succeeding the Dharma-lineage of Pháp Loa. It should be noticed that the chronicle of Pháp Loa's activities made in the *True Record of the Three Patriarchs* designates him as *Trúc Lâm Đệ Nhị Đại* (*of the Second Generation of Trúc Lâm School*). Consequently, that the Emperor Minh Tông called Master Kim Sơn *the Dhyāna Patriarch of the Third Generation of Trúc Lâm School* formally confirmed the latter to be the official successor of the Trúc Lâm school, at least until 1358 when the Emperor died. In this connection, after Huyền Quang's death in 1334 the Trúc Lâm school went on with its strong development under the auspices of the Trần house.

The presentation of the historical development of the Trúc Lâm school through the three Patriarchs Nhân Tông, Pháp Loa and Huyền Quang may be considered a distinctive creation of Vietnamese Buddhism in the 18th century, when Tính Quảng and his pupil Ngô Thời Nhiệm compiled the *True Record of the Three Patriarchs* based on many different materials. Studying this record, we see that the biography of Nhân Tông is originally cited from the *Recorded Sayings as the Lamps of the Saints*, except for an annex at the end of the record extracted from the *Quốc Sử* (*National*

History) concerning the fact that Master Trí Thông burned his arm on Emperor Nhân Tông's ordination and vowed to serve at the latter's stūpa in Yên Tử, and that the biography of Pháp Loa is a copy of his own one engraved on the tablet of the Viên Thông stūpa in the year of Đại Trị, Nhâm Dần (1362), which remains today at the Thanh Mai temple on Mount Tam Bản in what is now Hoàng Hoa Thám Village, Chí Linh District, Hải Dương Province.

As to the biography of Huyền Quang, it is cited from the *Tổ Gia Thực Lục (True Record of the Patriarchal House)*. This record has a rather strange history. When the Ming of China took control of our country in the years 1407-1428, they collected all of our country's writings and brought them to Chin-lêng, among which is the *True Record of the Patriarchal House.* This may be proved through a note at the end of the record:

This *True Record of the Patriarchal House* was brought to China by Shang-shu Huang-fu around the year Hsuan-te (1426-1435). For many years since then, [he] often dreamed a monk who asked him to return the record to its native country. Since his descendants did not yet have the opportunity to do so, they built a temple in their village for venerating it. Whatever prayer they had in front of the altar on which the Record was placed was effectively responded to; so they called the temple *The Temple of Annan Dhyāna Master Huyền Quang.* Around the year Chia-hsin (1522-1558), Tô Xuyên Hầu went to the Great Ming's court as a messenger and did not return until 19 years later. At his departure on returning home, he was seen off by Huang Chêng-tsu, a fourth-generation descendant of Huang-fu, who again dreamed the monk with his request for the returning of the Record. Huang Chêng-tsu then handed the Record to Tô Xuyên Hầu, telling him about the worshiping of it in the Ming country. When Trình Tuyên Hầu welcomed the messenger's return, he brought the Record home. Later, he composed a writing titled Giải Trào Văn about it.

Apart from the note just translated, at the end of the *True Record of the Three Patriarchs* printed in Thành Thái the Ninth, there is a comment by Ngô Thì Sỹ under the title *Huyền Quang Hạnh Giải* and noted to be an extract from the *Ngô Gia Văn Phái*:

As to the same action undertaken by different people if somebody has done it in a different manner, he would be doubted. Among many different words about the same fact, if somebody could confirm his own one, he would be trusted. Further, it is not quite scarce for people in the world to make their statements in an unreasonable and groundless manner. Therefore, if something has been written down, it must be elaborately examined.

Master Huyền Quang lived in the Trần's time. He cultivated the [Buddha's] Path at the Hoa Yên temple on Mount Yên Tử and was granted the title *The Third Patriarch of Trúc Lâm School*. As far as his practice of śīla and samādhi is concerned, there is no documentary evidence preserved today. It has been rumored, however, by some discursive people that the master had been the Honors Graduate [in a *đình* examination] before "taking refuge in Buddhism." One day, being doubtful of his monastic life [the king] Anh Tông gave the order for a concubine to test his purity. The concubine then could take [from the master] the amount of pure gold granted [to him] earlier by the king. At this, some verses and stories have been composed to record this incident so that the master's genuine practice of the Way can by no means be definitively determined.

Recently, in a writing of the style 'hạnh' [as to the master], Mr. Nguyễn of the Cổ Đô village[5] has omitted some unnecessary part [of the biography of the master] and pointed out the fact that the latter did give up wealth altogether and could eventually attain enlightenment. As for some alleged abuse on his violation of precepts, its authenticity has not yet been satisfactorily clarified.

Conventionally considered, female beauty is generally of most interest inside the Citadel. May it then be only because of some uncertainty that one could devote that which one loves most to testing somebody one does not trust? That a woman with her face beautified with pink powder appeared lonely in the long range of green mountains must be unequivocally considered to be something truly unreliable. Suppose [a certain woman had] appeared [with some charming words toward the master], the master, who was at the meditation seat in the midst of a serene temple late in the night, would be ready to respond with some instructions of the appearance of Buddha Maitreya in the future. For the chatter of a woman is not what a master needs to be concerned with. If the master, as being a monk of pure conduct, had been all of a sudden contaminated on his ears by some human voice, would he not have been able to act as a man of the State of

---

[5] By "Mr Nguyễn of the Cổ Đô village," the author refers to Nguyễn Bá Lân (1701-1785), a native of the Cổ Đô village, Tiên Phong district, former Sơn Tây province. He received the highest degree (tiến sỹ) in the 1731 examination and worked as Thượng Thư with the title Lễ Trạch Hầu. Well-versed in verses in the Nôm language, he was the author of Ngã Ba Hạc Phú, Giai Cảnh Hứng Tình Phú, and Vịnh Sử Thi Quyển. His writing on Huyền Quang has not yet been found. [LMT]

Lu? Would he not have been able to overwhelm it? Further, were there not a place in the vast meditation forest for a woman to stay overnight? If the graceful beauty of flowers early in the spring were not able to move the heart of a man on his first entering [the garden], how could he take pains to walk about in the corridor only to look at it, particularly as he had made so many efforts to purify his mind? Would the master not have been able to follow Liu Hsia-hue's good example even though he, whose heart has been so cooled as ash, might have lost his precaution due to some unmindfulness one morning? Naturally, the master was not interested in gold; ... Even though compassion is the very virtue of a monk, would he have been willing to give up his honor to some groundless abuse?

Consequently, it might happen that, being charmed in the first place by some graceful voice the master allowed her to stay. Then, in face of such a beauty he had some talk with her so that he, because of being joyful at her cunning words, finally decided to entrust all the gold to her. Only with such matters it would be hard for him to prove his untainted mind. As a consequence, the more we try to protect the master, the more he would be misunderstood.

Nowadays, I am living in a time some hundreds of years later than his. Yet, when thinking of unraveling some suspicions caused by false rumors of the world, why is it not possible for me to come to an openly fair judgment as to the master in terms of his very biography and verses? According to his biography, he was a native of the Vạn Tải village in Vũ Ninh of Bắc Giang Water Route. His home was on the southeast of the Ngọc Hoàng temple. His first ancestor Lý Ôn Hoàng was an official in the reign of Lý Thần

Tông. The descendant of the sixth generation named Quang Dụ worked as a *chuyển vận sứ* under the Trần dynasty. Quang Dụ had four sons, the youngest of whom was called Tuệ Tổ. The master was the latter's grandson. His mother gave birth to him after bearing him nearly twelve months. As a young baby, he appeared to be strangely intelligent and thus named Tải Đạo.[6] At the age of nine, he was already versed in literature. When he was 21-years-old, he passed the Đại Y examination. He had many achievements in receiving foreign messengers. He used to accompany the king to the Vĩnh Nghiêm temple in the Phượng Nhãn District, where, upon hearing Pháp Loa's discourse one day, he attained enlightenment. Thereafter, he submitted a memorial to the king, requesting to be ordained as a Buddhist monk. He was granted the monastic title Huyền Quang and appointed to be the abbot of the Hoa Yên temple on Mount Yên Tử, where he instructed more than 1,000 disciples. The Textbook with the annotation by him was commented by Emperor Nhân Tông that "if the book has been supervised by Huyền Quang, not a word may be added to or omitted from it." In such high esteem was he held by contemporaries.

His verses consist of the *Ngọc Tiên*, the *Trích Diễm*, the *Việt Âm*, in which there are the sentences like "nhất lãnh thuế y [kinh tuế hàn]" ([surviving the cold of winter] only with a light fur coat), "bán gian thạch thất" (half of the stone chamber), "đức bạc thường tàm kế tổ đăng" (shame at such little merit as to transmit the Patriarch's lamp), "dĩ thị thành thiền tâm nhất phiến; cung thanh tức tức vị thùy đa" (in meditation my mind has become one-

---

[6] Lit., "Conveying the Teaching."

pointed; for whom are the crickets making such laments?), and so on. The characteristics of mountain, forest, mist, evening sunshine are manifest in his wording, through which it may be assumed that he is a very plain and simple man. How would words of nonsense as falsely rumored by the world be able to proceed form such a man?

If it were asked by some that "the Master should give up that pure way of living, should he not?," let me answer with "should not". As to a monk of such highly pure conducts, it is hard to coin that he could not have led a righteous life or he could not help thinking about such as marriage. As his life has been so obviously known, the matter that a "tray of garlic" might be turned into a "tray of vegetarian food" becomes nonsense at once. If calmly and frankly considered, it may be said that "though the Trần king gave orders to test the master many times, the latter did not break his pure precepts. How could he, being the Third Patriarch of the Trúc Lâm Dhyāna school, exchange his honor for an act as such?

This comment is made by Chánh Tiến Sỹ Đốc Trấn Ngô Thì Sỹ, with the title Ngọ Phong Công, in the Tả Thanh Oai village of Thanh Oai district in the year of Tân Mùi, Cảnh Hưng, under the Lê dynasty (1751).

From the two endnotes of the *True Record of the Three Patriarchs*, it is clearly known that the *True Record of the Patriarchal House* Tính Quảng and Ngô Thời Nhiệm copied in their *True Record of the Three Patriarchs* is the text that was brought home from China by Tô Xuyên Hầu Lê Quang Bí in 1569, and later read by Trình Xuyên Hầu Nguyễn Bỉnh Khiêm (1491-1580) so that a writing titled *Giải Trào* was written as to it by the latter. Thereafter, it was copied and provided with an annex by Ngô Thời Nhiệm's father, namely, Ngô Thì Sỹ. Based upon Sỹ's comment, the compilation of the *True Record of the Three Patriarchs* may be supposedly to have been carried out as follows: First, Ngô Thời Nhiệm might read his father's copy of the *True Record of the Patriarchal House* where Huyền Quang is recorded to have been granted the posthumous title "Trúc Lâm Thiền Sư Đệ Tam Đại, Đặc Phong Tự Pháp Huyền Quang Tôn Giả" (Venerable Huyền Quang, Dhyāna Master of the Trúc Lâm Third Generation, Specifically Bestowed to Be the Dharma-Successor). From this, it might occur to Ngô Thời Nhiệm that he could compose a work named the *True Record of the Three Patriarchs*. Thereafter, he would discuss it with Tính Quảng, who might be the master of and grant the monastic name *Hải Lượng* to him if their monastic names were extracted from one and the same gātha representing the line of transmission of the Chi-Pan T'u-k'ung school of the Lin-chi lineage:

Trí tuệ thanh tịnh

Đạo đức viên minh

Chân như tính hải

Tịch chiếu phổ thông

Tâm nguyên quảng tục

Bản giác xương long

Năng nhân thánh quả

Thường diễn khoan hoằng

Duy truyền pháp ấn

Chứng ngộ hội dung

Kiên trì giới hạnh

Vĩnh thiệu tổ tông.

Then, following their discussion, a plan might be drawn up, that is, to cite the biography of Nhân Tông in the *Recorded Sayings as the Lamps of the Saints*, that of Pháp Loa on his memorial tablet at the Thanh Mai temple and what concerns Huyền Quang in the *True Record of the Patriarchal House*, to which some fragments of the three patriarchs' writings preserved somewhere in the temples under the title *Thiền Đạo Yếu Học* (*Study of the Essentials of Dhyana Doctrine*) were added, to constitute the *True Record of the Three Patriarchs*.

Since the *True Record of the Three Patriarchs* was published, these three patriarchs' lives and careers were widely known and further confirmed by another work titled *Fundamental Principles of Trúc Lâm Doctrine*, whose earliest edition was in Cảnh Thìn the Third (1795). In the foreword of this work, its author Ngô Thời Nhiệm presented the biographies of the first three patriarchs Nhân Tông, Pháp Loa and Huyền Quang of the Trúc Lâm school. The rest was an autobiography of the author himself under the heading "Trúc Lâm Đệ Tứ Tôn" (The Trúc Lâm's Fourth Honored-One). If tracing from the *Fundamental Principles of Trúc Lâm Doctrine* back to the year 1765, when the *True Record of the Three Patriarchs* was for the first time published, we can see that such a hypothesis as to the compilation of the *True Record of the Three Patriarchs* is not quite unreasonable and that Ngô Thời Nhiệm's supposed participation in the compilation of the work is not without any ground. Indeed, not only did he contribute to the literature of Vietnamese Buddhism but also helped throw light on a number of masters of the Trúc Lâm school such as Hải Âu Vũ Trinh (1726-1823), Hải Hòa Nguyễn Đăng Sở, Hải Huyền Ngô Thì Hành, Hải

Điển Nguyễn Hữu Đàm, and so on, who were the great intellectuals of the time, originating from the noble class in the latter half of the 18th century. In reality, owing to their influence and prestige that the notion of the Trúc Lâm Three Patriarchs has become popularly admitted. However, it is the popularity of this notion that has lent encouragement to some distorted view of the historical development of this school.

In effect, with the exception of the *True Record of the Three Patriarchs*, nowhere has Huyền Quang been considered "the Dhyāna Patriarch of the Third Generation of the Trúc Lâm School." As has been said above, this is the reverend title that the Emperor Minh Tông, before his death, employed to designate Master Kim Sơn. Accordingly, the Third Patriarch of the Trúc Lâm school must be Kim Sơn and not Huyền Quang. Earlier, we have suggested and proved in terms of documentary evidence that Kim Sơn may have composed the *Collected Prominent Figures of Dhyāna Garden*, a history of Dhyāna Buddhism in Vietnam, subsequent to the *Chiếu Đối Bản* of Thông Biện (?-1134), the *Chiếu Đối Lục* of Biện Tài, and the *Nam Tông Tự Pháp Đồ* (*Chart of Dharma-Successors of the Southern School*) of Thường Chiếu. As to the *Recorded Sayings as the Lamps of the Saints*, its composer is not known today; yet, from its content as well as style we may postulate that the author is none other than Kim Sơn. In addition, the *Cổ Châu Pháp Vân Phật Bản Hạnh* may have been composed by him, too.

Thus it may be said that in the middle of the 14th century a great movement of studying the history of Vietnamese Buddhism broke out widely. And Kim Sơn, as being an outstanding Dhyāna master under the reign of Minh Tông, must have conducted the task of compiling the afore-said history books. It is, however, unfortunate that we have not yet acquired any new information on this master so far, except for what is preserved in the *Recorded Sayings as the Lamps of the Saints.* Nevertheless, we may be sure that the Trúc Lâm school continued to exercise its strong influence on the court as well as the people until around the year 1358 at least. In all probability, the inscription of the *Chronicle* on the memorial tablet in front of the Viên Thông stūpa of Pháp Loa could be carried out by Kim Sơn himself. The sole question posed here is why it could not be engraved and erected at Pháp Loa's stūpa until 1362. Was there probably something wrong for the tablet to be made in memory of him during the Emperor Minh Tông's lifetime?

Whatever happened, Kim Sơn must have lived on for some more years after Minh Tông's death. However, due to the latter's successors who were only interested in sensual pleasures as Dụ Tông or who was so timid and hesitant as Nghệ Tông, the magnificent energy of Đông A gradually died out so that "the lamps of transmission" by various outstanding Dhyāna Masters were no longer recorded. This points out that such people of great prestige and high reputation as Kim Sơn passed away under the reign of Dụ Tông. Straightly stated, Master Kim Sơn might die between the years 1365-1370; and from this it may be speculated that he might be born at some time around the year 1300 so that he could be an immediate disciple of Pháp Loa's before the latter's death in 1330.

Subsequent to Kim Sơn's time, the Trúc Lâm school could certainly go on to develop well. For, even at Mount Côn where

Pháp Loa and Huyền Quang had the Tư Phúc temple built, there were some poet-monks who often visited Trần Nguyên Đán for the purpose of enriching their wording, as is mentioned in a poem of his:

As a state official I have worked for ten years.
Reading poems while walking with a stick under the pines,
I see no visitor coming in the dust raised by horses;
Only poet-monks often knock the door for words.
As I can no longer take care of the people,
May it be time for me to retire home soon?
If waiting for the accomplishment of my career,
This old body then would rest under a burial-mound.

In addition, Phạm Nhân Khanh, who is recorded in the *Recorded Sayings of as the Lamps of the Saints* to have brought the Emperor Minh Tông's letter to Huyền Quang some time before 1334, spoke of the National Master Lãm Sơn in a poem composed after he saw the master off the capital:

After some days' absence from the mountain, he hurried back.
For he felt more peaceful in his lonely life there.
In the pine-house the tea smelled so sweet when prepared;
In the crane-stream the cups were cleaned with so much water.
The virtues of Dhyāna spread by him prevailed for thousands of years;
The values of poetry displayed by him overwhelmed everything else.
Retiring to the secluded peak covered in clouds,
He quietly gave Dharma-rains to purify the world.

The most interesting event is that as the Cham Army under the command of Chế Bồng Nga attacked the capital Thăng Long for many times, an army composed of Buddhist monks was organized and commanded by Dhyāna Master Đại Than, whose secular name and Dharma-title are unknown. In the *Complete History of Đại Việt*, it is said that "in the 3rd month (of Tân Dậu, Xương Phù the Fifth, 1381) the National Master Đại Than was ordered to collect strong monks across the country, even those who were living in the mountains and had no monkish certificates, so as to serve for a time in the fighting expedition to Champa." On this occasion Phạm Nhân Khanh wrote a poem to praise Master Đại Than and his Monastic Army:

Dhyāna General Đại Than was like a tiger in the Dhyāna forest.
His strength could conquer tens of thousands of soldiers.
Holding the sacred flag uprightly, he smoothed out the enemy's rampart.
Driving the sword of wisdom lightly, he destroyed the brutal troops.
With the wind was his mantra recited for protection of the army.
In the air was his mandala drawn for destruction of the enemy.
Immediately submitted to the kings were his quick achievements,
Which truly constituted a picture of Lăng Yên by the National Teacher.

It may be said that this is the first and only time in the history of our country Buddhist monks have served as soldiers in the battle-fields. No doubt, this may be considered to be some echo or shadow of the voice or image of the renowned lay masters in the battle-fields of the 1285 and 1288 wars, such as Tuệ Trung, who, together with his brother Trần Hưng Đạo, commanded an army to liberate the capital Thăng Long in the spring of 1285. Thus, the fact that the number of monks in 1381 was large enough to be organized into an army under the command of Master Đại Than points out that the Trúc Lâm school was truly in its flourishing state by the end of the 14th century.

In reality, besides Master Đại Than's monastic army, an uprising which occurred in Quốc Oai was, too, led by a Dhyāna Master, namely, Phạm Sư Ôn, as recorded in the *Complete History of Đại Việt*. This master must have been of the Trúc Lâm school since, according to the *Chart of Dhyāna Lineage*, the Dhyāna schools of Vietnam, with the exception of the Trúc Lâm, declined early in the 14th century. By the end of this century, as a result of many ceremonies of transmitting monastic precepts held by Pháp Loa the Buddhist clergy, which numbered approximately 15,000 by 1329, could supply all the temples throughout the country with monks and nuns. Accordingly, it is rather easy to determine Phạm Sư Ôn's membership in the Trúc Lâm school. Yet, he has not been properly recognized so far, let alone the fact that some have blamed him for leading an uprising against the court. In effect, Pham Sư Ôn's action was simply a positive manifestation of Trúc Lâm Dhyāna Buddhism on the principle of "righteously serving one's lord, respectfully obeying one's father." Just as Đại Than undertook the organization and command of the Monks' Army for the purpose of saving the country, so Pham Sư Ôn took the leadership of the uprising for the sake of the suffering people. This is a characteristic of Buddhism in Vietnam. It has never been bound up absolutely with any dynasty even though that dynasty might be by all means supported or led by Buddhism. Instead, it is linked only with the welfare of the nation and the masses. In the 1360's the Trần dynasty's court led by Dụ Tông got so badly corruptive that they did not only fail to take care of the people's living but also showed indifferent to their sufferings. In face of that perilous situation of the country, a part of Vietnamese Buddhists did not demonstrate their attitudes in such a negative manner as of Chu Văn An, who did nothing but retiring home after his suggestions for reforming the court had been refuted by the Emperor at the time. Instead, they made a positive decision of taking weapons and siding with the masses in their struggle for vital reforms within the court and urgent improvements of the masses' living condition. It must be said that this is a typical attitude of Vietnamese Buddhists that the spirit of the "Worldly Life with Joy in the Way" has helped to produce.

No doubt, a question may be raised by some as to whether such an attitude would truly reflect the essentials of Buddhist teachings. And, from their own subjective reflections some then will make a reply on the spot that there is nothing to do with Buddhism in such an action, just as what was formerly stated recklessly by a Vietnamese writer: "The sole fact that [Buddhist] monks participated in politics or wrote verses is, in my opinion, neither in accord with the essential teaching of Śākya[muni], nor with such a doctrine of absolute nihilism."[7] From such a statement, we cannot know upon what sūtra its author's opinion has been based or whether it is merely a deluded reflection of his own ideas as to Buddhist monks that has been transformed into groundless, nonsense statements. For the past 100 years a number of critical studies on Buddhism have been made by prominent scholars in the

---

[7] Đặng Thái Mai, Mấy điều tâm đắc về một thời đại văn học in Thơ Văn Lý Trần I, Hà Nội: Nxb. KHXH, 1977, p.42. [LMT]

world where many problems have been put forward, among which is the most important question as to what the Buddha taught. Many circles of scholars on Buddhism have been founded to find out an answer to that question, the most prominent of which are those of England and Germany, France and Belgium, and Russia. In spite of this, there still remain some who claim that they could grasp "the essential teaching of the Śākya[muni]" so as to utter vague and groundless statements concerning Buddhism as mentioned above. Consequently, it is not easy at all to speak of the Buddhist teaching as many people have thought. Since the old days the study on the Buddhist teaching has ever been formulated that "if based on sūtras literally, any interpretation of the Three-Period Buddhas' teaching will be misleading; on the other hand, if not based upon even a single word of them, that will be identical with false doctrines."

Whatever it may be, there have been few cases in which the Buddhist clergy had to be engaged in military actions with regard to imperial courts in the history of Vietnamese Buddhism. If any, it was due to certain extremely urgent situations where they could not do anything else for the welfare of the people. Indeed, in the history of Vietnam Buddhism has played a much more extensive role, that is, fulfilling its cultural mission of assisting the masses to develop their good customs and abandon their bad ones so as to gain better and better living, both spiritual and material. It is with such a role that Buddhism has been able to make a strong impression on the Vietnamese people throughout their history. Even by the end of the 14th century that role of Buddhism went on to manifest itself distinctively. This may be proved through some of Buddhist devotees' achievements.

First, Nguyễn Trãi, a national hero of the Vietnamese people, ever received his own education from a Dhyāna Master for more than ten years, that is, Master Đạo Khiêm. In a poem whose inspiration was drawn from his reunion with the master the former said,

I remember being under your instruction for more than ten years;
Now this is the chance for us to spend overnight together.
Pleased that we are able to put aside secular affairs
So as to seek again the atmosphere of our former talks on the rock.
Tomorrow morning you will have to return to Linh Phố;
I know not when we can hear again the stream on Mount Côn.
Be not amazed at my "crazy" words when I am so old.
At your departure, I am still in the course of Supreme Dhyāna.

From it, it is obvious that Nguyễn Trãi lived together with Master Đạo Khiêm at the Tư Phúc temple on the Côn mountain and, under the latter's instruction, he studied many different subjects including Dhyāna Buddhism of the most transcendent type, that is, Supreme Dhyāna doctrine. The poem was written when Nguyễn Trãi was already in his old age. At that time the independence of the country was restored and Lê Lợi ascended the throne, but Nguyễn Trãi could not yet leave the court for his retirement on Mount Côn between 1435-1442.

Nguyễn Trãi was born in 1380. And he was already in his old age when he saw his master again around 1345. Thereupon, it may be assumed that the Dhyāna Master may have been born 15 years at least earlier than Nguyễn Trãi so as to be old enough to instruct Nguyễn Trãi for more than ten years when the latter was living at his maternal grandfather Trần Nguyên Đán's on Mount Côn, that is, between 1386 and 1400. For prior to the year 1400 Nguyễn Trãi had attended and passed the first examination in the reign of Hồ. In other words, Đạo Khiêm must have been born around 1370 and could have continued to settle on Mount Côn after the tragic law case in 1442. His date, therefore, may fall between 1370-1445.

In the time of Đạo Khiêm, there was another Dhyāna Master named Viên Thái, who translated the *Cổ Châu Pháp Vân Phật Bản Hạnh* written in Chinese by Master Kim Sơn into the Nôm language. Though the date of this master has not been determined so far, from his way of word-for-word translation as well as his wording we may postulate that he could not live later than the year 1550. Moreover, since the *Cổ Châu Pháp Vân Phật Bản Hạnh* was, too, paraphrased in verse by Pháp Tính, it has been assumed that as being translated in prose Viên Thái's translation certainly had to appear earlier than the translation in verse supposedly made by Pháp Tính, who lived between 1470-1550. Otherwise stated, Master Viên Thái must have lived before that date.[8]

In addition, there is an extant Nôm translation of the text *Phật Thuyết Đại Báo Phụ Mẫu Ân Trọng*, which may be dated around the first half of the 15th century in terms of an analysis of its following internal evidences. The first is about its avoiding the use of a character after which the Emperor Lê Thái Tổ was named owing to contemporary regulations concerning the names of the Emperor and other members of his family. This indicates that the translation could be put into circulation until this regulation was no longer in effect in 1469. So the translation and printing of its original had to be carried out between 1428-1469. The second is that the Nôm translation of the latter text is also worked on in the

---

[8] Lê Mạnh Thát, Viên Thái Thiền Sư Toàn Tập, Sài gòn: Tu Thư Vạn ạnh 77

method of word-for-word translation, and its style and wording are somewhat similar to those of the translation of the former text. In this connection, it may be assumed that these two translations could originate from one and the same translator, that is, Viên Thái. Thereupon, the date of this master must fall between 1400-1460.

Subsequent to Viên Thái is Master Hương Chân Pháp Tính (1470-1550?). He is the compiler of the most ancient Chinese-Nôm dictionary known today as the *Chỉ Nam Học Âm Giải Nghĩa*. Besides, he may possibly have paraphrased the *Cổ Châu Pháp Vân Phật Bản Hạnh Ngữ Lục* in a specific Vietnamese style of verse known as *lục bát*. Like most of Dhyāna Masters of the Trúc Lâm school, before leading a monastic life Pháp Tính ever passed the national examination and thus worked as an imperial official as in his own words:

In my prime youth I have passed the examination;
Now that I have been old, I decide to follow the Buddha's path.

Just like his First Patriarch Nhân Tông, Pháp Tính, even though he already lived a monastic life, did not abandon any of his services to the people. In face of the masses' difficulties in using the complex structure of the Nôm script at the time, he attempted to invent a much more simple way of transcribing the national speech, which would be easier for the public to read and write. Further, he strongly rejected the opinion that the Nôm script was nothing other than a vulgar language, not able to convey the sages' saying. In the words of Pháp Tính:

The spoken Nôm language may be allegedly considered vulgar;

Yet, as a written language, it can convey the sages' sayings.
Now I have its script divided into major and secondary characters
And widely popularized so that illiterate people can master it.
Formerly so many compound characters were created
That people of little education found it hard to read them.
Today simplified characters should be introduced
So that the people can read and understand them easily.

As a consequence, a great movement of applying the Nôm script to composing and recording in various fields of study grew up and flourished well due to Pháp Tính's achievement in the field of linguistics. A great number of Vietnamese authors began to employ the Nôm language in place of the Chinese language in their works, such as Thọ Tiên Diễn Khánh (1550-1620?) in his *Nam Hải Quan Âm Phật Sự Tích Ca*, Minh Châu Hương Hải in his more than 20 works of which the four complete ones have been preserved, Chân Nguyên, Như Trừng, Như Thị, Tính Quảng, Hải Lượng, Hải Âu, Hải Hòa, Hải Huyền, An Thiền, and so on. Most particularly, Chân An Tuệ Tĩnh (?-1711) did not only maintain *"the usage of traditional medicine for the Vietnamese,"* which had been studied and applied by himself, but also announced his scientific work in the Nôm language. These authors professed themselves to be members of the Trúc Lâm school in the 16th, 17th, 18th, and 19th centuries and actually made great contributions not only to Vietnamese Buddhism but also to the Vietnamese people in the common cause of building the country.

Thus, after Huyền Quang's death in 1334, the Trúc Lâm Dhyāna school, which was continuously succeeded by the outstanding figures who contributed a great deal to the country in many different fields, should not and cannot be considered "to have flourished for a short time" as falsely assumed by many people hitherto. Of course, such a mistake has taken its root deep in the past when Tính Quảng and Ngô Thời Nhiệm accomplished their compilation under the title *True Record of the Three Patriarchs* in 1765, and particularly when Ngô Thời Nhiệm introduced his writing *Tam Tổ Hành Trạng* (*Activities of the Three Patriarchs*), which was included in an edition of his *Fundamental Principles of Trúc Lâm Doctrine*. Nevertheless, in the middle of the 19th century, An Thiền, in his *Đại Nam Thiền Uyển Kế Đăng Lược Lục* printed around the year 1858, recorded a list of 23 Dhyāna Masters who consecutively undertook the patriarchal office of the Trúc Lâm Monastery on Mount Yên tử:

1. Patriarch Hiện Quang
2. National Teacher Viên Chứng
3. National Teacher Đại Đăng
4. Patriarch Tiêu Dao
5. Patriarch Huệ Tuệ
6. Patriarch Nhân Tông
7. Patriarch Pháp Loa
8. Patriarch Huyền Quang
9. National Teacher An Tâm
10. National Teacher Phù Vân (with the title Tĩnh Lự)
11. National Teacher Vô Trước
12. National Teacher Quốc Nhất
13. Patriarch Viên Minh
14. Patriarch Đạo Huệ
15. Patriarch Viên Ngộ
16. National Teacher Tổng Trì

17. National Teacher Khuê Thám

18. National Teacher Sơn Đằng

19. Great Master Hương Sơn

20. Great Master Trí Dung

21. Patriarch Tuệ Quang

22. Patriarch Chân Trú

23. Great Master Vô Phiển.

Later, some have adopted the list and named it "Yên tử tradition"[9] but not studied whether it has any historical value. Thereafter, some have cited it and claimed that "its authenticity is doubtful" and "the chronological order of the generations therein appears unreliable."[10] In spite of this they all admit that the generations prior to Nhân Tông are available for reference. For, in the*Collected Prominent Figures of Dhyāna Garden* Master Huyền Quang (?-1221) is recorded to have ever settled on Mount Yên tử. And in the preface to *A Manual of Dhyāna Teaching*, the Emperor Trần Thái Tông said that, on his arrival at Mount Yên Tử in 1236, he had met "the National Teacher, a Great Śramaṇa of Trúc Lâm," who is named National Teacher Phù Vân in the *Complete History of Đại Việt*. Besides, the *Recorded Sayings as the Lamps of the Saints*, the *Thiền Tông Bản Hạnh* and the *Đại Nam Thiền Uyển Kế Đăng Lục*, all record that the Emepror Trần Thái Tông met National Teacher Viên Chứng. Furthermore, since the*Collected Prominent Figures of Dhyāna Garden* mentions a disciple of Dhyāna Master Hiện Quang known as Đạo Viên, the latter is

---

[9] Nguyễn Lang, Việt Nam Phật Giáo Sử Luận, Sài gòn: Lá Bối, 1974, pp.397-398. [LMT]

[10] Viện Triết Học, Lịch Sử Phật Giáo Việt Nam, Hà nội: Nxb. KHXH, 1991, p.224. [LMT]

generally identified with Viên Chứng.

Suppose the names Viên Chứng and Đạo Viên would both refer to National Teacher Phù Vân, we may be assured that Viên Chứng lived until around the year 1278. For, according to the *Recorded Sayings as the Lamps of the Saints*, when Trần Thái Tông was about to die, his son, the Emperor Trần Thánh Tông, "gave the order for the two National Masters Phù Vân and Đại Đăng to expound the transcendental teaching" to him but he did not allow. For that reason, if Đại Đăng did succeed Phù Vân to be the abbot of the Yên tử Monastery, the fact would be dated from the year 1278 on, if not much later.

From the list above, subsequent to Đại Đăng is Patriarch Tiêu Dao, who is certainly not a disciple of the former. For, in the*Chart of Dhyāna Lineage* of the *Recorded Sayings of Thượng Sỹ* Tiêu Dao is recorded to have been a pupil of Layman Ứng Thuận. And Tiêu Dao must have died prior to the year 1291 when Tuệ Trung died. For, among the remaining forty-nine poems of Tuệ Trung there are four poems related to Tiêu Dao, that is, "Vấn Phúc Đường Đại Sư Tật," "Thượng Phúc Đường Tiêu Dao Thiền Sư," "Phúc Đường Cảnh Vật," and "Điếu Tiên Sư" ("A Funeral Lament to the Old Master"). Accordingly, the last poem points out evidently that Tiêu Dao had to die before the year 1291 so that Tuệ Trung could write the verse in memory of his master on his death.

Succeeding Tiêu Dao of the Yên tử Monastery is Patriarch Huệ Tuệ. But, who is Huệ Tuệ? Among the disciples of Tiêu Dao recorded in the *Chart of Dhyāna Lineage*, no one was named as such. However, based upon the way of identification of Đạo Viên with Viên Chứng, it is possible to identify Huệ Tuệ with Tuệ Trung though the latter was himself the celebrated General Hưng Ninh Vương Trần Quốc Tung. In addition, according to the list above the successor of Huệ Tuệ is none other than Điều Ngự Trần Nhân Tông himself. So, is it possible that Tuệ Trung ever took charge of the Yên tử Monastery? The life story of Tuệ Trung written by Emperor Nhân Tông in the *Recorded Sayings of Thượng Sỹ* tells us that the Emperor Trần Thánh Tông honored Tuệ Trung to be his monastic brother. If so, it is obviously possible that Tuệ Trung undertook the abbot's office of the Yên tử Monastery. And that the Emperor Nhân Tông succeeded Tuệ Trung to undertake the same office is not surprising at all although the latter died four years earlier than the ordination of the former. For the Emperor Nhân Tông was actually confirmed by Tuệ Trung to have attained enlightenment ever since 1278 as in his own words in the account just mentioned. Subsequent to Nhân Tông were Pháp Loa and Huyền Quang.

Such is what about the first eight patriarchs as enumerated in the list above, including Pháp Loa and Huyền Quang, whose dates and biographies are quite definitely known. As far as the remaining 15 ones are concerned, the fact that some of them bore the same monastic names has given rise to some doubt as to the authenticity of the whole list. National Teacher Quốc Nhất, the Patriarch of the twelfth generation, for instance, has the same name as a disciple of Master Ứng Thuận; and Great Master Hương Sơn, the 19th Patriarch, has the same name as a disciple of Nhân Tông. Naturally, Hương Sơn as being a disciple of Nhân Tông's could by no means be regarded as the 19th successor of the Yên Tử tradition.

In reality, the fact that some masters bear the same names should not be so surprising as to raise any doubts at all since it is quite ordinary in the history of Buddhism of a country as well as between some countries. In the history of Chinese Buddhism, for instance, a Buddhist master in the Chin dynasty and another in the Wei dynasty, which came into being more than 100 years later than the former, are both named Hui-yuan. In our country there are also many cases as such. For instance, Dhyāna Master Mãn Giác (1052-1096) in the Lý dynasty and a master of the same name in the reign of Lê Trung Hưng, who transmitted monastic rules to Chân Nguyên Tuệ Đăng (1647-1726); and Minh Châu Hương Hải of the 17th century and another master no less well-known than him, who are even of the same native locality, Nghệ An. For that reason, it is not necessary to have doubts as to such cases, especially when those who have the same names do not belong to the same period.

In addition, when the first eight patriarchs in the list above have been proved to be reliable, we may attempt to study the last one. This is the case of Dhyāna Master Vô Phiền, whose date has not been definitely determined so far. Based upon the 22nd patriarch who is known as Chân Trụ, however, it may be assured that he was Master Minh Nguyệt Chân Trụ, the first master of Master Chân Nguyên Tuệ Đăng. Though Chân Nguyên did not record the date of Chân Tru's death, we know that the former entered the monastery at the age of 19, that is, in 1665. Thus Chân Trụ must have lived until around the year 1665 at least. Further, according to Chân Nguyên, soon after transmitting Dharma to him, Chân Trụ passed away; and the former then had to undertake Bhikṣu precepts under Minh Lương Mãn Giác's transmission. In this connection, Chân Trụ must have lived between 1600-1670.

As a consequence, the presence of Chân Trụ may prove the authenticity of the list above. And the Yên Tử tradition did flourish on from the time of Hiện Quang up to Vô Phiền, that is, from 1200 to 1700. A question may be raised here as to why An Thiền did not record any more Dhyāna Masters prior to himself, that is, the period between 1700 and 1850. The reason is simple that he recorded their names in another place. To the *Ngự Chế Thiền Điển Thống Yếu Kế Đăng Lục* by Như Sơn, An Thiền added the list of the generations succeeding Chân Nguyên, including the Dhyāna Masters Như Trừng, Tính Huyền, Hải Quýnh, Tịch Truyền, Chiếu Khoan and Phổ Tịnh though they did not directly take charge of the Yên Tử Monastery.

Accordingly, the Trúc Lâm lineage beginning with the Emperor Nhân Tông has exercised great influence upon the history of country and of Buddhism and it has been continuously succeeded just so far. This is a Dhyāna school that is not only founded by a Vietnamese but also has many remarkable achievements in doctrine and practice so that it has been capable of fulfilling various requirements of development in the history of our country. For that reason, in order to unravel many historical and ideological problems in relation to this school, a certain study on it should be made on a far larger scale. What we have taken up so far is only an outline of it drawn up by chance in our discussion about the Emperor Nhân Tông's contributions to the history of country and Buddhism. It is unequivocally necessary to make a more intensive study in the future since without it there will surely be no hope of correcting a great deal of false views currently made as to the history and doctrine of this school.

Trans. into English by **Đạo Sinh**

THE MOVEMENTS
OF VIETNAMESE BUDDHISM
IN THE END
OF THE TANG DYNASTY

BY **TUE SY**

I. T'ANG'S POLICIES ON BUDDHISM

The movements that will be dealt with in the following imply both literal and figurative senses. Literally, they are real mass movements, even if taken in political meanings. They were started by Định Không (?-686), to say the least, as recorded in the *Thien uyen tap anh* 禪苑集英文 (The *Collection of the Eminents from the Dhyana Garden – abbr. TUTA)*. Figuratively they are stages of developing the distinctive character of Vietnamese Buddhism. When compared to Chinese Buddhism's activities, they would show us much more of a factor to come to a conclusion. For, especially from the aspects of practice and realization, Zen Masters are recognized to have eventually created a peculiar way obviously different from the Chinese.

Those movements could have been carried out only thanks to two factors. In the first place, communication was opened wide among Asian countries under the Tang. Secondly, measures taken by the Tang Emperors as to watch over activities of Buddhist clerical community had had some direct or indirect influence on activities of Buddhism in Vietnam. Owing to these measures, since the Ly dynasties onwards, in Vietnam there existed a regulation of monastic activities of which the most part has been taken after the above-mentioned measures.

*

Let us now mention the first, that is, the communication opened wide among Asian countries.

Up to the Tang epoch there existed at least three roads for the relation between China and India, according to biographies of pilgrim monks. The first was by land, passing through the Western Regions of China, i.e., the Central Asia. Monks from India to China or in the opposite direction mostly followed this road. The goal is either China or India. There existed, however, the longer itineraries. Jue-xian 覺賢 (Buddhabhadra), translator of an *Avatamsaka- sūtra* (398-421), the essential of Hua-yan School, is an instance. On the West, he from India passed over the Pamir, but then went back and took the sea-route. He moored in Giao-chi, and then, seemed to make use of the sea-route to land on China. Another instance is Fa-xian 法顯, a pilgrim before Yuan-Zhang 玄奘, and very renowned. He had taken off since 399AD, following the Dun-huang route, crossing the desert, and finally dropped in Afghanistan. It took him six years to reach the Central India. He later again took the sea route, passing by the Lion Island (Simha-dvipa, Sri Lanka today), finally reached Qingdao (Shandong today) by the year of Fire Dragon, the second year of Yixi Era (416 AC), under the Andi Dynasty of the Jin House 晉安帝. Such journeys brought about a considerably large knowledge of geography forming what we can give the name as "The Asian Buddhist World."

The second itinerary was running from Yunnan to India by the way through Burma. About this route, Yijing's *Tang Biographies of the Pilgrims to the West* 大唐西域求法高僧傳, in the biography of Huilun,[1] records a Chinese temple about 40 yi distant from Nalanda along the lower reaches of the Ganga River built, according to tradition, by King Sri-Gupta in dedication to Tang monks the number of which by then was about 20. They had set off from Shuquan 蜀川, following the Yanghua route. A note in the book writes: "From Shuquan to this temple (i.e., the Chinese) is about over 500 yi or post stations."[2]

Regarding the activities in the Yunnan Region, *Zi zhi tong jian* 資治通鑑 {The *Universal Mirror for Rulership*) records, under the Dynasty of Tang Dezong, in the seventh year of the Zhenyuan Era (791 AD), the King of Yunnan was appointed to be the King of Nan-zhao. The same work records that, in the second year of the same era (795 AD), Nan-zhao invaded Turfan, Tibet today. Later activities show Nan-zhao was getting stronger and stronger in the course of time. On the south, they many times launched attacks against An-nam, and the Tang had repeatedly to send relief troupes

---

[1] T 2066, p. 5a ff.
[2] ibd.

to raise the siege, but the intention would fail. Until under the Dynasty of Tang Xi-zong, the first year of the Qian-fu Era (874 AD), Gao-pian came to decapitate the King of Nan-zhao. Originally, Nan-zhao belonged to the White Thai clan who had settled down in the Yunnan Region.

The third route was by water, operating mostly between the seventh and eighth centuries. Yi-jing's *Pilgrimages to the West* records the biographies of fifty-six monks of which the great part followed the water route. We have seen from the number Tran Van Giap quoted twelve persons who had ever dropped in Giao-chi. The route consists of three starting points: 1) from Guang-zhou; 2) from Annam; 3) from Qingdao. They regularly pulled in to He-ling (Java), Lion Island, and then landed on India.

As the communication was opened wider, foreigners who came to reside in the China of Tang Dynasties, compared to other dynasties, are to be counted the most abundant. Nevertheless, the invasion of these ethnic clans caused much apprehension that *Zi zhi tong jian* ascribes to the barbarization of the Tang. That means traditional customs were rather imbued with the colours of barbarous tribes.

There are three factors that made the Tang Emperors show less racial discrimination than other dynasties. In the first place, Empror Tai-zong 太宗's mother is of Dou 竇 family whose ancestors are considered belonging to the Hu clan. In the second place is the "Hu soldiers" policy. Hu barbarians were to the most part the bellicose ethnic. In the first years of his pioneering work, Emperor Gao-zu of the Tang 唐高祖 owed much to their assistance. Accordingly, as early as in the second year of the Wude

Era (619 AD) of Tang Gao zu, twos years after the foundation of the Tang, a certain Hu was made General. Since then onwards up to the third year of the Qianlong Era of the Song Dynasty (962 AD), during nearly over 300 years of the Tang, there had been seventy-two Hu barbarians promoted to the rank of General. On the other hand, from the year Tian-bao (747 AD) up to Tang Zhao-zong 唐昭宗 (867 AD), passing by eleven Emperors, the Tang had had 85 Hus appointed as Governors. In addition from the first year of Wude (618) until the third year of Tianfu (903), there had been 23 Hus to be appointed as Prime Minister.

The third factor is perhaps of the most humanism. For the Tang dynasty is the period when the relationship between China and India on the field of thought came up to a high level. Had Buddhism succeeded not in developing a humanist attitude, it had not for sure have room to operate in China. As a result, even before the Tang, monks had motivated the humanist standpoint to justify the presence of Buddhism. The Chronological *Record of the Buddha and Patriarchs* 佛祖統紀, book 54,[3] recorded, in the second year of Jian-de (572), Emperor Wudi of the Zhou 周武帝 cracked down the policy of suppressing Buddhism. At that time, Dharma Master Hui-yuan 慧遠 led the monks' resistance. The Emperor justified his policy with three arguments, among which the second states that Buddhist scriptures are from the foreign, deserved to be get rid of. Hui-yuan retorted that Kong-zi 孔子 being of Lu 魯 origin was, with regard to Qin and Jin, a foreigner too; accordingly his teachings should have not been admitted. The Emperor replied, the countries of Lu, Qin, and Jin, although being

---

[3] T 2035, p. 471a13.

geographically different from each other, were influenced with a single imperial civilization, so the admission is justifiable. Hui-yuan opposed, if being so, both China and India share with each other the same Jambudvipa; that means both are on the same earth. Naturally they would have got through the same civilization. It is impartial to second either of them. The justification is obviously humanistic, differs not from Kong-zi's point of view in saying that why it is not to say a man has lost his bow and another man has fetched a bow, instead of saying a Chu citizen lost a bow and an another Chu citizen fetched a one. Later, Tang Wu-zong 唐武宗, in the fifth year of the Huichang Era (854) issued the order of eliminating Buddhism, sending monks and nuns back to the worldly life. Next year he passed away. Xuanzong 宣宗 succeeded the throne, revoked the banning Buddhism order. The event is recorded by *The Universal Mirror of the Sakya lineage* 釋氏通鑑 [4] together with the eulogy of the *Ancient History* 古史, to say in brief: "The idea of destroying religion has not taken Qin Shuihuang's as an example; only because of listening to the heresy's instigation to reject foreign religi

on. Besides, the religion introduced from India for more than 1,000 years has so far become part of the traditional customs deeply rooted in the people's mind. For all that, it is merely to make oneself laughing stock of average people by destroying holy images, throwing scriptures into fire, starting a feud with worshipers. Tang Wuzong's policy cannot be considered wise." As such, the humanistic argument has become the sociological argument. The development of Buddhism so far is to be said to

---

[4] T 1516, p. , 58c ff, 116a1, 119b.

have passed a very long distance. It is thanks to the Buddhist viewpoint as a humanistic doctrine that Chinese Buddhism has favorably exerted some influence on Vietnamese Buddhism, even to some extend on the latter's establishment of activity. As a result, the humanistic spirit of Buddhism has been spreading by means of the extended communication. This spirit would be the impetus behind the development of the self-determination consciousness.

Now let us deal with the second factor, that is, the measures the Tang dynasties were cracking down on Buddhism.

Since having been introduced into China till the Sui House, Buddhism had got for his own a rich literature. New schools, fit for Chinese traditional spirit, started taking shape.

Gaozu of the Sui 隋高祖 was a pious emperor. Just following the summarizing up of The *Universal Mirror of the Sakya Lineage* 釋氏通鑑[5] and the *General Commentaries on Longxing Chronology* 隆興佛教編年通論 (book 9)[6], it is made known that under Sui Gaozu's reign 30,000 monks and nuns had been given the full ordination; 5,000 temples and monasteries had been erected. By that time, there were 24 translators of Buddhist Scriptures. Among these translators Tì-ni-da-luu-chi 毗尼多流支 (Vinitaruci) is recorded in by *Universal Mirror*.[7] It is recorded that, by the second year of Kai-huang, under the reign of Sui Gaozu, in the first lunar month, the Emperor summoned Vinitaruci (translated in Chinese as Mie-xi 滅喜, Extinguishing Joy), together with Dharmaprajña 達摩般若, to do translation. Next month, the second of lunar

---

[5] T 1516, p. 64c ff.

[6] T 1512, vol. 75.

[7] T 1516, p. 64c16.

month, Vinitaruci finished his translation of *Sūtra in The Elephant Head Monastery* 象頭精舍經,[8] and Dharmaprajña his of *Sūtra on The Variety of Karma rewards* 業報差別經.[9]

Sui Gaozu's activities were not limited in China. They were extended to the countries under Chinese Dominion such as Gaoli (Korea today) and Vietnam. The fact is confirmed by *TUTA* through Thong Bien's quotation. According to Thong bien 通辯 (_1134), Sui Gaozu once talked to Dharma Master Tantien 曇天: "I am thinking of the compassionate teachings of Lord Buddha yet I don't know what to do to repay. I think myself unworthy of reigning over the people, so I have done my best to spread and support the Three Gems, having all the holy relics collected to worship in the forty-nine pagodas build up in the whole country, so that the world may have a place to take refuge in. Besides 150 pagodas I want in addition to have more built in Giao-chi 交趾 (Jiaozhi) countries too... wishing sentient beings all to attain the Enlightenment." These words are not found in the biography of Tantien as recorded in The *Sequel to the Stories of Eminent Monks* 續高僧傳 by Daoxuan 稻宣.[10] Yet they are not at all unreliable. First of all, the chronological histories of Buddhism in China such as The *Universal Mirror to the Sakya Lineage* 釋氏通鑑[11], The *General Record of the Buddha and Patriarchs through Generations* 佛祖曆代通載,[12] ... all have this fact in their record. According to it, in the first year of the Renshu Era (601), on the sixth lunar

---

[8] T 466, vol. 14.

[9] T 80, vol. 1, 佛為首迦長者說業報差別經, 隋洋川郡守瞿曇法智譯.

[10] T 2060, p. 571b ff.

[11] T 1516, p. 69c11 ff.

[12] T 2036, p. 560c4 ff.

month, Emperor Sui Gaozu issued an imperial edict stating that: *"I pay homage to the Enlightened One, the Infinitely Compassionate and Merciful Saviour of sentient beings, the One who makes himself bridge and shore for humble people. I have taken refuge in the Three Gems, promoting further the Holy Teachings. By means of which I have, together with people from four oceans, accumulated meritorious deeds as forever-good cause for acquiring the wonderful fruit. It is recommendable to invite thirty sramanas who are well versed in interpreting the essence of things, capable of preaching the Law. Each would bring with two attendants and an ex-office mandarin, a hundred and twenty jins of frankincense. They would take various directions to carry relics to thirty prefectures to build pagodas..."* Compared to the quotation of Thong Bien in *TUTA* as mentioned above, though some differences are found in term of phraseology, yet both are the same in general. According to this, the Emperor had pagodas for worshipping Buddha' s relics built in thirty prefectures. Each prefecture chose a sramana who was well versed in Buddhist doctrine, capable of undertaking preachment. A sramana was allowed to bring with two attendants and an ex office mandarin. The whole text of the imperial edict is collected into Daoxuan 道宣' s *A Large Collection of the Expansion of Light* 廣弘明集[13] Included in this original text is found a list of thirty prefectures in which Jiaozhou (Giao chau) is ranked as the 28th. Other prefectures are to the most part recorded with the place where pagoda was to be erected. Some others, Giao chau included, are not found registered with it. But in a memory of Wangchao 王邵 of the Sui Dynasty on *The Marvels of Relics* 舍利感應記, also

---

[13] T 2103, p. 213b3 ff.

collected by Daoxuan, one can find the registration of the place where the pagoda was built in Giao chau (Jiaozhou) is Thien chung 禪眾寺.[14] *TUTA*, however, has it located at Phap van Temple 法雲寺 (Fayun ji). The Phap Van temple was situated at Long bien (Bac ninh province) where Vinitaruci was dwelling during his staying in Vietnam to spread the teachings of Thien (Zen). The Thien Chung temple, on the other hand, is the one of Dich bang village, Thien duc prefecture, Bac ninh Province, which is the native locality of *Vạn Hạnh* 萬行 and Ly Cong Uan 李公蘊.

Sui Gaozu was reigning for 24 years (586-617). It took him ten early years to settle the remainder of the territory still under the control of the Chen. Moreover, he had in the South to conquer Giao chi (Jiaozhi), Chiem thanh (Champa). He nevertheless devoted the great part of his activities to Buddhism without a cease. Even Luu Phuong 劉方 (Luifang),[15] appointed as Generalissimo of the expedient forces to conquer the Champ between 603-605, was at the same time charged with conveying trunks of relics for Giao chau to erect stupas to worship as mentioned above. Viet Nam though being too remote, separated by boundaries, was counted among thirty prefectures of the Sui, submitted to the direct control under the Sui 's policy in all aspects. Being so, the measures that the Tang later set to the ecclesiastical institution cannot be considered as having no influence on Buddhism in Vietnam. However, the fact is that no trace of such influence on the Vietnamese ecclesiology of this period can be found in any available documents. It is until the dynasties of Ly and Tran that

---

[14] 廣弘明集. T 2103, p. 216b10.
[15] 資治通鑑卷 180.

the Vietnamese ecclesiastical institution began to take shape after the Tang 's, not to say thoroughly. Though it is known to us already that under Lê Đại Hành 黎大行's reign, the ecclesiastic hierarchy was established, but it does not seem so strict as later.

Generally speaking, during 38 years of the Sui, though the span of time was too short, there were left to the Tang several aftermaths. The first to be mentioned is that Sui Gaozu's policy of supporting Buddhism now turned out to be a menace for the Tang. A case shown below is enough to evidence for. The case is recorded in The *Sangha History* 僧史略[16] and The *Universal Mirror of the Sakya Lineage* 釋氏通鑑[17] takes down again after it. The account has it that in the fourth year of Kaihuang (548), Sui Gaozu treated Vinaya Master Lingzang 靈藏 so respectfully that he allowed the latter to get in the imperial palace at will, to be highly regarded the same as the Emperor, to share with him a seat, to go with him on the same imperial carriage. At the first sight, this shows no particularity. However, had it been carried on, monks would have become an element of defying the imperial orders, looking light the imperial law. They do not, of course, look light the imperial law in the same way brigands do, but it is because of their philosophy of life that underrates social positions and fame. Different in significance but likely in activity, therefore, charging it with activities of disobeying the Royal Court, as justified by Fuyi, head of historiographers of Tang Gaozu, is not totally unreasonable. The advocacy "Sramanas are unbound to show respect to the nobility" is a historical phenomenon of Chinese Buddhism. Let us note

---

[16] T 2126, p. 243b ff.
[17] T 1516, p. 65b16.

down some instances recorded in the *General Record of the Buddha and Patriarchs* 佛祖統紀[18] under the item "Excuse for not bowing down before Monarch and Parents."[19]

Jin Chengdi 晉成帝, the sixth year of Xiankang (340), Premier Yubing 庾氷 moved to compel sramanas to prostrate themselves before the noble. Nevertheless, Minister Hechong opposed it. The *General Survey of Longxing' s Chronology* 隆興編年通論 (Book 2)[20] gives an account of the matter in full details of both parts' controversy. Particularly the part that advocated sramanas are bound to prostrate themselves before the noble justified its standpoint in that It is yet unknown if the Buddha exists, but sure enough Buddhism is a foreign custom, for all that now people in the country follow it, to the extent that they change their form, alter their appearance, overlook the traditional code. Their talent is not better than an ordinary man but they dress up pretentiously with arrogance, consider themselves as equal to the monarch. That cannot be admitted.

Under the reign of Jin Andi, in the first year of the Yuanxing Era, Premier Wanxuan 桓玄 *(General Commentary on Long xing Chronology* 隆興編年通論 has it as Wanyuan 桓元)[21] moved to order sramanas to bow down before the noble. According to *Longxing,* this Wanyuan resumed from Yubing, and he had it that even Laozi 老子 was ranked no higher than a duke or a marquis. That the sramans were granted favor of the Emperor yet they did

---

[18] T 2035, p. 454b15; see also, 廣弘明集卷第二十五 T 2103, p. 291a14;

[19] T 2036, p. 580b22 ff:

[20] T 2035, p. 454b15; see also, 廣弘明集卷第二十五 T

[21] ibid., p. 125c23.

not pay respect to himis unacceptable. On account of this, Huiyuan 慧遠 wrote the *Essay on Sramanas' being unbound to bow down before the Noble* 沙門不敬王者論[22], composed of five chapters, for he saw this is the cause to corrupt the quality of Buddhism.

Song Xiaowu 宋孝武 (the year yet unknown, 454-464), stated sramanas were obliged to pay homage to the Monarch, but his successor, the First Dethroned Emperor 宋廢帝 (645), abolished it.

Sui Yangdi 隋煬帝, the fifth year of the Daye Era (609), wanted that when Taoist or Buddhist monks had anything to report to the Emperor, they should prostrate themselves. However, this order did not carried out. The Emperor questioned, and then monk Mingshan 明贍 gave answer that Buddhist clergymen observed Lord Buddha's precepts so it is inconvenient to them to prostrate themselves before laymen.[23]

Tang Taizong, the fifth year of the Jingguan Era, issued the edict to order monks and nuns to bow down before their parents. Some years later, this order was revoked.[24]

Tang Gaozong, the second year of the Xianqing Era (657), issued the order to prohibit Buddhist monks and Taoist priests to receive their parents and elders' bowing down.

Tặng Xuanzong issued Buddhist monks and Taoist priests to pay homage to their parents. Later he revoked this.

The *Universal Record of Lord Buddha* (book 52) gives in addition

---

[22]弘明集卷 5T 2102, p. 29c20 ff; see also 集沙門不應拜俗等事卷 2 T 2103, p. 449a2.

[23] T 2103, p. 280c20 ff.; see also T 2180, p. 452b18 ff.

[24] T 2108, p. 462a29 ff.

another matter: "Not to address himself as subject-monk," that means to say monks do not address themselves as subject to the monarch. The account runs as following:

Qi Wudi 齊武帝, the second year of the Yingming Era (484), monk Senggong had an audience with the Emperor. The former addressed himself "poor monk." The Emperor asked Wangjian 王儉. The latter replied, since the Qin and the Song onwards, most of monks addressed themselves "poor monk."[25] *Longxing Chronology* gives more in details. That year, an imperial made sramanas Faxian 法獻 and Xuanshang 玄暢 Heads of Buddhist clergymen. The other day, they had an audience with the Emperor, addressing themselves "poor monk," and having a talk with the latter while just sitting, not getting up from their seat. After having consulted Wangjian, the Emperor accepted the behavior. His permission became an usual practice.[26]

As it is seen, the attitude that holds monks would not pay homage to the noble was not a mere incident but a sensational affair in the history of Buddhism in China. In Vietnam, at the latest until the Nguyen Dynasty, the above-mentioned case did not take place. That means the clergy was by no means a community that went against the Royal Court as a menace to the monarchy. Ly Cao-tong' s attitude to order people to call him Buddha is but the pretentiousness of a moment. On account of such a fit of pretentiousness he did not hesitate to give monks and nuns *en mass* the sack. Being so, as the Chinese monarchs considered the claim of sramanas' being unbound to pay homage to the noble as a

---

[25] T 2035, p. 454b26 ff.
[26] T 1512, p. 136b12.

manifestation of defying the Royal Court's power, the act of sending monks and nuns back to the worldly life was justified legal. It is reasonable to say that this is one of the main causes that made Tang Gaozu, in the nine year of the Wude Era, took provisional measures to disqualify monks and nuns.

The *Universal Mirror*[27] records Tang Gaozu 高祖, on the fifth lunar month, in summer of the ninth year of the Wude Era, histographer Fuyi 傅奕 submitted a memorial to the Emperor moving an imperial ban against Buddhism. His justification can be summarized as follows: 1. Buddhism has its origin from the Western Regions. Its saying is vague, deceitful. 2. It urges people razing head, changing the clothing style to become unfilial elements. 3. They are the gangs that shirk work, do harm to the traditional morals and manners. Among three reasons, the main one implies that Buddhism approves of the approach to defying the Royal Court. As the argument runs, the birth and death or longevity is determined by the Heaven; the punishment or bestowing favor is decided by the monarch; richness or poverty is the outcome of one's own effort. For all that, Buddhism assigns all these to Buddha, is it not usurping the Creator's might? In fact, the *Large Collection of Expansion of Light* 廣弘明集 (book 7)[28] records Fuyi warned of eleven dangerous factors from Buddhism. Among which three factors are of the most importance: 1. Buddhist monks by nature held the attitude of defying the imperial power as it seen above; 2. Monks and nuns under the Tang at that time were numbered as much as 2,000,000. They were in cahoots with the

---

[27] T 1516, p. 75b8 ff.
[28] T 2130, p. 134a4 ff; 160a21 ff; 168b23 ff.

"barbarous mind," that is, disloyalty. Is it not unworthy of taking precautions? 3. Building temples and monasteries was but squandering people's resources, bringing forth damage to society. These three warnings were enough to arouse the emperor's suspicion about the community of Sangha; even though Chinese Buddhist Sangha hardly had had any relation to political activities. Charging them for all that with infidelity and seed of troubling seems overcritical.

Fuyi so far had seven times submitted memorials to the Emperor to move a ban against Buddhism. However, until then the Emperor was still uncertain. The only person who agreed with Fuyi's standpoint was General Squire Zhangdaoyuan 太僕卿張道源 .[29] Xiaowu 蕭瑀 denounced Daoyuan: Buddha is a Saint. Those who criticize a Saint deserve to be punished. Yuan retorted that in the way of humanity nobody could be looked up higher than one's monarch and father, nevertheless Buddha had disobeyed, run away from home and country. The average person as he was was bold enough to defy the Emperor' s power. At this point Xiaowu dared not to oppose. On the other hand, as noted by *The Universal Mirror*, the Emperor had in deed harbored hatred against Buddhist monks and Taoist priests, on account of their shirking military work. In addition they did not observe well the religious discipline; and Buddhist temples as well as Taoist shrines were seen everywhere... On the fifth lunar month, an imperial edict was issued to give the great part of monks and nuns the sack, having in the capital only three temples reserved, and one for each prefecture.

---

[29] T 2036, p. 564b5 ff.

Needless to say, the expulsion as such was not a good measure. Therefore, lots of regulations for the admission to the monastic life were set up, though the Tang originally showed tolerance towards religions. These regulations can be classed into two: conditions for becoming a monk, and hierarchy in the monastic order.

Conditions for becoming a monk. Here are four classes of monks as recorded in *The General Record of the Buddha and Patriarchs* 佛祖統紀 *(book 52).* Not to mention the class of monks who were admitted by way of an examination that had been the newly established regulation of the Tang, the other class of monks had been regulated by precedent dynasties.

a) *Monk by examination in the Scriptures.* Tang Zhongzong 唐中宗, in the Jinglong Era (707), issuing the imperial edict for carrying out the admission to become monk by way of examination. About the Era, works like *The Universal Mirror of the Sakya lineage* 佛祖統紀,[30] *A Historical survey in brief of the Sakya lineage* 釋鑑稽古略,[31] etc., all record the first year of Shenlong Era (706), on the eighth lunar month. These works give report that the Emperor issued an Edict to order novices have to get through an examination of reading well the Scriptures before they would be admitted as monks. The regulation to make a novice get through an examination for becoming a monk began since then.

Tang Suzong 唐肅宗, in the first year of the Qianyuan (758), conferred on laymen who had recited over 500 sheets of Scripture the title of *ming jing chu shen* 明經出身, that is, the monk who is

---

[30] T 2035, p. 414b,; 452c5: 唐中宗景龍初。詔天下試經度僧.
[31] T 2037, p. 822c24.

admitted through an examination on his understanding of the Holy Scriptures. The *A Historical survey in brief of the Sakya lineage* 釋鑑稽古略[32] records more in details: That year, the Emperor had a forum of preaching Dharma held in the Forbidden Citadel, convening highly virtuous monks from all over the country to form a jury to hear laymen reciting the Holy Scriptures and qualify the monkhood. Also on this occasion those who contributed a sum of money could be admitted to monkhood under the title of being admitted through reciting the Holy Scriptures.

Tang Daizong 唐代宗 (793-780), ordered an examination in Sūtras, Vinaya and Abhidharma to be held for the admission to monkhood.

b) *Monkhood by the special favor.* The class of monks who are granted by the Emperor's special favor. This has its precedent from the Sui.

c) *Monkhood by Promotion.* This has its precedent from Tang Suzong. In the first year of the Qianyuan Era (758), the Emperor had a forum held in the Forbidden Citadel by way of permitting those who contribute a sum of money to become monk as mentioned already above under the title of *monkhood by reciting.*

Therefore, there were three conditions for monkhood. Either by knowledge, by money or by favor granted by Emperor. It is seen right way the ulterior motive of the Tang's Emperors is to limit the status and ration of monkhood.

---

[32] T 2037, p. 827c17 ff.

2. *The Clerical Hierarchy,* classified into two categories: dignitary rank and clerical position.

a) *Conferring title.* Tang Taizong conferred the title of senior courtier 朝散大夫 on four monks.[33]

Tăng Gaozong did the same.

Empress Wuhou 武后 conferred the title of Duke the Prefecture 縣公 on nine monks.

Tang Zhongzong conferred the tile on monk Wanhui as the Duke of Dharma Cloud 萬回法雲公.

Tang Yuizong 睿宗 posthumously conferred the title of the Duke of Yu 虢國公 on the late Wanhui.

After his death, Dharma Master Fazang 法藏法師, third Patriarch of Huayan School, was posthumously conferred the title of Protocol Minister 鴻臚卿.

Tang Xuanzong 玄宗, Bodhiruci 菩提流志 was posthumously conferred the title of Protocol Minister 鴻臚卿.

Tang Suzong 肅宗 conferred on sramana Daoping 道平 the title of Jinyu General 金吾大將軍 charged with operating an expedition against Anlushan 安祿山.

Tang Dezong 德宗 appointed sramana Yuanzhao 圓照 as Protocol Minister for the Imperial Palace 充內供奉鴻臚卿.

Tang Xizong 僖宗 conferred the title on Sramana Miaoximg 沙門妙行 for his merit of reciting the Scriptures 誦經見佛大士.

---

[33] T 2035, p. 453c7 ff.

b) *Clerical Hierarchy.* Ranks of clerical hierarchy had been stipulated since the Dynasty of Jin Andi 晉安帝 (397-418). At that time Sengqi 僧[契-大+石] was mad Sangha Administrator 國僧正 and Faqin 法欽 Sangha Recorder 僧錄. Chen Wendi 陳文帝 (560-566) promoted Monk Baoxiong 寶瓊 to be the Sangha Leader 大僧統. Since the Tang there began the precedent of conferring the title of National Master on Zen Masters and offering them the posthumous name.

Besides, since Tang Xuanzong onwards, by the fifth year of the Tianbao Era (746), there began the precedent of charging the Minister of Protocol and Ceremony 祠部 which undertook the matters of ceremony and religion with responsibility of taking the census of clerical population.[34] On this matter, a note from the *Chronology of the Patriarchal Unity* 宗統編年[35] criticizes: "Since then there began the regulation of issuing the monkhood identification card by the Ministry of Ceremonies. But limiting the number of Sangha is not to understand the Buddha's Teaching." According to this notation, the Imperial Court 's issuing monkhood ID is but aiming at setting a limit to the population and activities of the clerical community.

General speaking, we see by and by the Tang cracked down lots of measures on activities of Buddhism.

Because of the communication was further open, Buddhism gradually exerted its influence on social behavior, altering by and by Chinese morals and manners, the measures as such were in

---

[34] T 2037, p. 827b13; T 1516, p. 99a19.

[35] T 1600, p. 1497c17.

need. They were bought forth not because of some discrimination of race and religion, but carried out because the sovereigns smelt something of menacing. As a result, the history of Buddhism in China witnessed four suppressions of which one took place under the Tang by Wuzong, by the year of 848. The main cause for it remains in that Buddhism had squandered a majority of national resources and man forces. About 100 years later, Emperor of the Post-Zhou re-operated another dread elimination with the same purpose of satisfying the conditions the then war required.

Comparing those mentioned above to the measures cracked down by the Vietnamese sovereigns through the dynasties of Ly and Tran, one could figure out the development of Buddhism in Vietnam. Under these two dynasties Buddhism was honored to the level of the so-called national religion, nonetheless its undergoing the Tang's measures is by no means without ulterior motives.

Now then, the measures that had been carried out under Ly and Tran are preferable to be summed up in the following, based on The *General Mirror of the History of Vietnam by the Imperial Order* 欽定越史通鑑綱目.

Conditions for admitting the Monkhood.

In the fifth year of the Thuần-thiện Era (1020), the Emperor had a ceremony of admitting the monkhood held at thể Vạn-tuế temple 萬歲寺.

In the eighth year of the Đại-khánh Era (1321), a nation-wide examination for monkhood was organized. Contents of exam were questions from the Diamond sūtras.

In the ninth year of the Quang-thai Era (1395) an examination was held for telling the authentic monks from the disguised ones. Those who were under fifty had had to get through this exam before his monkhood was admitted.

In the second year of the Thuan-thien Era (1429), an examination for monkhood was organized. The Royal Court ordered every monk all over the country had to attend the exam at the locality he belonged. If being qualified, he would be offered with a certification identifying his monkhood.

2. *The Grades of Monkhood.*

In the second year of the Thai-binh Era (971), Emperor Dinh-tien granted Sangha Leader Ngo Chan Luu 僧統吳真流 the title of Khuông Việt Thai Su 匡越太師, that means the Great Master who helps Vietnam. At the same time Truong Ma Ni 張摩尼 was appointed as the Sangha Administrator 僧正. (This title had been established since Tang Wenzong 唐文宗 (827-840) of China, consisting of the Administrator of the Left Rank and of the Right Rank; undertaking the role of advisor to the Emperor about the matters that concern to Buddhism and other religions). The *History of Sangha in Brief* 僧史略[36] has it that the title of the Sangha Administrator has as its origin the dispute on the grades at the Court between Buddhism and Taoism. If being so, under the reign of Dinh 丁 in our country, Buddhism and Taoism had had some equal influence on the Court.

In the fourth year of the Quang-huu Era (1088), Kho Dau was bestowed with the title of the National Master.

---

[36] T 2126, p. 242c14 ff.

In the fourth year of the Thien Chuong Bao Tu (1136), monk Minh Khong 明空 was bestowed with the title of the National Master.

Just seen, until the Dinh Buddhism in Vietnam started its system of organization. The fact shows that it is until then onwards that Buddhism began really exerting influence on the Court. Formally, during the times of the Chinese procrastinating dependence, every institution of activity of people from all walks of life had been certainly taking after the Chinese regulation. If, however, the record of *TUTA* is taken into notice, through Thong Bien' s quotation about the story of Tantien and Sui Gaozu as mentioned above, Buddhism in Vietnam yet far had been developed towards a direction of its own bearing no immediate influence from China. Moreover, according to it, the Chinese sovereigns, if of them some were pious, had but the role of assistants to the conditions of development that had already existed. Anyhow, one cannot deny to some extent the increasing influence of China. If in the earlier days Khang Tang Hoi 康僧會 set foot on China only after his having finished the Buddhist studies from Vietnam and was the first sramana who amazed people by his presence as recorded in the *Stories of Eminent Monks* 高僧傳[37]. However, it is seen in the later, under the Tang mostly Vietnamese had taken their Buddhist studies in China before they set off for their pilgrimage to India, taking Dai Thua Dang 大乘燈 for instance. On the contrary, also under the Tang, Vietnamese monks had aptly got the admirations from the Chinese. Yijing, in his *Tang Biographies of Pilgrim Monks*

---

[37] T 2059, p.325a13 ff.

to the West for studying the Dharma 大唐西域求法高僧傳[38], shows his high esteem for the Vietnamese monks who were studying in India. Take for another instance poet, Jiadao 賈島, a contemporary of Hanyu 翰愈. The former who had once been monk composed an inspiring poem dedicated to a Vietnamese monk with the words showing his high esteem, describing the unconventional behavior of a Buddhist from Vietnam.

As it is seen, the development of Buddhism in Vietnam has been going along with the progress of thought and learning in this country. They are the definitely indispensable elements to the consciousness of self-sovereign of a nation. The stages of development of Vietnamese Thien (Zen) school prove this. In the following we will deal with two branches of it in Vietnam existing before the Ly Dynasty, and their influence on the growing of Buddhism in Vietnam in the later dynasties.

II. CHARACTERISTICS OF THE FIRST TWO THIEN SECTS OF VIETNAM

After the Sui Buddhism in China was distinctively divided into two tendencies. The first is the doctrinal tendency absorbed in studying and thinking. The second is of contemplating devoted to practice and realization. The division was repeated by Thanh Bien as to outline the development of Buddhism in Vietnam. Thanh Bien's idea should be taken as exact. In the field of study and thinking Buddhism retained the less changed pattern of Indian tradition of philosophy. If there existed some variety, it was due to the natural endowments of the way of thinking. In the field of

---

[38] T 2066, p. 4b18 ff.

practicing and realizing, however, alterations are to be found in the concept of liberation among traditions. The ultimate end of Buddhism is liberation. However, each tradition aims at liberation from various directions. On account of these directions the end of liberation is recognized likely different among traditions. This idea is as well mentioned in Thanh Bien's quotation. Accordingly, Empress Mother Phu Thanh Cam Linh Nhan 符聖感靈仁 asked the difference of the Buddha from the Patriarchs. Buddha is a personification of liberation in the tradition of Indian Buddhism. In China, Buddha is a personification of liberation too, but in here He is an ideal personification. It is the Patriarch who personifies actually the liberation.

To say so means to say Buddhism has undergone some alteration in practice in each tradition. The essential condition for this alteration is the particularity in the way of living of the people in that tradition.

The study of Vietnamese Buddhism cannot merely rely on the way of learning to display its characteristics. The particularity of Indian Buddhism is *dhyana* or meditation. The one of Chinese Buddhism is also *dhyana* or *chan*. It is as well *dhyana* or *Thien* in Vietnam. Studying and thinking are simply the explanation and description of the experience realized by means of dhyana. Therefore as it is seen when the tendency of the phenomenology (Dharmalaksana-school) is developed in China, here exists at the same time a method of realization particular to this tendency, although it has not been expanded as an actual practice.

Being considered as such, then methodology of Thien or Zen should be taken in a broader sense that implies not only particularly the Zen School but the other schools as well. The most suitable word for it according to the Buddhist study in China is the School of Contemplation, as exactly as addressed by Thong Bien. The doctrinal school did not develop at large in Vietnam. On the contrary, just since the Sui Dynasty the contemplative school had established a distinctive system of transmission. It began with Ty-ni-da-luu-chi (Vinitaruci). Towards the end of the Tang, Vô Ngôn Thông set up another branch of Thien or Zen school. Each of both has its own tendency. They formed two movements of Vietnamese Buddhism before the Ly.

The Branch of Ty-ni-da-luu-chi[39]

TUTA has it:

"Thiển Master Tì-ni-đa-lưu-chi 毘尼多流支, the Southern Indian, is of the Brahmin class. In his childhood, he, cherishing the will of being freed from the ordinary life, had been travelling all over the West India in hope of finding out the Buddha's Seal of Mind. However, because of the favorable conditions for the True Dharma having been unripe yet, he was carrying the staff towards the Southeast. Under the reign of Chen Xuandi 陳宣帝, the sixth year of the Taijian Era (574), he came to set foot on Zhangan 長安 of China. In the meantime, Zhou Wudi 周武帝 was promulgating the policy of eliminating Buddhism, he put up his mind to get to Jianye 建鄴. Now then Sengcan 僧粲, the third Patriarch of Chinese Zen school on account of seeking asylum carried with the mantle and alms bowl and hid himself in the Sikong 司空

---

[39] Cf. Lê Mạnh Thát, Tổng tập văn học Phật giáo Việt nam, tập 3: Thiền uyển tập anh, 2002, p. 274 ff.

mountains. The Master went up there, met the Patriarch, finding in whom the uncommon behavior which aroused in him the admiration. He straightway folded his hands towards the Patriarch, standing on the very spot. As he did the same thrice, the Patriarch just sat closing his eyes without a word. After one or two second of reflecting, the Master suddenly found himself enlightened, as if he had just acquired something, then immediately he prostrated himself before Patriarch three times. The latter did nothing but just nodding thrice. The Master proceeded forward three steps and then backward three steps, saying: "Previously, I have had something unsettled in my mind. Now that thanks to your kindness, may I be allowed to attend on you." The Patriarch said: "You should as soon as possible go and do your association with people in the South. Don't stay here longer." He took leave and set foot on the way. Planting his Zen staff at the Chế chỉ (Zhizhi) temple 制旨寺 of Guang zhou, over a span of six year, he finished translating lots of sūtras, of The *Elephant Head sutra*[40], and The Sūtra on the *Variety of the Retributions of Karma* 報業差別經.[41]. Until the second year of the Dai tuong Era (580) of the Zhou Dynasty, he came to Vietnam, and resided at this temple. There again he finished another translation, *Dharani-sūtra*.[42] One day, he called Pháp Hiển 法賢, his advanced disciple, and told the latter: "Nobody can counterfeit the Buddhas' Seal of Mind. It is as round as the immensely large space, neither redundant nor deficient,

---

[40] It should be identified as 象頭精舍經, T 464; Cf. Le Manh That, ibid., p. 544, notes.

[41] Another translation was done by Dharmaprajna, T 80; cf. Lê Mạnh Thát. ibid., p. 545, notes.

[42] 大方廣總持經, T 275; cf. Lê Mạnh Thát, ibid.

neither going nor coming, neither obtained nor lost, neither identical nor different, neither eternal nor breaking-off, originally appearing from nowhere and disappearing to nowhere, neither detached nor non-detached. Only in relation to delusive conditions it is endowed with a false name. Therefore, Buddhas in the three periods of time had realized the same. Patriarchs through generations had realized the same. Moreover, I myself have realized the same. The same you do and the same all beings, sentient or non-sentient, do. Moreover, my Patriarch, Sengcan, has sealed on me that very mind, and told me to without delay go and do association in the South, being unfavorable to remain there by him longer. For years until the day I came to meet you, the prediction has been indeed justified. Take up yourself rather well. The time I have to take leave is coming." Having finished his admonishing, he passed away with hands folded. After having performed the cremation, Pháp Hiển collected his multicolored relics to store in a stupa. It is in the 14th year of Sui Khaihuang (594). Emperor Thái tông of the Ly 李太宗 composed a eulogy in reminiscence of him. The poem goes as follows:

Since having come to the South,
You have been known as to have
so far long practiced the dhyana.
You must have awakened the faith in the Buddha
And that must have to the far remote
agreed with the origin of the Mind-only.
Brightly bright is the moon of Lanka;
Fragrantly fragrant is the lotus of Wisdom.
When do I come to meet you

So that we may have a talk about the mystery of mystery.

The biography extracted above as recorded in the *TUTA* is the most detailed of those that are available to us at present. In this biography, however, are left some problems concerning the date, when compared to what is recorded in historical documents of Chinese Buddhism.

Probably the first account of Vinitaruci is to be found in FeiChangfang 費長房's *Record of the Three Gems through Dynasties* 歷代三寶記,[43] book 15, compiled under the Sui by the 17th year of Kaihuang (597), i.e., four years after Vinitarucuci's death.

Record of the Three Gems is a bibliography of Buddhist Scriptures translated into Chinese since beginning until the reign Sui Gaozu. Three years earlier before the *Changfang's Record*, i.e., by the 14th year of Kaihuang, there appeared already another biography named *Fajing's Biography* 法經錄 the original name of which is *Biography of all the sutras* 眾經目錄.[44] In the latter no mention about Vinitaruci is made.

Concerning the biography of Vinitaruci, *Changfang's Biography*[45] gives the report as follows: "Tripitaka Master Vinitaruci, from Wuzhang 烏場 (Udhyana), North India, having learned that our Emperor had reflourished the Three Gems, so he taking not care about the long distance carried along with the staff to come to the country. Having arrived, he was supported by the

---

[43] T 2034, vol. 49.

[44] T 2147, vol. 55.

[45] T 2034, p. 102c3.

Emperor to carry out his translations of the Sūtras. Right away at the Daxingshan temple 大興善寺 he started his work. Imperial Attendant Lydaobao 給事李道寶, and Tanpi 曇皮 who is Prajnaruci 般若流支's son, both took on interpretation. Faxuan 法纂 of the Daxingchan temple took the role of noting down, and correcting syntax, verifying the meanings as well. Mean-while, sramana Anzong wrote the Preface."

The Sūtras translated by Vinitaruci are recorded as:

1) *The Elephant Head Monastery Sūtra,*[46] one scroll, finished by the second year of Kaihuang (590). This is the second translation of the same original sūtra as *The Gaya Peak Sūtra.*[47] Both are of the same contents; different from each other only in name.

2) *The Mahāyānavaipulyadhāraṇisūtra,* one scroll, finished by the second year of Kaihuang.

The old biographies of Chinese Buddhism of later date seems merely copying the original text from *Changfang's Record* nearly without any alteration worth mentioning. To say in brief, take Daoxuan's *Great Tang's Buddhist Biography* 大唐內典錄[48] for instance, which written in the first year of Linde (664) under the Tang, likely copies the whole original text without making any skip. Up to the 18th year of Kaiyuan Era (730), Sramana Zhisheng 智昇 wrote the *Kaiyuan's Record of Buddhism* 開元釋教錄 yet no more detail is informed. Only in its notation there is mentioned the place of translation that will be dealt with later.

---

[46] 大方廣總持經, T 275, vol. 9.

[47] 伽耶山頂經 T 465, vol. 41.

[48] T 2149, p. 275a14

For the moment, let us look for Vinitaruci native home. Our *TUTA* reports that Vinitaruci is originally from South India., whereas *Changfang's Record* has it from Udhyana, North India. Udhyana was a small kingdom Xuanchuang had dropped in, and his *Pilgrimage for the West* transliterated it as Wu-zhang-na 烏仗那. The note at the end of book 2 of the *Pilgrimage for the West* makes it known that there are many other transliterations of the word, such as Wu-chang 烏場, Wu-cha 烏茶, of the North India. The same book gives report on its people that they were very timid, yet deceitful, anxious to learn but without taking pain, magic was their specialty... They worshipped the Buddha, the Dharma, having faith in Mahāyāna... moral was transparent yet well versed in incantation of magic. Of Vinayas, there existed five Schools: a) Vianaya of Dharmagupta, 2) of Mahisasaka, 3) Kaśyapa, 4) Sarvāstivada, 5) Mahāsaṅgika.

The date of translation, the *TUTA* as we have seen has it uncertain that it is six years before the second year of Zhou's Daxiang Era, i.e., in the interval of 574 and 580, whereas *Changfang's Record* gives out not only the year but even the month, that is, in the second year of Kaihuang (590), in the second and seventh lunar months.

Concerning the translations, the *TUTA* shows lots of mistakes. *The Variety of the karma retributions* according to *Changfang's Record* is a translation of Dharmaprajña. As we are told, in the same year, the second of Kaihuang, Dharmaprajña was summoned by Sui Gaozu to do translations at the Daxingshan temple, altogether with Vinitaruci. Dharmaprajña finished his translation of *The Variety of The Karma Retributions* in the third lunar month.

On the other hand, according to *Changfang's Record,* Dharmaprajña was well-versed not only in Sanskrit but as well in Chinese, accordingly when doing his translations he did not need the mediation of an interpreter and transcriptor as in the case of Vinitaruci. The fact shows that probably no sooner than his having just arrived in China he was rightway called up to do translations, and therefore he was granted no good chance to brush up his Chinese, that means not to travel as much over China as the *Collection* states.

About the place of translation, *Changfang's Record* has it at the Daxingshan temple. According to *The Ancient Record in Brief* 釋氏稽古略 *(book 2),*[49] by the year 582 AD (the 14th the year of Taijian of the Chen 陳大建, the 21st year of Tianbao of the Liang 後梁天保, the second year of Kaihuang of the Sui), the sixth lunar month, Sui Gaozu had at the Capitol Changan the Daxing Citadel built up, had the Daxing Hall and Daxingshan temple erected. Accordingly, *Kaiyuan's Record of Buddhism* shows its disbelief of the place where Vinitaruci and Dharmaprajña performed their translations and which *Changfang's Record* situates at the Daxingshan temple. For both did translations about the earlier spring of the second year of Kaihuang, whereas the temple until the sixth lunar month came to get the imperial edict for construction. If the translation was not been carried out at the Daxingshan temple, sure enough it was at some other temple situated at Chang an, the Capitol of the Sui, because the work of translation was organized by the Emperor himself. For all that, had the translation workshop been held at the Chế chỉ temple in Guangzhou as reported by The *Collection of*

---

[49] T 2037, p. 807c5

Eminent Monks, much would be left in uncertainty.

There remains another fact. *TUTA* has it that Vinitaruci translated the *Sūtras on Dharani* at the Pháp Vân, of Long Bien city (Bac Ninh Province), under the Chu (Zhou Dynasty), by the second year of Daxiang (581), that is, before Sui Gaozu would be made emperor and one year before the Kaihung Era. The place as well as the time, therefore, were far remote from what stated in *Changfang's Record.*

Out of these facts that contradict each other, we are likely bound to believe *Changfang's record* the better if we choose to resolute *Changfang's record*'s Vinitaruci and *TUTA's* are identical. Both are of the same person. That does not matter. For few are different in the date and place of the translation, otherwise the most part of the work is identical. It may happen that the author of TUTA gleaned information about Vinitaruci from hearsay that of course has its own value but in another sense is too groundless to verify. In this aspect of hearsay it is very difficult for us to make a search into the historicity of the problematic meeting of Sengcan and Vinitaruci.

Although we are encountering the problems of historicity that presently seem unresolved, but the Thien (Zen) branch of Vinitaruci has been transmitted, believed and practiced, accordingly this actuality has made him a personage so actual that goes beyond any dispute in term of the so-called historical facts. The only mistake the *TUTA* is supposed to commit is that it does not strictly follow the method of history taken in ordinary sense, but to the Thien (Zen) school 's point of view, the work has got a very precise conception of the pedigree of transmission of the Thien school. Take for example the Vinitaruci's transmission in which the second generation is Pháp Hiển, only a person; in the third generation, there are three, one of which is unrecorded and left vacant by *TUTA*. Only one figure from the fourth generation is mentioned in succession: Master Thanh Biện 清辨. Then in procession the fifth, sixth and seventh generations are left vacant. In the eighth generation, of the three persons two are left vacant. Three of the nine generations are all left vacant...

I. Vinitaruci
II.Pháp Hiển
III.Unknown
IV.Thanh Biện
V.Unknown
VI.Unknown
VII.Unknown
VIII. 1. Định Không. 2... 3....

It is seen, when compared to the Chinese *Transmission of the Lamp,* from the fourth Patriarch Daoxin backward the transmission was carried on by only a person. But since then onward there began appearing the sub-stream getting along with the main stream of the transmission. And it is since then onward that the vacancies in a generation are paid attention, although the transmission was kept continuous. Because of such bifurcation, the orthodoxy of the Thien (Zen) school is often urged to be ascertain as regards the Masters after the fourth Patriarch but not before.

The conception of continuous transmission, just as a lamp is shining only as long as its flame does not discontinue, is the crucial point of Chinese Zen School. This conception, on one hand, coincides with Chinese mentality of preservation of the ancient.

On the other hand, for the fact that the significance of transmitting the seal of mind cannot be transmitted by means of letters, the guidance of a clear-sighted teacher is extremely important. On both sides, the conception of transmission or *transmitting the lamp* of Zen school is a combination of the Chinese tradition and the Indian signification of liberation. Vietnamese Thien School inherited this conception of transmission, the trace of which is conspicuous in the presentation of *TUTA*. In addition to it is the particularity in the way of living of its people, Thien school of Vietnam has initiated its own special practice. The combination of these two factors will be seen later.

Because the objectivity of history is not held high esteem to Thien or Zen school, the ambiguity divulged in *TUTA* does not matter. What written in the latter, however, as regards the continuous transmission of Vinitaruci's branch of Thien (Zen), proves its unique way of persistence. At first, we should search for Vinitaruci's thought. Some conjecture is but categorical to the search. But depending on a few of given factors in his biography, then comparing to the development of Vinitaruci's Thien sect, in a way of conjecturing, we are in hope of obtaining a reliable ground to look into the persistence of this Thien sect.

To begin with, we deal at first with Vinitaruci native home. If we believe much more what is given out in *Changfang's Record* than *TUTA*, it would be better to recognize him as a native of North India, in Wuzhang or Wuzhangna (Skt. Udhyana). The mentality of its people and the customs of the country, as recorded by Xuanzhang's *The Tang's Pilgrimage to the West*, in term of way of thinking, was to the most part inclining towards Mahāyāna. The institution of Sangha's living was founded on the five traditions of monastic code. Xuangzhang and Vinitaruci were separated from each other around a half century, changes if any, therefore, were not too much different from what is written in The *Pilgrimage to the West*. Accordingly, Vinitaruci has somehow early in his native home been acquainted with Mahāyāna. And if he has been ordained, his monastic life sort of observed the discipline of Early Buddhism.

The tendency of Mahāyāna is conspicuous in his two translations. Nonetheless should both these translations be considered as representatives of his thought? Because it is unknown to us whether they were brought with him from India. Or someone else brought them to the Sui Court, and his work was but translating. In the chronological table of *Changfang's Record* is a fact to be noticeable. It was in the winter of the first year of Kaihung Era (581), the delegation of Zhizhou came back home from the Western Regions, carrying along with Brahmanist Scriptures consisting of 260 volume. The Emperor had the whole carried to the Capital and translated into Chinese. Perhaps out of which the original texts of Vinitaruci's translations could be found.

Although the exact origin of these two translations is left unsettled, at present it is better to review in here their contents for the purpose of completing what till now remains conjectural to us, and drawing out a conclusion on how far Vinitaruci's thought of Thien would have been influenced to some extend by them.

a) Sūtras in the Elephant-head Monastery. The sūtras were first translated by Kumarajiva, somehow in the Era of Huangshui, 401-409, having as its title The *Sūtra on Manjusri's Questions about*

Bodhi.[50] The various names according to *Changfang's Record* are: *Sūtras on Bodhi, Sūtras on the practice of Bodhi, Sūtras on the Peak Gaya.*[51] In the interval of 508-535, Bodhiruci 菩提流支 gave another translation under the title as *The Sūtras on the Peak Gaya.*[52] Vinitaruci's is the third. The fourth, around 639-724, under the reign of Tang, is another translation of Bodhiruci 菩提流志 titled as *Mahāyāna Sūtras on the Peak Gaya.*[53] All these translations are edited in the *Taisho Shinshu Daizokyo* (Taisho in brief), vol.XIV, numbers 464-467. Looking into the numbers of re-translations, we would see the Sūtra holds an important position in the Mahāyāna Buddhism. It is classified into the group of Vaipulya-literature, which means the extension of the deepest doctrine Buddha had ever taught. Sūtras belonging to this category are lying between Mahāyāna and *Hīnayāna*. The Gaya (i.e., Elephant) mountains is the place where Buddha realized the ultimate goal of enlightenment. In its introduction the Sūtra makes it known that the time of its delivering was no longer after Sakya-Muni 's Enlightenment. The number of bhikṣu who were attending the audience was around 1,000. Now then Buddha stated the meanings of Bodhi, i.e., enlightenment, saying that "The bodhi is found in nowhere. It is neither of the past, nor the present, nor the future. All the Dharmas are śūnya (empty, void). Though there is a language for it, but it is merely nominal, unreal. It is the non-

---

[50] 文殊師利菩薩問菩提經, T 464, vol. 14.

[51] T 2034, p. 78b1: 菩提經一卷(一名文殊師利所問菩提經。一名菩提無行經。一名伽耶頂經).

[52] T 2034, p. 86a7: 伽耶頂經一卷(第二譯。與秦世羅什菩提經同本別出異名。僧朗筆受).

[53] 大乘伽耶山頂經, T 467, vol.14.

created Dharma, which is empty, signless, desireless. It is neither being nor non-being. It is unmanifestable, unspeakable, unhearable..." By the way, Mañjuśri asked the Buddha: "If Bodhi is signless, where to dwell as to accomplish it?" Buddha taught: "The Bodhisattva who dwells in the non-dwell is dwelling in Bodhi. Dwelling in non-attachment is dwelling in Bodhi. Dwelling in the Voidness is dwelling in Bodhi. Dwelling in the Dharma of non-being is dwelling in Bodhi." In going on, the son of god Pure Flame by name asked about the dharmas the Bodhisattva would realize, and Bodhisattva Mañjuśri exposed the development of the spiritual realization, from the beginning with practicing good deeds up to awakening the great mind of loving-kindness and compassion, following the twofold path that composes of Skillful means and Wisdom.

b) *The Mahāyāna sūtras on dhāranani.* It is the second translation of the kind. The first by Dharmarakṣa 竺法護 was carried out in the interval 266-315, under the title *The Sūtra on Helping the extended studies.*[54] Both are edited in the *Taisho,* vol., IX. No 274-275, classified in the group of *Sadharmapuṇḍarīka.* The contents are of the same category with the *Sūtras on Immeasurable Meanings* that introduces into the doctrine of *Sadharmapuṇḍarīka* in which Buddha decided to deliver the teachings of the Only-way (Ekayāna). The place of preaching: Rajagṛha, the Capital of Magadha Kingdom, on the Vaulture mountains, the same place as *Shadharma*'s. The time of preaching: the years before Buddha's passing away. That is, before the time of preaching

---

[54]佛說濟諸方等學經, T 274, vol. 14. Cf. T 2034, p.63a06: 濟諸方等學經一卷(或無學字。見竺道祖晉世雜錄)

Mahāparinirvāṇasūtra. It is the period of *Saddharma.* In this period, Buddha makes a synthesis to assign all his previous various teachings into the only one. This ultimate teaching surpasses that of Sravaka, Pratyekabuddha, and Bodhisattva, going beyond both *Hīnayāna* and Mahāyāna. It is named as *Dhārani,* not because of any mystic meanings, but because it embraces all the teachings of Buddha without impartial to any one particularly. Not only recognizing Mahāyāna and other yānas as orthodox, it criticizes even those who esteems high this one and disregards others. Buddha said, once upon a very remote time when he was a bhikṣu Dharma by name, he then practiced the Dharma altogether with another bhikṣu namely Suddhajīva. The latter developed the practice of dhāraṇi, without disregarding any other practice. At that time, bhikṣu Dharma practiced and preached the śūnyatā, impartial to śūnyatā. As a result, he criticized bhikṣu Suddhajīva, blaming the latter as carrying out the frivolous heretic teaching. Consequently, as he reached the Buddhahood he should emerge in this ugly world. Meanwhile bhikṣu Suddhajīva accomplished his Buddhahood in the Pure Land. After having praised the practice of Dhāraṇi, Buddha preached four aspects of this method of practicing. They are four aspects of equality: equality of Boddhisattva towards every sentient beings; equality among dharmas; equality towards Bodhi; equality in preaching. So the Sūtra contains in it an embracing synthesis, recognizing the variety of views of various tendencies as equal to each other; recognizing the variety of practice that of Pure Land included. It implies the true meanings of the term *dhāraṇi.*

As designated in the title, the present sūtra belongs to the Vaipulya literature. This literature is a link between the genuine

Mahāyāna and the developed *Hīnayāna*.

The contents of two translations issued by Vinitaruci do, if not straightforwardly, make it known to us indirectly about his Mahāyāna tendency, and accordingly the particularity of his Thien or Zen spirit.

To some extend, as the way of thinking is concern, Vinitaruci's Thien sect reveals two major points: the one is the sunyata and undwelling from *Prajnaparamita*'s system of thought; the other is the synthetical tendency of *Saddharmapuṇḍarīka*. Both in him, however, do not partially incline to either Mahāyāna or Hīnayāna. Due to this characteristic, the way of practicing in Vinitaruci's Thien sect is eager to open wide its gate to the introduction of the popular faith intermingled with mysticism. This mixed popular faith tends to accept rather than reject, though not in a way of somewhat synthesis. As a result, Vinitaruci's Thien on account of its popularity was easily making its way to the mass movements. Thiền Master Vạn Hạnh is a successful figure emerging from this religious social movements.

2. The Branch of Vô Ngôn Thông[55]

As regards the story of Vô Ngôn Thông, *TUTA* records:

"Of the Tien Du 僊遊 prefecture (Bac Ninh Province), Phu Dong 扶董 village, Kiến Sơ temple 建初寺, family Trịnh 鄭, Vô Ngôn Thông 無言通 was in his youth firstly fond of studying Confucianism and negligent in his domestic affairs, later absorbed in studying Buddhism in Song Lam (Chuanglin) Temple 雙林寺 at

---

[55] Cf. Lê Mạnh Thát, op.cit. p.191.

Quảng Châu (Guangzhou). His personality is profoundly calm, talking less but remembering much, easily getting through whatsoever matter. For that reason he was called Vô Ngôn Thông by the contemporary. That means "understanding without a word." This name is recorded in the *Transmission of the Lamp* with a slight alteration: Bất Ngữ Thông 不語通, with the same meaning.

"One day, as he was just going out after a religious service, some Thien monk came to pay a visit and asked:

"-What did you bow down before?

" - I bowed down before the Buddha. He replied.

"The guest pointed to the Buddha image and asked:

" - What's that?

"He was unable to offer an answer. That night, neatly dressed, he approached the guest monk. And having paid homage to the latter, he asked:

" - I haven't grasped as yet the meanings of what you had uttered.

" - Since you have left home till now, how many rainy seasons did pass? Asked the guest.

" - For ten rainy seasons. He replied.

" - Does that mean you have really left home?

"Instantly he fell into bewilderment.

" - If you don't understand it, what's the use of it? The guest monk gave out a remark. He then made the Master going in company with him to present themselves to Mazu 馬祖. As he reached Jianxi 江西, Mazu had already passed away. So they went to Baizhang Huaihai 百丈懷海. At the moment they arrived, a monk were asking Baizhang:

"- What is the method of abrupt enlightenment?

"- Had the ground of mind become empty, the sun of wisdom would naturally shine. Replied Baizhang.

"The Master was awakened at these words. He later went back to Guangzhou, resided at the Hean temple 和安寺.

"- Are you a Thiền Master?" He was asked by someone.

"- I have never learned anything like Thien."

"For a moment, he called the man again. The monk responded 'Yes!' The Master pointed to the bolt. The man did not reply.

"Zen Master Yangshan 仰山 still being a mere novice was once asked by him:

"- Lo, Ji (i.e., Huiji 慧寂, religious nickname of Yangshan)! Bring the bed to here for me.

"Huiji brought it to him. The Master then ordered:

"- Put it back where it was as before.

"Huiji carried out the injunction. He then asked again:

"- What is there in the opposite side?

" - Nothing. Was the reply.

" - What is there in this side?

" - Nothing.

"- Lo, Ji! So called he again.

"- Yes! was his reply.

"- Go away! Thus he instructed.

"By the fifteenth year of Yuanhe Era (810) of the Tang, he arrived at this temple (Kiến sơ temple), settled down his Thien (zen) staff there. Besides taking meals, he enjoyed nothing but the taste of meditation. Whenever he sat down, he always faced the wall, without a word. Nobody knew a thing about him for years. Only a monk in the temple whose religious name was Cảm Thành 感誠 witnessed the scene and showed him the most respect, waiting on him. Gradually the latter in the silence came to knock open the door into the wonderful secret, getting through the essentials. One day, without being ill, after taking a bath and changing clothes, he sent for Cảm Thành and told the latter:

"- Once upon that time when my Patriarch Nam Nhac Hoai Nhuong 南嶽懷讓 (Nanyue Huairang) was passing away, he left the saying that all the dharmas are brought forth from the mind. If the mind is brought forth nowhere, dharmas will get no dwelling. If the ground of mind is gained, the dwelling is unobstructed. If you don't meet the noble man, don't be rash to divulge it.

"After having finished saying thus, he folded hands and passed away. Cảm Thành held cremation, gathered relics, and erected a stupa to worship on the Tien du mountains."

The story cited above contains lots of fact that are supposed to be extracted from *The Transmission of the Lamp*, (book 9), in the anecdote of Zen Master Tong (Thông thiền sư)[56], successor of Baizhang Huaihai. In this record no mention is made to the

---

[56] T 2076, p. 268a28 ff: 廣州和安寺通禪師.

conditions under which Vô Ngôn Thông was enlightened. The condition related by *Thien Uyen Tap Anh* is found in another anecdote from the story of Baizhang Huaihai in *The Transmission of the Lamp* (boo 6).[57] A certain monk asked Baizhang what is the method of abrupt enlightenment of Hināyāna.

To this Baizhang replied:

"You must at first exhaust all conditions, stop everything. Don't keep in mind, think of all dharmas, the good and the bad, the worldly and the out-worldly. Set free, give up your mind and body so that they would get along at ease. Your mind should be similar to wood and stone. There is nothing in it to discriminate. Had the ground of mind have been vacant, the sun of wisdom would shine in a natural way. Just as clouds are dispersed and the sun appears."

Finally, the original of Nanyue Huairang's saying Vô Ngôn Thông quoted to Cảm Thành is found in the story of Huairang as recorded by *The Transmission of the Lamp*, book 5.[58]

No anecdote of the history of Zen in China is found to record much more details than the *Transmission of the Lamp* concerning the story of Vô Ngôn Thông. Due to this missing, nothing is learned towards the end of his life. Therefore, the date he came to Vietnam as reported by *TUTA* cannot be ascertained. Only the *Collection of Finger and the Moon* gives out in addition a statement to the end of the story. Nonetheless not only no new detail is added, it contains even lots of skipping and errors in transcription. In a way of reading one may be lead to the idea that Vô Ngôn

---

[57] ibid., p. 249b26 ff.
[58] ibid., p. 240c7 ff.

Thông eventually died of being poisoned. The information is of course groundless, and meaningless. *The Collection of Finger and the Moon* 指月錄[59] means simply, and exactly, to say that in the pedigree of Vô Ngôn Thông no orthodox transmission is recognized, but there is only an unorthodox transmission to Yangshan. Probably Yangshan was ordained as novice under Vô Ngôn Thông but later he was enlightened under Weishan Lingyou 潙山靈祐 and then he founded the Zen branch known as Weiyang sect 潙仰宗. His sect is not found having successor in Vietnam.

Another history of Zen titled as *The Store of the Universal Light* 大光明藏 written by Baotan 寶曇 under the Tong Dynasty.[60] Besides the story of Vô Ngôn Thông, the work pronounces an a eulogy on Vô Ngôn Thông to the end of the latter's story. The eulogy runs: "The ancients, from men of sharp intelligence and high wisdom to the simpleton, all are alike in general. Their ways of searching for the Truth do not seem to match each other, but their practical use is the same. Take for instance Buyutong (Bất Ngữ Thông 不語通) onwards, up to The Masters like Daan, they themselves went out from Baizhang's furnace, being forged into unalloyed gold without a bit of ore. But that merely aims at meeting with conditions in an instant. One should inspect their energy as they are set antagonistic towards each other, as the sharp and the blunt touch each other. Who other than brothers dare to have a touch in a rash?"

In this way, in China Zen Master Thong or Tong was not

---

[59] T 1578, p. 520b18 ff.
[60] T 695a9.

identified as Vô Ngôn Thông. But only Buyutong or Bất Ngữ Thông was recognized. Then, since when did the name Vô Ngôn Thông appear? In our present conditions no searching for it could easily be carried out.

The fact he from Guangzhou came to Vietnam can be inferred from another instance. It is the case of Jizang 吉藏, founder of Sanron school 三論宗. According to *Biographies of Eminent Monks*, in his youth Jizang very often frequented the regions of Jiao and Guang, i.e., Jiaozhou (Giao chau) and Guangzhou. A conclusion can be drawn from this account is that under the reign of Tang Jiaozhou or Guangzhou to some extent were the ground of intellectual activities. Therefore, that Vô Ngôn Thông in the first place resided at the Hean temple of Guang zhou and later then arrived at Vietnam is believable.

When comparing the story of Vô Ngôn Thông to Vinitaruci's we find out a similarity. Both came to Vietnam before Chinese Zen school started branching off. Chinese Zen after Sengcan, since the fourth Patriarch Daoxin 道信 onwards, was divided into two lines. The main line was flowing down to Huangren 弘忍 then to Huineng 慧能. The second was down to Farung 法融 in the name of Niutou Zen 牛頭禪. Niutou is the name of a mountain where Farung resided. This second line, according to *Transmission of the Lamp*, was handed down to six generations. Bodhidharma also has by-successors, of which three are mentioned.[61] The second Patriarch, Huike 慧可, besides Sengcan considered as principal successor, have also 17 others. Concerning Sengcan's, *The*

---

61 景德傳燈錄卷第三: 菩提達磨旁出三人.

Transmission of the Lamp dealt with Daoxin as the only principal successor. Little is known about in what occasion the transmission to Vinitaruci was carried out.

From Nanyue Huairang onwards, the transmission was going on down to Mazu, and then to Baizhang; from Baizhng downwards to Weishan Lingyou; from Lingyou down to Yangshan Huiji and by the latter the Weiyang Zen sect was founded. Another line from Baizhang was carried down to Linji Yixuan 臨濟義玄, and since then the Linji (Rinzai) sect was founded.

That Vô Ngôn Thông as we were told is Baizhang's successor in the pedigree of Chinese Zen is credible. But that Vinitaruci himself belongs to this lineage as well remains uncertain. For much is left to farther research, and what recorded in *TUTA* seems to be gleaned from hearsay though not so necessarily groundless that we would like to take it for pseudograph. Anyway, if we believe *TUTA* has its own justified intention when it puts both two founders of Thien or Zen school in Vietnam into a position somewhat loose against the China soil that is very often considered to be its origin. The intention is clear enough as to represent a lineage in this country independent of China. But the transmission of the seal of mind is similar to the continuation of a lamp, therefore the tradition of Zen does not allow to place them outside the continuous transmission from Lord Buddha and the first Patriarch Kaśypa downwards. If Thien or Zen is to be taken in a broader sense that refers it to the tendency of meditation, apart the other tendency devoted in studying the doctrine, then, *TUTA*'s effort of legitimizing the Vietnamese lineage of Zen transmission is willingly accepted.

In our historical research into Vinitaruci, we know though incompletely some outline on his natural endowments, altogether with other details in his living, his native home as well as what he had realized in the field of thought. As regards his counterpart, Vô Ngôn Thông, in the pedigree of Chinese Zen, is counted among the disciples of Huairang. This lineage later brought forth the Linji sect, well known in the history of Chinese Zen for its literature works. Scions of Vô Ngôn Thông were carrying with them something of the like. The most part of them hold a high esteemed position in the history of Vietnamese literature. The figures very often mentioned among them are Viên Chiếu, Thông Biện, Cứu Chỉ, Ngộ Ấn, Mãn Giác, and many others. In contrast to this, in the lineage of Vinitaruci emerged the monks of mysticist tendency blended with magical belief that to some extent held a significance in the movements of populace.

Consequently, though being in short and vulnerable to dubiousness, the givens we have got from the founders before the Ly have offered us a rather embracing sight into both branches of Thien (Zen). Their truthfulness is reliable.

III. ACTIVITIES OF THIỀN MASTERS

Based on what was recorded by *TUTA,* from beginning downwards to Vạn Hạnh generation, we can have a list of the successors of two sects as follows:

Vinitaruci branch. This branch diffused since the Sui up to the end of the Tang. Because of the long course of four centuries, successors in this branch was rather large. Among them, however, only nine are related in *TUTA.*

Tì-ni-đa-lưu-chi   (Vinitaruci, ? 594)
Pháp Hiển   (- 626)
Thanh Biện   (- 686)
La Quý   (- 936)
Pháp Thuận   (915 – 991)
Ma Ha   (- 1029)
Thiền Ông   (- 979)
Vạn Hạnh   (- 1025)

Vô Ngôn Thông branch. Because of its being found only until the 11th century, the list of successors in this branch is comparatively short.

- Cảm Thành   (- 860)
- Thiện Hội   (- 900)
- Vân Phong   (- 956)
- Khuông Việt   (- 1011)

Of the successors belonging either sect listed above, as regards their activities, three from the Vinitaruci's and one from the Vô Ngôn Thông's are deserved to be studied. As regards Vạn Hạnh, a special study should be carried out.

Now, to begin with, let's read into *TUTA* to have a look at the monks we are interested in.

The Story of Thiền / Zen Master Định Không 定空 （730-808） [62]

Thiền Master Định Không, of the Chúng Thiện Temple 眾善寺, Dịch Bảng village 驛牓鄉, Thien Duc 天德 prefecture, was born in Cổ Chau 古洲, into a family of Nguyễn 阮, a rich powerful

---

[62] Cf. Lê Mạnh Thát, op.cit. p. 281.

descendant. He was good at telling the destiny of the world. His deeds were all in conformity with regulations. Villagers respected him and addressed him as Elder. In his old age, he studied Buddhism in the Long Tuyền 龍泉 congregation at Nam Dương 南陽 g. On hearing the preaching, he grasped the essentials. Henceforth, he inclined toward the teaching of Sakya.

In the Era of Jingyuan (784-805) of the Tang, he had the Quỳnh Lâm Temple 瓊林寺 built in the native village. As starting to lay the foundation, the workers unexpectedly exhumed an incense burner and ten inverted bells. He had them brought to water to wash. One of them sank to the bottom. He deciphered: "Ten items (十 口) refers to the character cổ 古 (ancient). Sinking down to the water (水 去) refers to the character pháp 法. Earth is the ground on which we live. Everything are brought forth from the earth." On account of this event, he proposed to change the name of the village as *Cổ Pháp*. Its former name was Diên Uẩn 延蘊. He then composed a stanza:

地 呈 法 器
一 品 精 銅
致 佛 法 以 興 隆
立 鄉 名 古 法

Earth presents the Dharma instruments.
An artifact is made of refined copper.
In order to develop the Teaching of Buddha,
The village is given the name Cổ Pháp.

He then uttered some divinations:

To the door of Buddha appear ten copper bells;

King Lý Hưng has got success in three artifacts.

An item was sinking down to the ground;

Henceforth the village has been renamed as Cổ Pháp.

Cock was singing to the crescent moon. It is later the omen for the development of Buddhism.

On the deathbed, he gave the last instruction to his disciple Thông Thiện 通善, saying:

"I was anxious to have enlarged the village, only I have had a fear that in the interval of time a disaster will take place. (Later, in fact, Cao Biền 高駢 of the Tang came and incanted some suppression against the country). After my passing away, you must protect well this Dharma. If you meet a person of the Đinh 丁 family, then hand it over to him. In doing so, you are supposed to successfully carry out my will."

On these words he took leave forever, at the age of 79. It is in the third year of Yuanhe Era (808) of the Tang. Thông Thiện built up a stupa to the west of Lục Tổ Temple 六祖寺 wherein he inscribed Định Không's last will.

The Story of Thiền Master La Quy 羅貴 (852-936)[63]

Elder La Quy, of the Song Lâm Temple 雙林寺, Phù Ninh 扶寧 village, Thiên Đức 天德 prefecture, had been, in his youth, setting foot to the outworld, paying visit lots of Thiền Masters all over the country. Years passed, yet he remained unenlightened. So he was likely frustrated at his approaching the Dharma. Later, on hearing a saying in the congregation of Thông Thiện, suddenly the ground

---

[63] op.cit. p. 283.

of mind opened, hence he did his best to serve the master.

At the moment Thông Thiện was laying on his deathbed, he told La Quý:

"In former days, my teacher once told me: 'You have to protect well my Dharma. Hand it over to nobody but the man of Dinh 丁 family.' The word now comes true in deed; for you are the man. Now I'm going to pass away."

Having attained the Path, he propagated it according to favorable conditions, chose the ground to build temples, and whatsoever he had ever said later turned out to be augury. At the Lục tổ temple, he had the statue of the Sixth Patriarch Huineng cast of gold. Later for fear of its being stolen away, he hid it underground before the front gate of the temple, and left word with his disciples, saying: "Exhume it up if you live under brilliant monarch. Hide it away if it is the reign of a fatuous and self-indulgent ruler."

As he was about to pass away, he told his disciple Thiền Ông:

"Formerly, Cao Biền had the citadel built up by the Tô Lịch 蘇歷 River. Seeing our Cổ Pháp conceal the royal atmosphere, he tried to suppress it by discontinuing the sweet stream, to exorcise it by digging ponds and lakes in about 19 places. Now that I have examined and restored the places that had been not in good order. I then planted at the Châu Minh Temple 珠明寺 a cotton tree to keep the spot that had been cut off. For I know a king of prosperity will appear to support our True Law. After my passing away, you should by skilful means build up a large stupa to conceal the True Law in it, letting nobody see."

On finishing these words he passed away. He was 85 then.

In addition, in the third year of Qiangtai Era (936) of the Tang, while planting the cotton tree, he composed a stanza:

大 山 龍 頭 起
虯 尾 隱 珠 明
十 八 子 定 成
棉 樹 現 龍 形
兔 雞 臘 月 內
定 見 日 出 清

The dragonhead rises on the grand mountain;
The dragon tail keeps hidden at the Châu Minh temple.
The eighteen seeds are destined to fully grow,
When the cotton tree takes form of a dragon.
On the month of rabbit and cock,
The sun will rise sure.
The Story of Thiền Master Pháp Thuận 法順 *(592-990)*[64]

Thiền Master Pháp Thuận, of the Cổ Sơn Temple 鼓山寺, Thừ 蜍 village, Ải 隘 prefecture. His native home is unknown. His family name is Đỗ 杜. Learned, well versed in composing poems, endowed with the talent to assist the monarch, he had got a thorough understanding of the contemporary problems. Being ordained in his childhood, he was a pupil of, and waiting upon, Long Thọ Phù Trì as his master. After his acquiring the knowledge of the Dharma, what he uttered out turned out to be oracles.

When the Lý Dynasty got the start of its foundation, in drawing up plans, devising stratagem, he showed to be a capable assistant. When the country was at peace, he refused honors and rewards.

---

[64] op.cit. p. 284.

Therefore, Lê Đại Hành doubled his respect toward him.

He took responsibility for royal documents and correspondence for the king.

In the seventh year of Thiên Phúc Era (942), the Song's subject Nguyễn Giác 阮覺 was delegated to Vietnam on a mission of friendly relations between two nations, the king made Pháp Thuận changing clothes in disguise of a steersman with purpose of watching Giác's moves.

Now that at the sight of a couple of swans swimming over the river, Giác recited for fun two lines he himself composed through improvisation:

鵝鵝兩鵝鵝
仰面向天家

Swan and swan, a couple of swans
Are raising their head upward to the corner of heaven.

Pháp Thuận was, while one hand punting the boat, immediately joined reciting two lines he also composed through improvisation:

白毛鋪綠水
紅棹罷清波

Their white feather are displaying on the green water,
Their talons are rowing against the blue waves.

Giác appreciated him highly.

Once being asked by the king about the national stability, he replied in a poem:

國祚如藤絡

南天裏泰平
無為居殿閣
處處息刀兵

The throne of the kingdom is like the twine of wisteria;
Peace will reign on the South Heaven.
Royal noninterference will reside the palace.
War will not be found all over the country.

In the second year of Hưng thống (991), he took leave forever, at the age of 76. He had written a liturgical book namely *Bồ tát hiệu sám hối văn*, names of Bodhisattve for repentance.

Thiền Master Khuông Việt 匡越 (930-1011)[65]

Thiền Master Khuông Việt, belonging to the fourth generation in the line of Vô Ngôn Thông, of the Phật Đà Temple 佛陀寺, Cát Lợi 吉利 village, prefecture Thường Lạc, was born into the Ngô 吳 family of the Cát Lợi village, descendant of Emperor Ngô Thuận 吳 順帝. He was a man of stalwart build, free in behavior. In his childhood he made his study in Confucianism. As growing up, he inclined to Buddhism. Together with his fellow students he received the full ordination under Master Vân Phong 雲風, at the Khai Quốc Temple 開國寺. Since then, he devoted himself to studying Buddhism, reading Buddhist Scriptures, searching into the essentials of Thiền (Zen Buddhism). At the age of forty, his name had been well known to the Royal Court. Emperor Đinh Tiên 丁先皇帝 summoned him to the Court to have an audience, and appointed him as the Sangha President.

---

[65] op.cit., p. 200.

In the second year of Thái Bình Era (791), the king offered him the title of Khuông Việt Thái sư 匡越太師, "The Grand Master who assists Vietnam."

Emperor Lê Đại Hành paid respect to him ever more. To whatsoever matter of the Court, military as well as political, he was asked for giving his advice.

At a time when he was making a tour for sightseeing, attracted by the stillness and beauty of the landscape, he took it in mind to build up in here a cottage. At night he dreamed a deity in golden armor, with a golden spear in right hand, a small pagoda in left hand, approached him and told him:

"I am God King Vaiśravana. My retinue is yakṣas as a whole. His Majesty of gods sends me to this country as its guardian, protecting its boundaries with purpose of flourishing Buddhism. Because of our predestined relations, I come to make your acquaintance."

The Master then woke up with a start, hearing the shout echoing from the mountains. He took it weird. At daybreak, he went into the mountain, and found out a huge tree, about thirty five meters high, luxuriant with branches and wigs, shaded with auspicious clouds above. He henceforth had workers felled it down, and according to what he had seen in dream he had a statue sculpted to worship.

In the first year of Thiên Phúc Era (980), the Tống (Song) invaded the country. Having heard the account in details of what had taken place, the king ordered to hold a service to pray for a victory. Invaders all of a sudden got started, withdrew and laid camp at Chi giang 支江. Here again they had to meet with so violent wind as if dragons and snakes were up-heaving, so they fled in panic.

In the seventh year, Nguyễn Giác of the Tống (Sóng) came ơn a mission of peaceful relations. At that time Dharma Master Đỗ Thuận had got equal great reputation. Đỗ Thuận and he were ordered by the king to disguise as a river watcher to welcome the Chinese envoy.

Giác appreciated the Master as being well-versed in literature. So the former composed a poem dedicating to him, in which a line is read as follows:

天外有天應遠照

It should shine farther to the other sky beyond the (Chinese) sky.

The king showed this line to the master. He explained:

"That means the envoy honors Your Majesty the same as his Lord."

When Giác was on the point of being back home, the Master composed a poem after the tune of "Seeing off Wanglang" to see him off. The poem runs as follows:

祥光風好錦帆張
神僊復帝鄉
千重萬里涉滄浪
九天歸路長
人情慘切最離觴
攀戀使星郎
願將深意為南邦
分明報我皇

The sail is going to spread against propitious winds, under the auspicious light.
The noble one is returning his homeland.
He will cross the deep blue, some ten thousand miles away.
The way back home is as far as the highest heavens.
Human feelings are deadly heartbreaking as they are facing over the cup of bidding farewell.
I feel attached to him, the envoy, reluctant to be away.
Hope he would bring the profound meaning,
For the sake of the southern boundary,
Give a brilliant report to His Majesty.

As he grew older, he took leave to return to his native home, on the Du hí 遊戲 mountains. There he built a temple and settled down. Students of Buddhism came in crowds.

One day, Đa Bảo 多寶, disciple of his confidence, asked:

"From beginning to end, how does the search for truth proceed?"

"There is nothing from beginning to end. It is as marvelous as empty space." If the Suchness were understood, the essence would be seen identical." He replied.

"What is the responsibility to uphold it?"

"No room to show your hand." was the reply.

"Do you finish talking?"

"What do you understand?"

Đa Bảo shouted.

On the 15th, second year of the Thuận thiên Era (1011), the Lý

Dynasty, on his deathbed, he instructed the disciples:

木中元有火
有火火還生
若謂本無火
鑽燧何由萌

Fire is inherent in wood.
There fire exists, so fire takes place.
If you say there is no fire inherent in wood;
How does fire appear as you rub wood?

After finishing the stanza, he passed away in position of crossed-legs; at the age of 52. Some say 79.

IV. CONCLUSION

Before drawing out from the biographies as cited above a possible conclusion, it is recommendable to review their reliability in term of history.

1. Master Định Không died in 808, at the age of 79, accordingly his birth can be in 730. At that time Vô Ngôn Thông had not arrived yet. The former belongs to the eighth generation of Tì-ni-đa-lưu-chi line. Its fourth generation according to TUTA is Thanh Biện who died in 686. From then up to Định Không, as is seen, only three generations are mentioned, yet the time was lasting over a century and a haft. As a result, each generation owned its existence at least fifty years. The figure is likely, but not reliably, to be accurate. The chronology of TUTA remains incomprehensible to us, and it is not easy to justify its truthfulness.

2. Định Không studied Thiền/Zen under Long Tuyền Nam Dương 龍泉南陽. The latter can be the locality where Zen Master

Nam Dương Tuệ Trung 南陽慧中 (Nanyang Huichung). Tuệ Trung (Huichung) is the sixth generation in the transmission of Ngưu Đầu (Niutou), a subsect branching out of the fourth patriarch Đạo Tín 道信 (Daoxin). Tuệ Trung was flourishing around 683-769. Its biographies as recorded by *The Transmission of the Lamp* (book 3) and *The General Record of Buddha and Patriarchs* (book 13). Nowhere in these records were found as an assembly of Dharma-talk of Tuệ Trung. Nevertheless, both Nam dương (Nanyang) and Long tuyển (Longxuan) are the names of place in China. Among the Chinese contemporaries of Định Không, no one was found residing at Long tuyển but Tuệ Trung at Nam dương.

3. Cổ Pháp originally was a prefecture. The name has been known since the pre-Lê. Under the Đinh, it was named as Cổ Lãm. Nevertheless, TUTA ascertained that the name was assigned by Định Không. The possible suggestion is that previously it was a nickname of the village Diên Uẩn acknowledged only among villagers, until under the Lê it came to be used as an official name of the prefecture. Diên Uẩn or Cổ Pháp is the native home of Lý Công Uẩn, founder of the Lý Dynasty. The official history records Diên uẩn located in the prefecture Cổ Pháp, having no hint of Cổ Pháp as a name of the village.

4. It is not clear whom the three terms *Lý hưng vương* 李興王 (the flourishing king of the Ly) in the biography of Định Không refer to. In the story of La Qúy, *hưng vương* is also related, but there it could be taken not as a person name, rather denoting a flourishing noble. Accordingly, it could be a reference to Lý Công Uẩn who would be flourishing in the time to come.

5. As regards the oracles disclosed on the bark of the cotton tree at the Châu Minh Temple previously planted by La Quý, something of the kind can be read in the *Đại Việt sử ký toàn thư* 大越史記全書 (The Complete History of Dai Viet). The latter is said spreading in the year of Thái Bình the fifth (974), under the reign of Emperor Đinh Tiên. Its prediction relates the fall of the Đinh House, sucessfully the pre-Lê House, and then the rise of Lý.

6. The story of Khuông Việt records the fact that his prayers were successful in repelling the invasion of the Song army commanded by Hầu Nhân Bảo 侯仁保 in the first year of Thiên Phuc. Something of the kind relating to the two gods of Long nhãn is also found in the legend of *Lĩnh Nam trích quái* 嶺南摭怪. The same legend is related also in *Việt điện u linh tập* 越甸幽靈集, in which, however, the background of events was in the time of Nam Tấn cương, of the Ngô House. Probably it was a very popular legend spreading orally among people to the extent it turned out to be inconsistent.

Generally speaking, the data given by TUTA can only be considered as unofficial ones, the legends narrated among the people. Nevertheless, they harbour a great value in term of history, giving us factual traditions among them, the relations of Thiền Masters with people of the time and their role as well.

The first to be noticed is the then public opinion about Cao Biền's making the canal Thien Uy and constructing the citadel Dai La. In the *Đại Việt sử ký toàn thư*, the work of Cao Bien was officially admired as heavenly, supernatural, done with the assistance of gods. Ngô Sĩ Liên, a royal historian, gave his comments without hesitation: "How strange was Cao Biền's construction of the canal!

It is on account of its conformity to reason that it was aided by the Heaven. The Heaven is but the reason..." The work, which the official historian valued as godly, was not given in the least any admiration by TUTA, rather being considered as the undermining one, and Cao Biền was but a brigand. Accordingly, Bao Biển had not left any good impression to the people, if not the horrible one, which TUTA wanted not to tell in details. In the eyes of the people, what Cao Biển had been doing were aimed at a sole purpose, the long lasting dominance of the North. Therefore, TUTA disclosed the evil performance of Cao Biển in the constructions of canal and citadel as the way of exorcism intending to destroy the auspices of independence prosperity of Vietnam. To this point, to some extent, TUTA has related the social and political movements that generated the consciousness of self-sovereignty of Vietnam heralding a new phase in the history of Vietnam.

EMPEROR TRẦN NHÂN TÔNG'S MONASTIC LIFE

BY PROF. **LÊ MẠNH THÁT**

As various attempts to keep peace and improve the people's living in the postwar period were proceeding, the Emperor Nhân Tông decided to hand over the imperial throne to his son Trần Anh Tông in the third month of Quý Tỵ (1293). In the year that followed, i.e., the seventh month of Giáp Ngọ (1294), on an excursion in the Vũ Lâm Valley he made up his mind to be ordained a Buddhist monk. The Complete History of Đại Việt says, "The Emperor-Father then was going on a cruise in a cave in Vũ Lâm. The mouth of the cave was narrow and he was seated in a small boat. The Queen-Mother Tuyên Từ, who was sitting at the rear of the boat, told Văn Túc Vương to move to the bow and had only an oarsman employed. Later, when the Emperor-Father was about to leave [the citadel] for his ordination, he summoned Văn Túc to the Dưỡng Đức House in the Thánh Từ Palace to take part in a feast of seafood...”[1]

Thus, the Emperor's ordination was formally held in the year Giáp Ngọ (1294). In the Imperial Condensed History of Đại Việt, however, it is dated the sixth month of Ất Mùi (1295), that is, after his fighting expedition to Laos: "After his return from Laos, the Emperor-Father was ordained at the Vũ Lâm Palace but then went back to the Capital."[2] In so recording, the work definitely connotes that the Emperor would not have taken any more military actions after his ordination. As it will be seen below, however, even when he already became a monk, Nhân Tông went on to have activities for the sake of the country. And he was, too, often consulted by imperial officials for crucial decisions of the court. Before his arrival in Champa as a messenger, for instance, Đoàn Nhữ Hài is said to have waited nearly a day to meet with Nhân Tông at the Sùng Nghiêm temple on Mount Chí Linh. Accordingly, the fact that the Emperor was ordained on Mount Vũ Lâm certainly took place in 1294, as in the words of the Complete History of Đại Việt.

Vũ Lâm is a beautiful valley in what is now Ninh Bình Province.[3] On the east is the Ngô Đồng River, and on the other sides are limestone mountains. There remains today a shrine named Thái Vi built by the Emperor Nhân Tông's order for worshiping his grandfather the Emperor Thái Tông, his father the Emperor Thánh Tông, and his mother the Queen Hiếu Từ, which may be precisely recognized in terms of inscriptions on the three stone tablets preserved inside the shrine.

---

[1] Vol. 6, p. 2b2-4.

[2] Khâm Định Việt Sử Thông Giám Cương Mục, vol. 8, p.23b1

[3] Ninh Hải village of Hoa Lư district. [LMT]

The first tablet titled Tu Tạo Thái Vi Cung Thần Từ Thạch Bi (Stone Tablet [Recording] the Restoration of the Thái Vi Sacred Shrine) and engraved on the 10th of the third month of Vĩnh Thịnh the Tenth (1715) was erected by the villagers, their chiefs, and local functionaries of the two villages Trung and Cật of Ô Lâm when the shrine was in time of repair. The tablet runs, "In the autumn, the eighth month, of Giáp Ngọ (1715), having seen the magnificently precious shrine handed down by the preceding reign to be in such badly ruined condition, [the local inhabitants] made a decision to restore it (...)

The Thái Vi Precious Shrine,
An ancient relic from the days
Of sacred ancestors in the Trần dynasty,
Who were, for generations, interested in Dhyāna,
Keeping the nation's security,
Protecting the people..."

The second tablet of the same title records the merits of those who contributed to the restoration of the shrine. It was erected six months later of the same year and by the same people. These two tablets are engraved on the front and back only. But the third is engraved on its four sides, the three sides of which record merits and the other titled Tu Lý Thái Vi Điện Bi Ký (Stone Inscription of the Restoration of the Thái Vi Shrine) records the date of construction of the shrine, that is, the years between 1273 and 1278 of Era name Bảo Phù of the Trần house, and those of its restorations in the years of Quang Hưng, Kỷ Sửu (1598), and of Bảo Đại, Bính Dần (1926). This tablet was engraved in the latter restoration.

From the inscription dated Bảo Đại, Bính Dần it is known that the shrine was built in the year Bảo Phù. That is to say, before mounting the throne in the 10th month of Bảo Phù, Mậu Dần (1278) the Emperor Nhân Tông had learned of Vũ Lâm. Then, in the war of 1278 when he was commanding the South Army to halt T'o-huan's troops from the north and So-tu's troops from the south, he might have chosen that valley to be his headquarters where he could hold swift and urgent conferences with prominent generals Trần Quốc Tuấn, Trần Quang Khải, and so on. Being situated in the midst of Hoa Lư, Vũ Lâm was naturally a remarkably strategic position. Further, the landscape there has a fantastically attractive beauty as is described in one of his poems:

The splendid bridge is horizontally reflected on the stream,
Beyond which comes the ray from the sun in the evening sky.
Quietly in the endless mountains red leaves are falling;
Like in a dream are the wet clouds and the bell from afar.

Tuệ Trung and the Emperor Nhân Tông

Thus, Vũ Lâm was definitely chosen by the Emperor to be the place where his ordination would take place. Yet we do not know how the ordination was held and by whom it was ritually conducted. From the Recorded Sayings as the Lamps of the Saints, however, it is known that Nhân Tông was "capable of penetrating into the essentials of Dhyāna doctrine under Tuệ Trung Thượng Sỹ. Therefore, he treated the latter as his master." Accordingly, he who transmitted the mind-seal to him was none other than Tuệ Trung Thượng Sỹ, who had formerly liberated the capital Thăng Long from the Yuan occupation in the war of 1285 and had ostensibly negotiated with the enemy at the base of Vạn Kiếp in our army's plan of counteroffensives in the war of 1288.

As has been said before, the Emperor Nhân Tông received an education of various branches of his time and, according to his family's tradition, came in contact with the Buddhist teachings very early in his life. In spite of this, he professed in a poem that he did not so early experience Buddhism profoundly:

Form-Emptiness was incomprehensible for me at such an early age.
Spring came and my mind was among a variety of flowers.
Now that I have realized the 'face' of Spring,
From the meditation seat I can contemplate falling flowers.

On Tuệ Trung Thượng Sỹ's death, the Emperor Nhân Tông himself composed a biography of his master and, simultaneously, his uncle, in which he accounted for his experience of enlightenment:

Formerly, when I was going into mourning at my Queen-Mother Nguyên Thánh's death, I once visited Tuệ Trung Thượng Sỹ and was given two records of Hsüeh-tou and Yeh-hsüan. Rather doubtful of his secular way of living, I pretended to ask him, "How is it possible for those who have had the habit of eating meat and drinking wine not to be exerted by the effect of such unwholesome actions?" "Suppose somebody who does not know the king to be passing by his back has thrown something at him, would he be frightened in that case? Should the king get angry with him? [Certainly it does not matter anything at all] because the two facts have nothing to do with each other," he explained. Then, he read two stanzas to express it:

All saṃskāras[4] are impermanent.
Faults proceed from doubt alone.
Nothing has arisen so far;
Neither seeds nor sprouts are.

And again,

In our everyday perception of all things,
They arise just from our mind.
Both things and mind have not truly existed.
Nowhere is no-pāramitā.[5]

Whereby I could comprehend his implications, so asking, "Though it is so, how should we act as faults and merits have been definitely distinguished [in the sūtras]?" He went on with his instruction in another stanza:

Eating grass and eating meat,
That depends on beings' consciousness.
All kinds of grass grow when spring comes.
What may be called faults and merits?

"If so, what is the use of observing Brahmacarya[6] strictly?" I asked. He smiled without saying. At my repeated question, he read two more stanzas:

Observing precepts and cultivating patience,

---

[4] Skt.; referring to both the activity of forming and the state of being formed. Here it is used in the latter meaning (saṃskṛta), that is, all things that arise upon dependent conditions.

[5] Skt.; the other side (of the ocean of birth-and-death), denoting the ultimate liberation in Buddhism.

[6] Skt.; holy conduct, referring to what constitutes the noble lifestyle of a Buddhist practitioner.

That is to gain no merits but faults.

To realize merits and faults are all of śūnyatā,[7]

Do not observe precepts nor cultivate patience.

And again,

Like a man who is climbing a tree,

Thus seeking for danger from safety;

If not climbing the tree,

Why must he be concerned with moon and wind?

Then he instructed me secretly, "Do not tell those who are not

worthy."

Such was the Emperor Nhân Tông's process of studying and realizing the Buddhist teachings under Tuệ Trung Trần Quốc Tung. From his account we know that the two records he was given are named Hsüeh-tou yü-lu and Yeh-hsüan yü-lu respectively. TheRecord of Yeh-hsüan is lost now; even his name is not found in any Ch'an books of China except for a poem of his collected in theCh'an-tsung sung-ku lien-chou-tung.[8] In this connection, he could probably live in the years 900-1050. As far as the other record is concerned, its author, Ch'an Master Hsüeh-tou, is Ming-chiao Ch'ung-hsien (980-1052), who lived on Mount Yehtou in Ningchou. He was a disciple of Chih-men Kuang-tsu of the Yün-men lineage of Ch'an in China. His record, namely, Hsüeh-tou Ming-chiao yü-lu, has been popularly in vogue.

---

[7] A Buddhist term of various meanings. Here it means the state of being without self-nature. As being things that proceed from dependent conditions, merit and fault are conventionally considered to be existing. Yet, nothing within them may in essence be truly 'merit' or 'fault'.

[8] Selection 1, p.128c5-6 (256a5-6).

According to the Recorded Sayings as the Lamps of the Saints, it was ever taught many times in the meditation halls of Vietnam after the Emperor Nhân Tông's time.

Still from the account cited above we can now determine the date the Emperor Nhân Tông attained enlightenment, that is, the spring of Đinh Hợi (1287) when our country was preparing for the third invasion of the Yuan court and when the Emperor-Queen Nguyên Thánh Thiên Cảm departed. At his mother's death, the Emperor himself invited his mother's brother Tuệ Trung Thượng Sỹ Trần Quốc Tung to attend her funeral. And it was on this occasion that he got awakened under Tuệ Trung Thượng Sỹ as in the words of the dialogue above. Also from this dialogue we may acquire some knowledge of the doctrinal basis on which his thought was formed, which was later formulated by himself in a long verse titled "A Worldly Life with Joy in the Way," and further developed to be a guiding principle of the development of Buddhism in Vietnam for nearly 400 years at least, i.e., from 1300 to 1695. This is the period when Buddhism was introduced and practiced just in the midst of worldly life; otherwise stated, there were then no distinctions between monastic and lay devotees. They lived together at peace, and at times both ways of living could manifest themselves within one and the same practitioner, which is typified by Hương Chân Pháp Tính (1470-1550?), Thọ Tiên Diễn Khánh (1550-1610?) and Minh Châu Hương Hải (1628-1715). They had all passed national examinations, worked as imperial officials, and undertaken various national affairs before they became Buddhist monks, as what is expressed by Pháp Tính in the following lines:

In the prime of youth I ever passed national examinations;

Now in my old age I decide to tread on the Buddha's path.

It should be borne in mind that the doctrinal basis mentioned above must not be neglected in any research in the teachings of the Trúc Lâm school founded by the Emperor Nhân Tông. For, though he had been ordained Buddhist monk in the seventh month, the Emperor actually commanded an army to attack Laos in the eighth month of the same year as in the words of the Complete History of Đại Việt: "In the 8th month [of Giáp Ngọ, 1294] the Emperor-Father himself marched an army into Laos, capturing alive numerous people and animals. In this campaign the spearhead General Trung Thành Vương (name unknown) was once besieged by Laotian troops. Shortly thereafter, Phạm Ngũ Lão launched a sudden thrust to break the ring and then attack them. Being defeated, they dedicated a golden tally to Ngũ Lão."[9]

Receiving the mission of Li-hsin and Chiao T'ai-teng

By the first of the fifth month of the year that followed, the Emperor Nhân Tông received a Chinese mission headed by Li-hsin and Chiao T'ai-teng. They had left China in the sixth month of Chih Yuan the 13th (1294), i.e., a month after Yüan Ch'eng-tsu's enthronement, and reached our country in the second month of the following year. At their departure, Chang Po-shun is said to have warned them of some difficulties in this mission: "Why is it said to be difficult? Formerly it was widely known that a decree once delivered to that country (Đại Việt) always represented our sovereignty, implying some favor or misfortune brought about for them. If they showed anxiety in receiving it, it meant they would

---

[9] Vol.6, p.3a1-3.

obey it easily. Otherwise, our task was simply to return and report everything to the court for their own solution. Now, it may be somewhat difficult for you to have to cover thousands of miles to persuade them to reform their country only with the help of an ordinary letter. Remember that you are not assigned to go and return without anything achieved. It is natural that when one is aware of one's innocence after so much anxiety, one will be extremely satisfied. But satisfaction is normally the very cause of pride and contempt. So, take advantage of their pride to persuade them to follow the new way [of reform]."

Obviously, the Chinese mission's difficulty was in that behind the Yuan kings' requests remained no compelling forces, which might be conducive to some contempt from the Đại Việt's side. Nevertheless, Nhân Tông treated them in an unexpectedly polite manner, offering them a very formal reception, which was probably the most pleasant of his after he had been successful in smashing their plot of invasion as expressed in his poem at their departure:

By the deep pool is a farewell feast warmly held.
The wind of Spring cannot hinder their departure.
No one knows for how long the two 'stars'[10] of fortune
Would be able to shine in the sky of Đại Việt.

Simultaneously with the Chinese mission's departure, Trần Khắc Dụng and Phạm Thảo, by the Emperor's order, went to the Yuan court with his letter of applying for the Chinese Buddhist Canon.

---

[10] Referring to the messengers. In Chinese literature, a messenger is sometimes respectfully called 'messenger-star'.

The letter, which was signed by Nhân Tông himself, is extant in the An-nan Chih-lüeh[11] where it is further mentioned that his application was approved of by the Yuan court. Thus, this may be the edition of the Buddhist Canon that Nhân Tông's work Thạch Thất Mỵ Ngữ (Words in Sleep in the Stone Chamber) was later added to by Trần Anh Tông's order as in the words of the Recorded Sayings as the Lamps of the Saints.

By the sixth month of the same year (1295), "the Emperor-Father returned to the Capital from the Vũ Lâm Palace where he had been ordained Buddhist monk," as is recorded in the Complete History of Đại Việt.[12] The fact that the Emperor was ordained in Vũ Lâm, therefore, might take place in approximately the seventh month of Giáp Ngọ (1294), that is, more than a year after his transferring the throne to his son. In the Section "The Emperor-Father's Return from Laos in the Summer, the 6th Month, of Ất Mùi (1295)" of the Imperial Condensed History of Đại Việt, it is said that "after his return from Laos, the Emperor-Father was ordained Buddhist monk at the Vũ Lâm Palace; but soon he went back to the Capital."[13] Thus, according to the Office of Historiographers of the Nguyễn dynasty it was not until the summer of Ất Mùi that Nhân Tông's ordination was held.

Concerning his ordination, however, the Complete History of Đại Việt, in an account of the Emperor's excursion in Vũ Lâm in the autumn[14] of Giáp Ngọ (1294) and his determination to become

---

[11] Vol.6, p.80.

[12] Vol.6, p.3a7-8

[13] Vol.8, p.23a7

[14] the seventh month.

a monk there, mentions his affectionate attitude toward Thái Sư[15] Trần Quang Khải's son, Trần Đạo Tải:[16]

The Emperor-Father then was going on a cruise in a cave in Vũ Lâm. The mouth of the cave was narrow, so he was seated in a small boat. The Queen-Mother Tuyên Từ, who was sitting at the rear, told Văn Túc Vương to move to the bow and had only one oarsman employed...When the Emperor-Father was about to leave [the Citadel] for ordination, he summoned Đạo Tải to the Dưỡng Đức House in the Thánh Từ Palace for a feast of seafood. There he wrote the poem:

The deliciously red skinned "qui cước,"[17]
And the sweet-smelling yellow "mã yên"[18] when toasted.
The mountain-monk with precepts purely observed
Sat at the same table but ate not the same food.

The similar fact was, too, written down in Hồ Nguyên Trừng's Record of Nam Ông's Dreams. According to the style of these two accounts, it is evident that the poem cited above is doubtlessly composed by Nhân Tông. On the other hand, the third line "The mountain-monk with precepts purely observed" points out explicitly that the poem might not be written by Trần Đạo Tải. For, from his great respect for the Emperor Nhân Tông and his determination to give up traveling in a chariot upon learning that the Emperor always went on foot ever since his ordination, it is obvious that Trần Đạo Tải hardly dared to mention the Emperor

---

[15] The chief of the imperial tutors

[16] Vol. 6, p.2b4-6

[17] lit. "turtle legs", a dish of seafood.

[18] lit. "horse saddles", a dish of seafood.

Nhân Tông in terms of mountain-monk. Thus, no one other than Nhân Tông could call himself mountain-monk, particularly when his peculiar interest in mountain and forest was frequently expressed in many of his verses.

Though his ordination in Vũ Lâm has been so definitely recorded, the Recorded Sayings as the Lamps of the Saints says that Nhân Tông could have been ordained "in the 10th month of Kỷ Hợi, i.e., Hưng Long the Seventh, when [the Emperor-Father] moved to Mount Yên Tử, diligently cultivating the Twelve Ascetic Practices,[19] calling himself Great Ascetic Hương Vân, having the Chi Để Temple built where so many students as 'clouds' gathered to study the Buddhist teaching expounded by him." It seems most likely that from the 6th month of Ất Mùi (1295) to the eighth month of Kỷ Hợi (1299) the Emperor might settle in Vũ Lâm since nothing in relation to his activities, monastic and secular, in this period is mentioned in the extant historical documents. This, too, may be the period when the Emperor is said in the Recorded Sayings as the Lamps of the Saints to have been training himself through the Twelve Ascetic Practices. In the poem "The Vân Yên Temple" by Lý Tải Đạo, who then was Dhyāna Master Huyền Quang and living with the Emperor on Mount Yên Tử, described the daily living of the Great Ascetic Hương Vân as follows,

Wearing kṣāya,[20] sitting behind the paper-curtain,

---

[19] Skt., dhuta; lit. "shake off" (passions). Twelve such ascetic pratices are wearing patched robe, wearing a robe made of three pieces, eating begged food only, only one meal a day, taking no further food, taking only one portion, living in seclusion, living in a charnel ground, living under a tree, living in the open, living in whatever place presents itself, sitting only.

[20] Skt.; a monk's robe.

Not concerned with stores full of pearls and cases full of jades;
Forgetting delicious food, giving up sweet wine, Only a pot of egg-
fruit and a jar of soy left.

This is truly an unimaginably simple lifestyle of a hero, a talented emperor who just gained a glorious victory over the invaders. According to the Complete History of Đại Việt,[21] not until the fifth month of Kỷ Hợi did Nhân Tông return from Thiên Trường to Thăng Long where, seeing the Emperor Anh Tông to be drunk, he gave orders for all the Court to move to Thiên Trường. After getting sober again, the Emperor Anh Tông told Đoàn Nhữ Hài to write a memorial of apology, with which the former personally came and saw the Emperor-Father Nhân Tông in Thiên Trường to ask his pardon. Still in the words of the Complete History of Đại Việt, by his order a temple named Ngự Dược was built on Mount Yên Tử; and "in the 8th month, the Emperor-Father left Thiên Trường Prefecture again for Mount Yên Tử where he went on with his ascetic practice."[22] Thus, it was by the eighth but not the 10th month as recorded in the Recorded Sayings as the Lamps of the Saints that Nhân Tông returned to his monastic life.

What then were Nhân Tông's activities after his ordination? The Recorded Sayings as the Lamps of the Saintssays: "At the Phổ Minh Temple in Thiên Trường Prefecture the Emperor-Father had eminent monks invited and large halls built for preaching Buddhist teachings for many years. Thereafter, having wandered everywhere, he arrived at Camp Bố Chính, staying at the Tri Kiến Temple." In reality, according to the Complete History of Đại

---

[21] Vol.6, p.6a1-b9.
[22] Vol.6, p.7a6-7.

Việt,[23] it was in the period of Nhân Tông's practice of asceticism on Mount Yên Tử that the Emperor Anh Tông together with Trần Quốc Tuấn once paid a visit to him. Later, in the third month of Tân Sửu (1301) Nhân Tông went preaching as far as Champa and did not come back until the 11th month of the same year. Then, still in the words of the Complete History of Đại Việt, on the 15th of the first month of Quý Mão (1303), "while staying in Thiên Trường Prefecture, the Emperor-Father had a Dharma-assembly held at the Phổ Minh Temple, preaching Buddhist teachings, transmitting precepts, donating gold, silver, money and silk to the poor in the country."[24]

All these accounts indicate that after his return to Mount Yên Tử, Nhân Tông could have settled there for some time. By the third month of Tân Sửu (1301), he went to the south and stayed at the Tri Kiến temple in Camp Bố Chính. According to the Latest Record of Ô District, Tri Kiến is the administrative office of Camp Bố Chính: "Tri Kiến is the site of the old district."[25] Therefore, the Tri Kiến Temple is probably the temple of the Tri Kiến District of Camp Bố Chính. It may be said that this is the first temple to have been known so far in the areas named Địa Lý, Ma Linh and Bố Chính, which were annexed to Đại Việt by the Emperor Lý Thánh Tông in 1069. Today they pertain to Quảng Bình Province and the two districts Vĩnh Linh and Gio Linh of Quảng Trị Province, where many other temples unknown today must have been built.

---

[23] Vol.6, pp.7a7-8a2.

[24] Vol.6, p.17a9b2.

[25] Viet., Ô Châu C?n L?c, vol.3, p.45a5: "? ? ? ? ? ?", which may be translated as "Tri Ki?n is the old district of Ki?n" in which Ki?n may be the local name of Tri Ki?n.

Nhân Tông's Journey to Champa

It was from Camp Bố Chính that the Emperor set out to Champa. In Ch'ên Kuang-chih's prefactory characters to the painting Chu-lin ta-shih chu-shan-t'u, it seems that his journey could be that of a missionary and he had been welcomed as such by the Cham king: "Sometimes, to teach Buddhism to the neighboring states he wandered as far as Champa where he often went on begging rounds in the Inner City. Learning of this, the king respectfully offered him vegetarian food, had ships and other ritual objects prepared for his return home. On his departure, the king personally saw him off. Further, the king conceded him the two districts, which are Thuận District and Hóa District today."

Through the diplomatic relation between Đại Việt and Champa in the period when Nhân Tông was ruling the country, we may be assured that the King Chế Mân of Champa must have learned of and had some good feeling for him. For, as has been said before, when the Yuan-Cham war took place in 1283, the Emperor Nhân Tông sent 20,000 men and 500 warships to Champa as reinforcements. Though it is natural that his reinforcement then was aimed at ensuring a long peace for the people of Đại Việt, our troops actually devoted their lives to the Cham people's victory over Yuan invaders. It was their devotion to the peaceful relationship between Champa and Đại Việt that caused the Cham king to have such great respect and admiration for the leader of Đại Việt.

Factually, the Complete History of Đại Việt[26] tells us that before

---

[26] Vol.6, pp.17b7-18b4.

his mission to Champa, Đoàn Nhữ Hài went to consult the Emperor Nhân Tông at the Sùng Nghiêm temple on Mount Chí Linh. Though having to wait for him there all day, Đoàn Nhữ Hài could after all meet with the Emperor just in his excursion, and spoke with him for more than two hours. After their talk, the Emperor said to his followers, "It is naturally reasonable for the Court to employ such a competent man as Nhữ Hài." This fact points out that though he had not been on the throne, Nhân Tông actually concerned himself with the relationship between our country and Champa.

According to the Complete History of Đại Việt,[27] in the third month of Giáp Thìn (1304) a Cham monk well versed in yoga, whose peculiar habit was to have milk for daily food, arrived in our country. Still in the words of the Complete History of Đại Việt,[28] in the second month of Ất Tỵ (1305) "Champa ordered Chế Bồ Đài together with more than a hundred men to come to our country, offering gold, silver, rare things for the purpose of asking for the date of marriage [between their king and our country's princess]. Though the marriage was mostly protested by the Court, it was eventually passed owing to Văn Túc Vương Đạo Tải's proposal for negotiation and Trần Khắc Chung's approval."

In the sixth month of Bính Ngọ (1306), still in the words of the Complete History of Đại Việt, "Princess Huyền Trân was married to Chế Mân, the Cham king. For, formerly in his journey to Champa the Emperor-Father had promised to do so. Most of the intellectuals inside and outside the Court, who relied on an old

---

[27] Vol.6, p.19b1.
[28] Vol.6, p.20a3-6.

story as to the Han king's Chao-chün being married to Hsiung-nu, wrote verses in the national speech to laugh over [this incident]."[29] In the spring, the first month, of the year that followed, "Đoàn Nhữ Hài was ordered to rule the people of the two districts Ô and Lý, which then were renamed Thuận and Hóa respectively. Formerly, when the Cham king Chế Mân conceded these districts as a proposal of marriage, the inhabitants of the villages La Thủy, Tác Hồng and Đà Bồng protested his concession. For that reason, [our] king ordered Nhữ Hài to go there to proclaim the Court's policy, according to which local inhabitants would be selected to be officials and land would be allotted without any tax collected for three years for the purpose of allaying them," as recorded in the Complete History of Đại Việt.[30]

In the fifth month of Đinh Mùi, Chế Mân died. In the ninth month, Huyền Trân's son, Chế Đa Da, ordered the messenger Bảo Lộc to offer white elephants to our Court, probably for the purpose of requesting our Court to receive Princess Huyền Trân back to our country. For "it is customary in Champa that when a king dies, his wife has to be cremated alive together with him." Therefore, by the 10th month, Trần Khắc Chung and Đặng Văn went to Champa to receive Princess Huyền Trân and her son. The Complete History of Đại Việt says, "On the pretext of attending the Cham king's funeral service, Trần Khắc Chung came and suggested that 'if the princess is cremated at the same time [with the king], no one will be in charge of his funeral service. The best way, therefore, is to have the ceremony for evoking the king's soul held at the seashore.

---

[29] Vol.6, p.21a8b1.
[30] Vol.6, p.22a7-b2.

After the ceremony the princess will come back onto the cremation together with his soul.' The Chams agreed to his suggestion. [When arriving at the seashore, however,] Khắc Chung managed to flee with the princess in a small ship, on which they coupled with each other for a rather long time before returning to the capital."[31]

In the words of the Complete History of Đại Việt: "On the 18th of the 8th month of Giáp Thân (1308) Princess Huyền Trân returned from Champa. By the Emperor-Father's order, the chief of Hóa District led three hundred Chams back to their country by ship."[32] Accordingly, it took nearly one year for Trần Khắc Chung to take Princess Huyền Trân back to Đại Việt. And not more than three months before his death, the Emperor Nhân Tông went on with his care about the issues of Champa. Today, we cannot know who then was appointed the chief of Hóa District and why 300 Chams had to be returned to their country. Was it likely that they were those who had followed the princess to the seashore for the rites of evoking their king's soul? Whatever happened, the Emperor was eventually able to see his beloved daughter again. Though a slender princess, she had effectively fulfilled the mission of annexing the two districts Ô and Lý to the map of Đại Việt, which later became a well-known area named Thuận Hóa and the imperial capital of a unified Vietnam for a long time.

Geographically, Ô District was the region called Ô Mã by the Chams, which had been reported by So-tu in his 1283 invasion to

---

[31] Vol.6, pp.32a7-33a2.
[32] Vol.6, p.33b3-4.

be the area "bordering Annan," as recorded in the Yuan Shih 209.[33] And Lý District, i.e., the area of Việt Lý, was the place where So-tu had passed on their way of attacking Camp Bố Chính and Hoan Ái of Đại Việt. It was due to So-tu's Army rushing from the south that the Emperor Nhân Tông and his father had commanded the South Army to fight against them and had finally put down their attack, in which So-tu's head was cut off and nearly 10,000 Yuan men were captured alive.

Thus, Ô and Lý were a strategically decisive position with respect to the security of Đại Việt. Just in the early years of war, the Emperor Nhân Tông, from the view of such a gifted militarist as him, thought of some control of these two districts to make possible the safety of Đại Việt. It was doubtlessly from such a view that a series of measures was put into action, including the decision of marrying Princess Huyền Trân, the only daughter of the Emperor, to the Cham king Chế Mân. As a consequence, the annexation of the districts Ô and Lý to Đại Việt was peacefully accomplished, in quite a different manner from the Emperor Lý Thánh Tông's in his annexation of the three districts Địa Lý, Ma Linh and Bố Chính more than 200 years earlier. In order to gain these districts, the latter had then forced the Cham king Chế Củ to surrender them in return for his own life. But, not so the former. Thanks to his ingenious policy, the Cham king Chế Mân had a Vietnamese wife and his wife further bore him a son. Indeed, the Emperor Nhân Tông's peaceful diplomatic policy actually brought about unexpectedly great achievements in politics and security of Đại Việt. Accordingly, we become aware that the advance to the

---

[33] p. 9b.

south by the Vietnamese in the past took place so increasingly swiftly as a tide was rising violently. Less than 100 years after Ô and Lý had been turned into Thuận District and Hóa District respectively, the southern borderland of Đại Việt was extended with Thăng Hóa and Tư Nghĩa by Hồ Quý Lý. And about half a century after that, the Emperor Lê Thánh Tông succeeded in having boundary posts erected on Mount Đá Bia in Phú Yên Province. Hence, it may be said that the annexation of the two districts Ô and Lý in such a peaceful manner laid a foundation for the extension of the border of the Fatherland—a great contribution by the Emperor Nhân Tông to the country, which will be forever remembered with gratitude by all the Vietnamese.

Thus, even in his last days the Emperor Nhân Tông proceeded to pay his special attention to Champa. This attention alone, however, did not hinder him thoroughly from other national affairs. According to the Recorded Sayings as the Lamps of the Saints, in Giáp Thìn (1304) the Emperor "wandered through villages, teaching the people to practice the Ten Good Things[34] and give up superstitious beliefs." The fact that the Ten Good Things were introduced to the people reflected evidently the political view of Buddhism in Vietnam, which had been formulated and collected in the Collected Teachings of the Six Pāramitās more than a 1,000 years before. It may be said that it is the most ancient Buddhist text known in our country, in which Buddhist thought and national tradition have been successfully mixed. Since its propagation, the

---

[34] Refraining from (1) killing, (2) stealing, (3) sexual misconduct, (4) lying, (5) slander, (6) coarse speech, (7) frivolous chatter, (8) greed, (9) hatred, (10) false views.

text has unceasingly called for the leaders of the nation to apply the Ten Good Things as the basis of "national law" and "national policy".[35] And the Emperor Nhân Tông was the first seen to respond to this appeal.

In the winter of the same year, "Anh Tông submitted a memorial to the Emperor-Father, applying for the latter's transmission of Bodhisattva mind-precepts. As the Emperor-Father was about to enter the citadel, the officials held a ceremony for welcoming him. They were all exhorted to undertake the precepts, too." Thus, the entire imperial court of Đại Việt determined to lead a living in accordance with the Buddha's teachings. The transmission of Bodhisattva mind-precepts to the Court demonstrated so obviously the thought of "Worldly Life with Joy in the Way" that the Emperor Nhân Tông had inherited directly from his father, Vô Nhị Thượng Nhân Trần Thánh Tông, and his master, Tuệ Trung Thượng Sỹ Trần Quốc Tung.

Just before the Emperor Anh Tông's undertaking Boddhisattva precepts, the imperial court of Đại Việt might have been a Buddhistic court and all the people the Buddhist followers. For, in a mission of his in 1293 Ch'en-fu composed the verse "An-nan chi-shih" written down in the Collected Poems of Ch'en Kang-chung,[36] where it is known that the court of the Trần House, "in spite of many temples built, did not hold anniversaries for the departed. Instead, they held only the ceremonies of offering to the Buddha very respectfully," and "the people were for the most part Buddhist monks." Still in the words of Ch'en-fu, even Trần Hưng Đạo "was

---

[35] Viet. "quʔc pháp" and "quʔc chính" [LMT]
[36] Vol.2, pp.24a3-37b2.

so interested in Buddhism that he named the district Vạn Kiếp[37]." Further, Buddhist thought was expressed in a poem of Đinh Củng Viên, composed in his seeing Ch'en-fu off. The poem, which was written down in the Collected Poems of Ch'en Kang-chung,[38] has been recorded neither in the most ancient books of our country nor in the collections of poetry and prose under the Lý and Trần dynasties. It therefore is now published for the purpose of supplementing the literary heritage of Lý and Trần dynasties in general and of Đinh Củng Viên in particular:

The "messenger-star" flies down together with a "good cloud,"
Without fear of the perilous way through nine heavens.
The two sleeves can sweep away the bad climate of the South Sea.
A single shout can break the lower level of Dhyāna.
Though young but able to surpass Chung-chün,
And precede Liu-che in eloquent controversy.
On return to the Court, remember to report
That the people of this remote place always wish the king longevity.

According to the Recorded Sayings as the Lamps of the Saints, after the rites of transmitting Bodhisattva-precepts to the Emperor Anh Tông and his subjects in the winter of Giáp Thìn (1304), "the Emperor-Father settled at the Sùng Nghiêm temple on Mount Chí Linh, expounding the Buddhist teaching." In effect, it was not by the end of Giáp Thìn that the Emperor began to settle at the Sùng Nghiêm temple. In the words of the Complete History of Đại Việt[39]

---

[37] lit. the "Ten Thousand World Ages," implying the eternal existence of the land.

[38] Vol. 2, p.27b3-6.

[39] Vol.6, p.17b8-9.

he had lived there from the year Tân Mão (1303) when Đoàn Nhữ Hài came to consult him before a mission to Champa. The date recorded above by the Recorded Sayings as the Lamps of the Saints might probably be set forth to lay some stress on the fact that the propagation of Buddhist teachings had been actually performed by the emperor just at that point of time.

Indeed, after so dating the Recorded Sayings as the Lamps of the Saints devotes more than six pages to Nhân Tông's discourses at the Sùng Nghiêm temple:

In the beginning of his discourse at the hall, the Emperor-Father mounted the platform, burning incense to show gratitude [to the Buddhas and the Patriarchs]. Thereafter, the head monk struck a board to invite him to the seat. The Emperor-Father said, "On behalf of a great deed Buddha Śākyamuni appeared in the world. For forty-nine years he moved his lips but not a word was ever spoken. As to me, present here in this seat in front of you all, what may I say?" He sat down for a moment on the dhyāna-bed, then saying,

The cuckoos are singing away in the bright moonlight;
Let not the spring pass so idly.

With a slap given [on the bed], he said, "Nothing at all; go out! go out!"

Of the discourse above only a passage is cited here to show partly how its procedure and content started and proceeded. We may be sure that in each of the beginning of the discourse, which is termed "opening the hall"[40] in the original text, there must have been an announcement for all the students to attend. When they were all present, the Dharma-Master mounted the platform, burned incense for showing gratitude to the Buddhas and Patriarchs, and went to the seat. There, the organizer and conductor of the assembly, who is called the "head monk"[41] in the Recorded Sayings as the Lamps of the Saints, struck a board as the signal for beginning the discourse and invited the master to start preaching.

In accordance with Dhyāna tradition, the Emperor Nhân Tông's opening words at the discourse by the end of winter in Giáp Thìn (1304) were to remind the audience of the fact that the World-Honored One spoke nothing in his forty-nine years' preaching on earth. Then, he concluded that even an Enlightened One could not say anything about the ultimate truth, much less anyone like him. It was after those opening words that he could sit down on the dhyāna-bed and began his discourse with an exhortation that everyone should not let time pass at leisure, just like what the World-Honored One had exhorted his immediate disciples before his parinirvāṇa: "Vayadhammā samkhārā appamādena sampādethāti" (All composed things are impermanent; strive on with diligence.) Thereafter, his preaching turned into a Dhyāna dialogue of master-and-student. It may be said that such dialogues have represented a particular feature of the preaching of Buddhist teachings in Vietnam in the old days. A student raised the questions to which the master would accordingly give his answers. It may be said that this was the first discourse recorded in full in the history of

---

[40] Viet., "khai du?ng."
[41] Viet., "thu?ng th?".

Buddhism in Vietnam that could provide us with an example of the activity of preaching Buddhism in our country in the 13th century, if not earlier. An intensive study of it may help us acquire some rather proper knowledge of the activity just mentioned. There were at least three students who had posed their questions in the discourse just cited. And the following is the dialogue between the first student and the Emperor Nhân Tông:

The monk asked, "What is Buddha?"

The master said, "Understanding as before is not possible."

The monk asked, "What is Dharma?"

The master said, "Understanding as before is not possible."

The monk asked, "What does it mean after all?"

The master said,

The 'eight words'[42] have all been openly spoken;
Nothing left for me to demonstrate to you.

The monk asked, "What is Saṃgha?"

The master said, "Understanding as before is not possible."

The monk asked, "What does it mean after all?"

The master said,

The 'eight words' have all been openly spoken;
Nothing left for me to demonstrate to you.

The monk asked: "What is the task that helps go upwards?"

---

[42] Referring to the essentials of the Dhyana doctrine.

The master said: "Keeping the stick up to tease the sun and the moon."

The monk asked: "What is the use of setting forth an old 'công án'[43]?"

The master said: "Once repeated, once renewed."

The monk asked: "What is the meaning of 'the special transmission outside the teaching'?"

The master said: "The frog fails to leap out of the peck."

The monk asked: "What about leaping out but then submerging?"

The master said: "That depends on the length of its jumping in mud or sand."

The monk asked: "What about failing to leap out?"

The master said: "What does that blind man see?"

The monk said: "What are you playing tricks for, master?"

The master uttered a sigh. The monk stood thinking. The master hit him. He was about to pose another question when the master shouted. So did the monk.

"What then do you mean when shouting at me again and again?" asked the master.

---

[43] Chinese, kung-an; Japanese, koan. In Dhyana teaching and practice, the term usually refers to a phrase from a text or teaching on Dhyana realization, an episode from the life of an ancient master, a question-answer—whatever the source, each points to the nature of ultimate reality, which transcends the logical or conceptual ability. Thus, a công án cannot be solved by reason but by some level of intuitive comprehension only.

The monk thought over it. The master shouted again, "Where is the cunning fox that has just come?"

The monk bowed and went out.

A full translation of the dialogue is produced here to present partly the style and content of Nhân Tông's discourse at the Sùng Nghiêm temple by the end of winter in Giáp Thìn (1304). Its theme explicitly deals with the three precious ones, i.e., Buddha, Dharma, saṃgha, the way of enlightenment, and the 'transmission outside the orthodox teaching'. And just in the style of Dhyāna teaching, the answers appear by no means to correspond with the student's questions, which are to be grasped by the people involved only. That is because the language of Dhyāna has its own characteristics, requiring that the listener has to possess some level of knowledge, some resolution of penetrating into the matter in question in a certain way. Though making use of the same words as the everyday language, its structure is quite different from the latter.

According to the Thiền Uyển Tập Anh (Collected Prominent Figures of Dhyāna Garden), the dialogues in such a pattern came into existence in the time of Master Pháp Hiền (? - 626) and remarkably popular in the time of Master Viên Chiếu (999–1090) when the latter composed the Tham Đồ Hiển Quyết, which has been completely preserved so far. The work consists in analyzing the 'công án' for the practitioners of Dhyāna to grasp their meaning. For instance, the Collected Prominent Figures of Dhyāna Garden records one of the first phrases like this:

"What is the meaning of Buddhas and [Confucian] sages?" asked a monk.

"The chrysanthemum blooms under the hedgerow in the autumn; the bird sings on the branch early in the spring," the master said.

From the question-answer above, it may be interpreted that the relation between Buddhism and Confucianism is likened to that of a chrysanthemum, which blooms in September, and the bird singing in the early spring. That is to say, Buddhism and Confucianism have their respective tasks that are to be implemented according to their own circumstances.

The language of Dhyāna, therefore, has its own semantic structure that can only be comprehended and grasped by the people involved. This structure is at times interpreted as a device to awaken and give rise to some potential capacity of getting enlightened inherent in each being. The language of Dhyāna, however, is not always confined within its semantic or grammatical structure. In effect, it often goes beyond the verbal language to embrace even such bodily actions as gazing, shouting, striking, etc., that is, the body language. In the above-cited dialogue the language of the latter type is known to have been applied by Nhân Tông when he shouted and struck the monk. Today, we cannot know how many people could comprehend his teaching and how many people got truly awakened through his instruction in the discourse just mentioned. Yet, the point is that they were after all capable of gaining some understanding of Buddhist teachings.

Here a question may be raised as to whether such a way of preaching may be influenced by that from China. Naturally, as a cultural movement Dhyāna, or Ch'an(-na) as transliterated in Chinese, has inevitably absorbed various factors during its development. For that reason, even in the history of its development in China, Dhyāna has really undergone some changes through the ages. This is evidently proved by the dialogues of Hui-neng and I-hsuan recorded in the Ching-te ch'uan-teng-lu (Record of the Transmission of the Lamp in the Ching-te Period). In the time of Hui-neng, a Dhyāna discourse in the form of question-answer is usually rather comprehensible; that is to say, a reply is to be found in exact accordance with the meaning conveyed in the question. It has, however, become quite a different style in I-hsuan's time, when shouting and striking began to make their appearance in the language of Dhyāna.

In Vietnam, Dhyāna has developed in quite a different course. It came into being to set forth some solution to a problem of thought; that is, "why cannot the Buddha be seen during one's practice of his teaching?", which was put up in the middle of the fifth century C.E.[44] Factually, it is for answering that question that Dhyāna of Vietnam made its way. Thus, together with the appearance of Dhyāna a new concept was produced in Vietnam with regard to the Buddha. Not only is the Buddha conceived as a historical one or a certain being outside of us but he further becomes 'something' inseparable from our nature. In this connection, to practice the Buddha's teaching is to make possible the manifestation of this 'Buddha' within ourselves. From such a starting-point, Dhyāna of Vietnam has inevitably been exerted by some impact of concrete requirements of Vietnam. If in the course of its development, Dhyāna of Vietnam is found to have had some similar or even

---

[44] Lê Mạnh Thát, Lịch Sử Phật Giáo Việt Nam I, NXB Thuận Hóa, 1999, pp.574-578. [LMT]

identical features with the other traditions of Dhyāna, they should be regarded as an utterly natural demonstration of the same universality and humanitarianism of a particular tradition of Buddhism in the Far East.

The just-cited preaching of Dhyāna at the Sùng Nghiêm temple by the end of Giáp Thìn may in some measure supply us with a view of Buddhist activities of our people as well as of the Emperor Nhân Tông himself. Besides, the True Record of the Three Patriarchs, a record composed by Tính Quảng and Ngô Thì Nhiệm and based upon historical documents of the Trần dynasty, gives us another discourse by the Emperor. It was held at the Kỳ Lân Hall on the ninth of the leap first month of Bính Ngọ (1306) and recounted by the True Record of the Three Patriarchs as follows:

On the ninth of the leap first month of Bính Ngọ, the Most Venerable Trúc Lâm came to the Kỳ Lân Hall to open the preaching. Pointing at the Dharma-seat, he said, "This is the cane bed, the precious Seat of Golden Lion; yet, it is impossible to determine the words of the Buddhas and the Patriarchs in such a narrow seat." Then, burning incense, he uttered his prayer:

"This incense, which can produce sweet-scented smoke and pleasant atmosphere, is composed of the five attributes of the Dharma-kāya and offered marvelously to the ten directions. May the heat arising from the incensory grant fortune to the ten directions, consecrate the nine temples, prolong the king's life and consolidate the heavenly throne!

"This incense, which is pure at the root and born from a precious seed, is grown up not by tending but by understanding. May the heat arising from the incensory bring about favorable weather, make the country at peace and the people at ease, the Buddha-sun increasingly bright and the wheel of Dharma constant in motion!

"This incense, which does not become cooked when toasted nor fire when burned nor open when knocked nor move when pulled, can split the brain into two if smelled and exhaust the pupil if looked at. May the heat from the incensory be dedicated to the Superior Man Vô Nhị and the Great Man Tuệ Trung, whose 'Dharma-rains' have permeated through subsequent generations!

Thereafter, the Emperor-Father walked to the seat. When he was seated, the head monk struck the board, inviting him to preach. He said, "Venerables, if our presentation is centered on the transcendental truth, we would go wrong when forming a certain idea and false when opening our mouths. In such a case, how should we grasp the truth? How should we master meditation? Is it then possible to base our presentation on the conventional truth?"

Then taking a glance from right to left, he said, "Is it true that no one in the very place has a sufficiently big eye? If he does, not even a hair of his eyebrows is lost. If not, I, a poor monk, find it hard to avoid from moving my mouth and uttering wasteful nonsense. Today, in virtue of you, let me draw out some mixed and blended part. Listen! Listen!

"Look, the Great Way is devoid of anything, neither tying nor binding. The original nature is transparent, neither good nor evil. Due to picking and choosing, numerous ways emerge; owing to a shadow of delusion, everything becomes greatly set apart. Saints and fools are of the same path; no distinction can be found between right and wrong. Remember that faults and merits originally do not exist, that cause and effect are devoid of essence.

From the very beginning, nothing is lacking within everybody, all is inherent in everybody. Just like form and shadow, Buddha-nature and Dharma-nature occasionally appear and disappear, neither being attached to nor detached from each other. Obviously, just on the face the nostrils turn down and the eyebrows cross above the eyes; yet it is not easy for you to get an insight into it.

"Thus, seek for the Way that can by no means be sought. Concentrated in only one 'inch of intestines'[45] are the 3,000 Dharma-gates. And from just the source of mind are numerous marvelous functions. What is called the threefold gate of precept, meditation and wisdom is not lacking within yourselves.

"Dharma is nature; Buddha is mind. Not any nature is no Dharma. Not any mind is no Buddha. Mind is Buddha, mind is Dharma; Dharma is essentially no Dharma. Dharma is mind, mind is essentially no mind; mind is Buddha.

"Venerables, time passes so fast, human life is not stable. Eating gruel and eating vegetables, why do you understand nothing about the bowls, the spoons, the chopsticks?"

The opening passage of the discourse delivered by Nhân Tông at the Kỳ Lân Hall is here translated in full to make up what is left unwritten down in an account of the Recorded Sayings as the Lamps of the Saints concerning the same discourse at the Sùng Nghiêm temple. In the latter account, Nhân Tông is recorded to "have mounted the platform, burning incense to show gratitude [to the Buddhas and the Patriarchs]. Thereafter, the head monk struck a board to invite him to the seat..." but nothing is mentioned as to

---

[45] denoting a practictioner's heart or mind.

how he burned incense. From the passage just translated, we are aware of how his ritual conducts of burning incense were performed and what meaning his actions conveyed.

Further, another reason for the passage above to be cited here is to prove that the prologue in his preaching at the Kỳ Lân Hall has quite an identical content with that at the Sùng Nghiêm temple. However long and of rather different words, the former mainly consists in affirming that the ultimate truth cannot be expressed by means of language and exhorting the assembly to practice Buddhist teachings diligently. It is the identification of the two prologues that helps us determine that he who conducted the discourse at the Kỳ Lân Hall is none other than Nhân Tông.

Besides, if analyzing the content of the entire discourse, we can easily see that it has the same theme and style as those of the discourse at the Sùng Nghiêm temple. This may be proved by the following short dialogue:

Then, a monk stepped out, asking, "It is an ordinary affair for having meals and putting on clothes. Why should one be so much concerned with them that one has to raise doubt?"

Having prostrated himself, he stood up, asking again, "We do not ask about the Realm of Dhyāna without Desire. We put up only a question as to the Realm of Desire without Dhyāna."

Thereupon the master pointed to the air.

The monk asked, "What is the use of employing the ancient people's saliva and sputum?"

The master said, "Once raised, once renewed."

The monk: "The ancient people used to speak about what the Buddha is, what the Dharma is, what the Saṃgha is. What did they mean by 'what'?"

The master said, "What!' 'What!"

The monk said, "The sound of a lute without strings is scarcely understood; yet its tune becomes highly appreciated when the father plays it for his son."

The passage just cited from the True Record of the Three Patriarchs comes to an end with the words "and so on". That is to say, the discourse did prolong some more but it was not entirely written down in the work. In spite of this, from the above passage it becomes evident that the main ideas and linguistic structures of the discourse are for the most part similar to what was preached at the Sùng Nghiêm temple by the late winter of Giáp Thìn. And this is a particular feature of Nhân Tông's way of preaching.

The Last Days of the Emperor

On the first day of the New Year festival of Mậu Thân (1308), the Emperor Nhân Tông moved to the Bảo An temple in Siêu Loại District. There, he sent for Pháp Loa, who was later chosen as his official Dharma-successor of the Trúc Lâm lineage and appointed the abbot of the temple. By the fourth month, Nhân Tông spent his summer retreat at the Vĩnh Nghiêm temple in Lạng Giang. This time he summoned Pháp Loa and asked him to take charge of the Báo Ân temple. There, during his three months' retreat he preached the Ching-te ch'uan-teng-lu whereas the National Teacher Đạo Nhất expounded the Lotus Sūtra. After the summer retreat, he entered the Yên Tử Mountain, allowing the eunuchs and those who had served him in his daily life as a preacher of Buddhist teachings to go home, with the exception of ten servants who later often followed him in the last days of his life. Thereafter, he went to the Tử Tiêu temple where he expounded the Ching-te ch'uan-teng-lu to Pháp Loa. Later, the servants gradually left the mountain, except for Bảo Sát, an intimate disciple of his, who stayed there to take care of him.

Since then, Nhân Tông wandered in all the caves where he often stayed for several days. Seeing that, Bảo Sát said to him, "What will the life of Buddhism be like if you go on wandering in the severe weather at such an old age, Master?" "My time has come. I am planning for my 'long journey'," said Nhân Tông. On the fifth of the 10th month, some boy-servants of Princess Thiên Thụy, who was suffering a serious illness, went to the mountain to inform him of the princess's wish to see him again before her death. Sorrowfully, he said, "The time has come." Together with only a servant, he went down the mountain. After ten days' journey, he arrived at Thăng Long on the 15th of the 10th month. After talking and advising his sister, he went back to the mountain. On the way back, he stayed overnight at the Bảo An temple in Siêu Loại District. Early in the following morning, he went on with his journey. When arriving at a temple in Cổ Châu Village, he wrote a stanza on the wall of the temple:

A lifespan comes to an end in such a confused state of mind;
And human feelings close at the same time with the eyes.
How narrowly the Maras' Palace is confined!

But the Buddhas' land is in Spring at all times.[46]

On the 17th, he stayed overnight at the Sùng Nghiêm temple on Mount Chí Linh. Thereafter, the Great Queen Tuyên Từ invited him to a vegetarian dinner at the Bình Dương temple. He pleasantly said, "This is the last meal offered to me." On the 18th, he walked to the Từ Lâm Temple on Mount Kỳ Đặc in Yên Sinh, where, having a headache, he called the monks Tử Doanh and Hoàn Trung, saying, "I would like to go to the Ngọa Vân Mountain but I cannot lift my legs. How should I do now?" The monks said, "We can help you." On reaching the Ngọa Vân Mountain, he thanked them and said, "After going down the mountain, try your best to cultivate the way; do not disregard the cycle of birth-and-death." On the 19th, at his request, the attendant Pháp Không went to the Tử Tiêu Temple on Mount Yên Tử to ask Bảo Sát to see him immediately. On the 20th, when reaching the stream named Doanh, Bảo Sát saw a line of black clouds spreading from Mount Ngọa Vân to Mount Lôi over the Doanh stream. The water of the stream then rose several feet high but soon lowered. On the surface of water suddenly appeared two dragons, raising their heads as big as horses with their bright eyes like stars. They raised themselves several feet high and then disappeared. That night, Bảo Sát stayed in a hermitage on the mountain and he dreamt of unlucky omens.

On the 21st, he reached the Ngọa Vân Mountain. Seeing him, Nhân Tông smiled, saying, "I am about to go. Why have you come so late? Tell me what you have not yet comprehended of Buddhist teachings."

---

[46] 大方廣總持經, T 275, vol. 9.

Standing up, Bảo Sát asked, "When the Great Master Ma was not well, the abbot asked him, 'How have Your Venerable been?'. Thereupon, he answered, 'I see the Buddha every day; I see him every month.' What did he mean in so replying?"

Nhân Tông spoke loudly, "What is 'Three Nobles and Five Emperors'?"

Standing up again, Bảo Sát asked, "What is the meaning of 'it is just like flowers blooming so colorfully as brocade; bamboo in the south and trees in the north'?"

Nhân Tông said, "Are you already blind?"

But Bảo Sát spoke nothing more. Since then, it is recorded that during the period of four days the sky became gloomy, the wind blew violently, the snowy rain covered all the trees, the monkeys and gibbons walked around the temple crying and screaming, the birds sang in grief.

On the first of the 11th month, when the morning star was shining bright at mid-night, Nhân Tông asked, "What time is it?" "It is the Tý, Master,"[47] answered Bảo Sát. Opening the window, he looked out and said, "It is time for me to go." "Where are you going, Master?" asked Bảo Sát. He said,

All dharmas do not arise;
All dharmas do not pass away.
If it is so understood,
The Buddhas are always present.
What is the use of asking 'going and coming'?

---

[47] the period between 11 p.m. and 1 a.m.

Standing up, Bảo Sát asked, "What about non-arising and non-destruction?" Nhân Tông suddenly covered his mouth with his hand, saying, "Do not talk wildly." Then he lay down in the lion-posture and quietly passed away.

According to Nhân Tông's will, on the evening of the following day Bảo Sát had his body cremated in the grounds of the temple where he had spent his last days. It is said that during the cremation the space was permeated with fragrance and from the sky came down the heavenly music with a five-colored cloud covering the cremation. By the following fourth day, the Venerable Phổ Tuệ hurried back from Mount Yên Tử. He sprinkled the cremation with perfumed water and held a ceremony of gathering sacred bones where more than 500 śāriras and numerous smaller ones were collected.

Soon, the Emperor Anh Tông, the Highest Minister and courtiers came with an imperial ship from the capital. To show their respect, they unceasingly prostrated themselves while walking along the mountain path to the cremation. Thereafter, Nhân Tông's sacred bones and śāriras were brought to the capital where his funeral service would be officially held. For many days in every street of the capital was all the time sounding the cries of the courtiers and the common people. The Emperor Nhân Tông was bestowed the sacred title Đại Thánh Trần Triều Trúc Lâm Đầu Đà Tịnh Tuệ Giác Hoàng Điều Ngự Tổ Phật (The Great Saint of the Trần Dynasty, the Great Ascetic of Trúc Lâm, the Enlightened Emperor of Pure Wisdom, the Buddha-Patriarch in Guiding All Sentient Beings). His sacred bones were contained in a precious case. His śāriras were divided into two parts, which were placed in golden boxes each. After the funeral service, the sacred bones were buried in the imperial tomb named Nhân Tông. One case of śariras was worshiped in the Precious Stūpa in the Long Hưng Prefecture; and the other was worshiped in the Golden Stūpa at the Vân Yên temple on Mount Yên Tử.

Such were the last days of the Emperor Nhân Tông as in the words of the Recorded Sayings as the Lamps of the Saints. In the Complete History of Đại Việt the event is somewhat briefly and variedly recorded:

On the third (of the 11th month), the Emperor-Father passed away at the Ngọa Vân temple on Mount Yên Tử. Earlier, he was ordained Buddhist monk under the title Great Man Trúc Lâm on the Tử Tiêu Peak of Mount Yên Tử. Once, learning that his sister Thiên Thụy was getting a very serious illness, he went down the mountain to see her. "If it is time for you to leave, pass calmly. In the realm of the deceased if asked about something, remember to answer, 'Please, wait for a moment; my brother, Great Man Trúc Lâm, is coming,'" said he. Then he came back to the mountain where, having given Pháp Loa some instructions about his own funeral service, he sat quiet and passed away. At the same time Thiên Thụy departed, too.

After the Emperor-Father's cremation Pháp Loa gathered more than 3,000 pieces of śariras, which were by [the king's] order brought to the Tử Phúc temple in the capital. The king showed suspicions and most of the courtiers asked him for punishment on Pháp Loa. The Crown Prince Mạnh, who was just at the age of nine and was then standing aside, felt on himself something like pieces of śariras, which he took out to see. It was truly the pieces of śariras which had not been found in the case. Deeply moved by this, the king (Anh Tông) swept, showing no more suspicion [about Pháp Loa].[48]

Thus, according to the Complete History of Đại Việt Bảo Sát was not mentioned at all with respect to the Emperor Nhân Tông's death; whereas, in the words of the Recorded Sayings of the Saints, he was named the "outstanding disciple" of the Emperor's and was said to serve the latter during the last days of his life. It was Bảo Sát who carried out the cremation according to Nhân Tông's instructions without waiting for Pháp Loa. When the latter came, his task was simply to sprinkle perfume on the cremation and collect sacred bones and śāriras. Through the above facts it seems that, in spite of having been appointed by Nhân Tông to be his Dharma-successor, Pháp Loa's role showed rather indistinct during the last days of the Emperor Nhân Tông's life.

Further, in the Complete History of Đại Việt the fact that Nhân Tông's śāriras were brought to the stūpa for worshiping is said to have taken place more than a year later: "On the 16th of the 9th month of the year Canh Tuất (1310) the Emperor-Father's coffin was carried to the Quy Đức Tomb in the Long Hưng Prefecture for burial, where the body of the Queen-mother Khâm Từ Bảo Thánh was again buried nearby. His śāriras were worshiped in the Precious Stūpa at the Ngọa Vân temple. The temple where he was officially worshiped was named Nhân Tông and he was posthumously bestowed Pháp Thiên Sùng Đạo Ứng Thế Hóa Duyên Long Từ Huyển Huệ Thánh Văn Thần Vũ Nguyên Minh Duệ Hiếu Hoàng Đế. Before the burial service, his coffin was

---

[48] Vol.6, pp.23b4-24a4.

temporarily placed at the Diên Hiển Palace. Thereafter, although the good time came for his coffin to be moved into the tomb, the officials and the common people remained crowded in the grounds of the palace. The head minister had to drive them with sticks but could not open up the road. Sending for Trịnh Trọng Tử, the king (Anh Tông) said to him, 'How can the coffin be moved when the people are gathering so crowdedly?' Trọng Tử commanded his troops to come and sit everywhere in the grounds of the Thiên Trì Temple, where they were ordered to sing some phrases of the song Long Ngâm. Extremely amazed, the masses rushed there to watch, leaving enough room for the coffin to be moved to the Quy Đức tomb...″[49]

Such were the last days of the Emperor Nhân Tông's life as recorded by the Complete History of Đại Việt. In the history of our country, few emperors received such a full account concerning the people's admiration for them after their deaths. This is the life of an emperor who, only within fifty years, could make extremely great contributions to the country and the human kind. His life has ended but left so much regret for contemporaries as well as subsequent generations. A life was closed with an extremely plain but noble end. Today, whenever we read all that our ancestors wrote about the Emperor Nhân Tông, we cannot help feeling deeply moved as if we were in the presence of his genuine body, the embodiment of a national hero who went beyond the limits of time to exist forever with our country and our people.

*Trans. into English by **Đạo Sinh***

---

[49] Vol.6, pp.25b9-27a8.

TRẦN NHÂN TÔNG'S POSITION
IN THE HISTORY
OF VIETNAMESE LITERATURE

BY PROF. **LÊ MẠNH THÁT**

The spoken language of our people must have come into existence long ago. It is, however, not until the Hùng dynasty, i.e., around the first centuries of the Common Era and earlier, that this language can leave some trace of its own in a short text entitled the *Việt Ca* (*Song of Việt*) and in some linguistic structures of the Buddhist texts *Lục Độ Tập Kinh* (*Collected Teachings of Six Pāramitās*) and *Tạp Thí Dụ Kinh* (*A Miscellaneous Collection of Parables*).[1] Of these seemingly most ancient works the last two, which may be regarded as the earliest Buddhist texts known to us today, might be in circulation during the first centuries of the Common Era, at least for some time prior to their translation into

---

[1] Lê Mạnh Thát, Lục Độ Tập Kinh Và Lịch Sử Khởi Nguyên Dân Tộc Ta, Tu Thư Đại Học Vạn Hạnh, 1972, pp.254-321; Khương Tăng Hội Toàn Tập I, Tu Thư Đại Học Vạn Hạnh, 1975, pp.172-188. [LMT]

Chinese by Khương Tăng Hội (?-280). In those days, the Vietnamese language was already so richly developed that Shih-she (137-226) is said to have compiled the first Chinese-Vietnamese Lexicon, consisting of two volumes and known today under the title *Chỉ Nam Phẩm Vựng*. By the end of the fourth century its development was once more marked with the circulation of the *Tá Âm* and the *Tá Âm Tự* by Đạo Cao (370-450?) in the form of dictionaries provided with some directions about the method of transcription.[2]

Thereafter the Vietnamese language continued to be widely used as script. It was employed by the common people to confer the title *Bố Cái Đại Vương* on the hero Phùng Hưng. And when the national independence was restored, it could have been used by imperial courts in issuing administrative ordinances. Such a hypothesis may be unhesitatingly put forward on the grounds of an incident concerning Đinh Củng Viên, a scribe of the Imperial Academy, and Lê Tòng Giáo, an administrative functionary, in 1288, according to which an imperial decree is known to have been announced in both Vietnamese and Chinese. Thus in the middle of the 13th century the Vietnamese language as a script was made possible to perform all of its functions. Unfortunately, on account of wars and natural disasters a great number of works composed in the speech of our people, including the earliest text *Lục Độ Tập Kinh*, some imperial decrees and literary works such as the *Tiều Ẩn Quốc Ngữ Thi Tập* of Chu Văn An, etc., are lost.

The first verse in Vietnamese, which is known today under the

---

[2] Lê Mạnh Thát, Lịch Sử Phật Giáo Việt Nam, Tập I, Nxb. Thuận Hóa, 1999, pp.474-490. [LMT]

title "Giáo Trò" and was composed for folksong theater, is attributed to Dhyāna Master Đạo Hạnh (?-1117). Some questions as to its authenticity, however, have been posed since, as being a short verse of thirty-two words only, it has not been determined in the bibliographical aspect so far. It is not until the Emperor Nhân Tông's time when his two verses the "Worldly Life with Joy in the Way" and the "Song of the Realization of the Way," Huyền Quang's "A Depiction of the Vân Yên Temple" and Mạc Đỉnh Chi's "Educating Children" were put into circulation that literature in Vietnamese with its complete works began to be preserved. The influence of Emperor Nhân Tông in the field of literature, therefore, is extremely great.

Historically considered, it is not by chance that such an honor is ascribed to the Emperor Nhân Tông. In the preceding chapters we have seen how great his career and personality are so that they have had strong impressions on the minds of the Vietnamese people in spite of the wear of time and the enemy's destruction. It is none other than the people who have undertaken the task to preserve the afore-said literary works among hundreds or thousands of others that may be known today under their titles alone. Otherwise stated, the Emperor's contributions to our people are so great that his works such as the "Worldly Life with Joy in the Way" and the "Song of the Realization of the Way," and so on, have been enjoyed and preserved so far.

Yet it is not only because of his own prestige and merit that those two works have been preserved. Indeed, a reason why they have been able to stand so well with the Vietnamese people is their intrinsic values, particularly the "Worldly Life with Joy in the

Way." It may be said that the "Worldly Life with Joy in the Way" is a proclamation with respect to the way of living in accord with the Way that Buddhism in Vietnam set forth and that truly exercised a remarkable influence on millions of Vietnamese Buddhists in the Emperor Nhân Tông's time and in the centuries that followed. Further, it is one of a few works of Buddhism in Vietnam that was referred to as an authority in Master Chân Nguyên's presentation of Buddhist problems, which are cited in the *Kiến Tánh Thành Phật (Seeing into Nature and Becoming a Buddha)*,[3] to the Emperor Lê Chính Hòa around 1692. Accordingly, it is the thought of the "Worldly Life with Joy in the Way" that helps partly with the existence of the verse in its course of circulation.

For the past three centuries the"Worldly Life with Joy in the Way" and the"Song of the Realization of the Way" have been published and put into circulation widely. Their earliest edition, which is extant and dated the year 1745, was reprinted by Śrāmaṇerikā Diệu Liên under her master's instruction, and their printing blocks have been preserved at the Liên Hoa Temple in the imperial capital Thăng Long. These verses were printed in addition to the latter part of Master Chân Nguyên's *Thiền Tông Bản Hạnh* (*Fundamental Activities of the Dhyāna School*) on pages 47-57. In this edition are also included Huyền Quang's verse "A Depiction of the Vân Yên Temple" and Chân Nguyên's gātha "The Conditions of the Realization of the Way." That the two verses of the Emperor Nhân Tông are printed in addition shows that the texts employed by Bhikṣuṇi Diệu Liên must certainly proceed from a certain

---

[3] Lê Mạnh Thát, Kiến Tính Thành Phật Lục in Chân Nguyên Thiền Sư Toàn Tập, Tu Thư Đại Học Vạn Hạnh, 1982, p.72. [LMT]

edition of Master Chân Nguyên, that is, that of the late 17th century. Before that date we have no information on what happened to the "Worldly Life with Joy in the Way".

Though no information is given about the circulation of the "Worldly Life with Joy in the Way" and the "Song of the Realization of the Way" prior to the 17th century, what may be known about their circulation in the 18th century, that is, following the edition by Bhikṣuṇi Diệu Liên, is rather reliable. In the foreword to the 1930 edition of the *Thiền Tông Bản Hạnh*, Master Thanh Hanh (1840-1936) says that this work was reprinted in Gia Long the Twelfth (1814), in which the "Worldly Life with Joy in the Way" and the "Song of the Realization of the Way" must have been included. Further, when making a list of Buddhist texts published in the first half of the 19th century in the *Đạo Giáo Nguyên Lưu*, An Thiền records a work entitled *Trần Triều Thập Hội Lục* (*Record of the 'Ten Sections' in the Trần Dynasty*), which obviously refers to the ten sections of the verse "Worldly Life with Joy in the Way".

The fact that the "Worldly Life with Joy in the Way" and the "Song of the Realization of the Way" have been reprinted many times during the past 300 years proves that the thought of the former verse has continued to be studied and spread though Buddhism and the country have undergone many important changes. The value of reasoning of the verse, therefore, still has its strong influence, particularly in relation with military achievements of Tây Sơn troops and civilians in the battles of Ngọc Hồi and Đống Đa by the end of the 18th century, among whom some prominent figures such as Master Hải Lượng, Master Hải Âu, and so on, professed themselves to be inheritors of the Trúc Lâm tradition.

For the past more than 300 years the "Worldly Life with Joy in the Way" and the "Song of the Realization of the Way" have been appreciated, studied and preserved as such; so it may be supposedly known that in the more than 300 years earlier, they must have received the same admiration from our people. For, without such an admiration these two works might be burned down together with other works of our people prior to the Lý and Trần dynasties during the nearly 20 years' occupation by Ming invaders from China. Furthermore, Buddhism under the reigns of Early Lê and Mạc was strongly revived during the movement of cultural nationalization, the greatest achievements of which were the translation of Buddhist texts into Vietnamese such as the *Đại Báo Phụ Mẫu Ân Trọng Kinh* by Master Viên Thái, the reprinting of some history books of Buddhism such as the *Nam Tông Tự Pháp Đồ* (*Chart of Dharma-Successors of the Southern School*) of the Honors Graduate Lương Thế Vinh, the *Recorded Sayings of the Saints* of Master Chân Nguyên, and especially the foundation and encouragement of the usage of the Vietnamese language by Master Pháp Tính in the *Chỉ Nam Ngọc Âm Giải Nghĩa*.

In a period full of such influential and enthusiastic activities of Buddhism, the study and application of the two works of the Emperor Nhân Tông mentioned above must have been carried on. The sole regret is that we have not yet acquired any information on their circulation of the time. In spite of this, they had surely been somehow spread so that they could eventually be cited in Master Chân Nguyên's *Kiến Tánh Thành Phật* by the end of the 17th century. Otherwise stated, they were ever present in the main course of literature and thought that was successfully implemented in terms of our people's own script. Therefore, as has been said above, it is actually an honor for our people's literature in the mother language to have been initiated with the pen of such a national hero of glorious military achievements as the Emperor Nhân Tông and with the works that have exercised such a deep influence not only on Buddhism but further on the national tradition as the "Worldly Life with Joy in the Way" and the "Song of the Realization of the Way."

These works are of the type of argumentative literature; that is to say, they are the texts of political reasoning consisting in presenting questions of thought and logic, in which the Vietnamese language has been employed to formulate abstract ideas in a skillful and intelligible manner. As a consequence, the Vietnamese language has since then grown into a language that is capable of conveying any of various thoughts in its most colorful style. It is due to those linguistic characteristics that the two works did not only attract contemporaries' attention but also had an interesting impact upon the subsequent generations. The Vietnamese language itself has become a literary language. And this is, so to speak, one of the great achievements that the two works of the Emperor Nhân Tông's could bring about for Vietnamese literature.

For these works to have been composed in such a colorfully literary style by the end of the 13th century, the Vietnamese language had to be employed for many generations, that is, for more than 1,000 years, as a language of literature. No doubt, it could inherit the achievements and essentials of age-long national literature so that, when we read these verses today, we still feel their beauty, intimacy, and intelligibility in quite a different manner from what we have in contact with a great deal of puzzling and unnatural sentences recorded by foreigners just about 300 years ago. In effect, to produce a style of reasoning as exposed in the "Worldly Life with Joy in the Way" and the "Song of the Realization of the Way," the Vietnamese language has doubtlessly undergone thousands of years' of trial and usage, not merely in the time of Emperor Nhân Tông.

Indeed, if the Vietnamese language had not survived those more than 1,000 years to stand opposite to the Han language of China and thus to become one of the ramparts obstructing the plot of Hanization resolutely carried out by the contemporary Chinese, the Vietnamese people could not have existed so far, much less their own language and national independence. In this connection, it may be said that the "Worldly Life with Joy in the Way" and the "Song of the Realization of the Way" truly represent a combination of our people's extraordinarily painstaking efforts in their tragic struggles for the country's territory and ownership. Consequently, the literary value of these two works may be doubly increased.

It is due to some combination of such a kind that no language of the world has been able to jump all of a sudden onto the arena of literature to become a literary language. Even some great languages like Chinese, Sanskrit, Greek, etc., with their age-old texts have had to undergo a process of combination such that they can step by step grow from the rude texts of divination or simple folk songs into the well-known languages in the world. So has the Vietnamese language. For colorfully literary works like the "Worldly Life with Joy in the Way" and the "Song of the Realization of the Way" to have been composed, the Vietnamese language, too, has to go through a long process of combination--from the earliest text known as the *Việt Ca*, the short stories in the *Lục Độ Tập Kinh* and the *Tạp Thí Dụ Kinh* to the *Giáo Trò* of Master Đạo Hạnh. As a consequence, it is the whole process of using the Vietnamese language in a skillful and fluent manner that has actually given the opportunity for the appearance of the two works mentioned above.

Thus the appearance of Vietnamese as a language of literature proceeds from a series of struggles full of hardship and uncertainty. Yet, it is through those struggles in blood and tear that the Vietnamese language has proved its superiority, its ability to serve as the premise for the appearance of the "Worldly Life with Joy in the Way" and the "Song of the Realization of the Way." Without such a process, any works like them can hardly be produced. This is the point that all researchers in Vietnamese literature have never paid their attention to. Instead, they often occupy themselves with seeking after the origin of the Nôm script in the amount of stone inscriptions preserved from the Lý and Trần dynasties, and thence shifting the birth-date of it to between the eighth and the 13th centuries. They forget that for such works as the "Worldly Life with Joy in the Way" and the "Song of the Realization of the Way" to have been produced by the end of the 13th century the Vietnamese language, both spoken and written, must have come into being between 500 and 700 years earlier at least. It is an objective, indispensable process not merely for the Vietnamese language but also for any other languages. In this connection, to study these two works is nothing other than to study its process of combination.

Nowadays, we cannot know accurately when the Emperor Nhân

Tông worked on these two works. From its content, however, the "Song of the Realization of the Way" had to be composed in the period when he was settling on Mount Yên Tử, that is, after the eighth month of Kỷ Hợi (1299), which the *Complete History* refers to as the time when "from the Thiên Trường Prefecture the Emperor-Father returned to Mount Yên Tử for ascetic practice." For the verse mentions the fact that

Content with life in poverty,
I have sought a place for training.
Secluded in the high mountains,
Hiding in the wilderness,
Where gibbons alone are pleased
To make friends with me.
In the quiet forests and mountains,
I let go of mind and body.

And

I would seclude myself
In the quiet mountains
To concentrate all my mind on practice,
However poor life therein might be.

These lines are most similar to what Huyền Quang depicts of the Vân Yên temple and Nhân Tông's life there:

Looking like a painting,
The landscape is peaceful.
It is so fantastically created by the Holy Heaven
That the Buddha-King cultivates the Way there.
Taking flowers in their beaks, the birds offer;

Embracing their young by the door, the gibbons listen to sūtras.
In the serene temple, the Buddha manifests compassion.
In the light breeze and thin clouds,
The master sits meditating by the window.
The bright moon, the blue mountains

And

Wearing kṣaya, lying behind the paper curtain,
Not concerned with stores full of jades, cases full of pearls.
Forgetting delicious food, giving up sweet wine,
Only a pot of egg-fruit and a jar of soy.

And

Practicing earlier, the master has attained Buddhahood;
Just initiated in the Way, the disciple is still a Bhikṣu.

As to the "Worldly Life with Joy in the Way" it is really difficult to determine in what phase of his life the Emperor Nhân Tông wrote it. Some have hold that it might be written before his ordination to be a Buddhist monk, that is, before 1299. No doubt, in so saying their hypothesis is based on the first two lines of the verse:

Though settling in the city,
The way of living I take is of forest and mountain.

Accordingly, they have come to a conclusion that the Emperor then was settling in the capital Thăng Long and his mind was perfectly cleansed of defilement of all kinds. Yet some lines of Section 5 of the same verse read,

With five phrases from Dhyāna teachings I can lie in Ho-yu

leisurely;

With three recitations of sūtra I can sit in Hsin-lo at ease.

To comprehend the Buddhist teaching, to penetrate into its essentials,

One has to go through patriarchal gates and Dharma-halls.

To rid oneself of praise and blame, to detach oneself from sound and form,

One has to cease seeking pleasures in recreation of all kinds.

The compassionate Buddha,

May I be with Him in many lives!

Out of the king's favor,

May people be exempted from hard labor!

Whether robes and blankets are patched or tattered,

They help me survive the cold of winter.

Whether rice and gruel are plain or somewhat rotten,

They help me overcome everyday hunger.

Being so described, it is obviously not of life in the city but in the mountains. For that reason, it is really difficult to determine the date of the verse in terms of its content alone. A definite point, however, is that it had to be composed after the Emperor had more or less concerned himself with the Yên Tử Mountain. It is well known that Yên Tử occupied a central position in Buddhist activities under the Trần dynasty. For his grandfather, the Emperor Trần Thái Tông, ever arrived there, and in his youth the Emperor Nhân Tông himself had the desire to settle there. Whatever happened, the thought of the "Worldly Life with Joy in the Way," which was formally confirmed by Tuệ Trung Trần Quốc Tung to have been realized by the Emperor Nhân Tông in 1287, became more and more manifest. In other words, the "Worldly Life with Joy in the Way" could hardly be composed until 1287 when the enemy had been completely swept out of our country and our people were making great efforts to build the Fatherland.

The glossary of the "Worldly Life with Joy in the Way" contains 1688 terms, including those of the verse-title and section-subtitles as well as the concluding quatrain in Chinese. In the entire sections proper there are 1623 terms, some Vietnamese words of which are employed rather frequently such as *lòng*, mind or heart (18 times), *cho*, give (13 times), *chẳng*, never (13 times), *mới*, just (11 or 12 times), *Bụt*, Buddha (10 times), etc. Of these 1623 if proper terms, specific terms, and terms of transliteration are separately listed, the number is reduced to approximately 1400 terms.

For example, the number of terms like *Thích Ca* (Śākya), *Di Đà* (Amitābha), *Di Lặc* (Maitreya), *Bát Nhã* (Prajñā), *Chiêm Bặc* (Campaka), *Chiên Đàn* (Candana), *Bồ Đề* (Bodhi), *Bồ Tát* (Bodhisattva), *Đàn Việt* (Dānapati), *Ưu Đàm* (Udumbara), *Câu Chi* (Koṭi), *Diễn Nhã Đạt Đa* (Yajñadatta), which number 26 as transliterated from Sanskrit, remains 12 when classified. So are specific terms *bát phong* (eight kinds of wind), *bát thức* (eight consciousnesses), *Cực Lạc* (the Land of Bliss), *đại thừa* (mahāyāna), *tiểu thừa* (hīnayāna), *hữu lậu* (āsrava), *kim cương* (vajra, diamond), *vô lậu* (anāsrava), *lục căn* (six faculties), *lục tặc* (six enemies), *tam độc* (three poisons), *tam thân* (three bodies), *tam tạng* (tripiṭaka), *tam huyền* (three unfathomable things), *tam yếu* (three essentials), *tam nghiệp* (three actions of mind, speech and body), *Tịnh độ* (the Pure Land), *thái bình* (peace), *thượng sỹ* (superior man), *trí tuệ* (wisdom), *tri âm* (bosom friend), *tri thức* (knowledge), *tri kiến* (view), *tri cơ* (knowledge of capability), *trượng phu* (great man), *trưởng lão* (the elders), *viên giác* (perfect enlightenment), *vô thường* (impermanent), *vô minh* (avidyā, ignorance), *vô sinh* (non-arising), *vô tâm* (no-mind), *vô vi* (the Uncomposed). If classified by their respective items, there remain 32 instead of 64 terms. So are proper names *Cánh Diều, Yên Tử, Hà Hữu (Ho-yu), Hùng Nhĩ (Hsiung-erh), Tân la (Hsin-lo), Thiên trúc (T'ien-chu), Thiếu lâm (Shao-lin), Tào Khê (Ts'ao-ch'i), Thiếu Thất (Shao-shih), Lư lăng (Lo-leng), Phá Táo (P'o-t'sao), Thạch Đầu (Shih-tou), Lâm tế (Lin-chi), Bí Ma (Pi-ma), Thuyền Tử (Ch'an-szu), Đạo ngô (Tao-wu), Thiều dương (Shao-yang), Triệu Lão, Thiên cang (T'ien-kang), Thái Bạch (Thai-pai).*

With the amount of approximately 1400 terms the "Worldly Life with Joy in the Way" may be considered to be a relatively sufficient glossary for us to make a study of the Vietnamese language in the reign of the Emperor Nhân Tông. And they are just terms included in the "Worldly Life with Joy in the Way" alone. If combined with the terms used in the "Song of the Realization of the Way," in which the number of 238 terms is obtained from the classification of its 336 terms according to their respective items, the total amount may make up a glossary of nearly 2000 terms, that is, equal to a small-sized dictionary, which may supply us with a rather perfect knowledge of the Vietnamese language in the Emperor Nhân Tông's time, that is, nearly 700 years ago.

Here, it is naturally necessary for us to make an intensive study on these two works. However, it should be kept in mind that the Emperor's literary career is not confined in the works composed in Vietnamese. Also he is the author of thirty poems and stanzas, 22 letters written to Yüan emperors and their officials, and two discourses delivered at the Sùng Nghiêm temple and at the Kỳ Lân Institute. In these discourses there are also some poems and stanzas, given as his answers to some questions posed by his students, which have not yet been included in the amount of Nhân Tông's poems and stanzas. That is to say, the works Nhân Tông has left for us are not of small number though most of them are written in Chinese.

In regard to his literary works in Chinese, most of Vietnamese researchers in the past and the present alike have agreed on considering him to be *an outstanding author* in this field. Indeed, reading his poems written in Chinese none of us can fail to form in mind various beautiful pictures of the country. The following poem, for instance, is a depiction of a serene evening in a village close to the imperial residence at the Thiên Trường Prefecture in the delta of the Red River:

村 後 村 前 淡 似 煙
半 無 半 有 夕 陽 邊
牧 童 笛 裏 牛 歸 盡
白 鷺 雙 雙 飛 下 田

The front and rear of the hamlet are covered in mist like a dream.
In the evening sunshine it appears both existent and non-existent.
The buffalos are turning back in the sound of the herdsman's flute.
And on the rice-fields the pairs of herons are flying down.

And a temple in Lạng Châu in the highlands of northern Vietnam:

古 寺 淒 涼 秋 靄 外

漁 船 蕭 瑟 暮 鐘 初
水 明 山 静 白 鷗 過
風 定 雲 閑 紅 樹 疏

The old temple looks gloomy in the mist of autumn.
A fishing-boat is floating lonely in the first sounds of the evening bell.
Over the clear water and quiet mountains the white sea-gulls are flying.
The wind subsides, the clouds are moving leisurely over a few trees of red leaves.

Even in everyday life, the moonlight in the evening, the sound of dew-drops falling on leaves in the yard and the sound of washing clothes from a certain village could touch the poet's heart slightly and help him recognize the beauty of the country at peace.

半 窗 燈 影 滿 床 書
露 滴 秋 庭 夜 氣 虚
睡 起 砧 聲 無 覓 處
木 樨 花 上 月 來 初

On the bed full of books I sat under the lamp by the window,
Knowing not where the sound of washing clothes came.
In the yard the transparent air was permeated with the mist of autumn,
And on the cassia-flowers began to come the first moonlight.

Unlike some emperors who were born, grew up and then enjoyed a country already at peace, the date Nhân Tông was born was the very time when the Emperor Thái Tông had just smashed the Mongol-Yüan Army in their first invasion of our country under the command of the notoriously brutal General Wu-liang-ho-thai (Uryangqadai). And during the 20 years that followed was a hard struggle for him on the diplomatic front so as to maintain the country's ownership, bring about peace for the people and prepare national strength for fighting against the enemy's coming invasions.

Upon ascending the throne in the 10th month of Mậu Dần (1278), Nhân Tông had to confront the messengers who "sticked out their 'barn-owl' tongues to disregard our imperial court, exposed their 'goat-dog' bodies to show pride before the Emperor." as in Trần Hưng Đạo's account. Accordingly, the whole people started a movement of killing the enemy to save the country. Though the war of Đinh Tỵ (1257) had ended long before, its impressive atmosphere seemed to remain somewhere when he paid a visit to his grandfather's tomb on a Spring day before the war of 1285.

貔 虎 千 門 肅
衣 冠 七 品 通
白 頭 軍 士 在
往 往 説 元 豐

Solemnly at the thousand gates are brave guards,
Together with officials of all the seven ranks.
There remain the soldiers whose hair already turned white,
Occasionally recounting the victory of Nguyên Phong.

And the most remarkable thing is that the Emperor himself ever commanded an army to advance on the battle-fields. In reality, he fought in some violent battles, beside his officers and soldiers so that he could deeply feel great sympathy for those wives whose husbands were fighting on a certain front of the fatherland.

睡 起 鈎 簾 看 墜 紅
黃 鸝 不 語 怨 東 風
無 端 落 日 西 樓 外
花 影 枝 頭 盡 向 東

Raising the blind and watching falling flowers after getting up;
Being angry at the spring wind, the orioles cease singing.
Beyond the western pavilion the sun is indifferently setting.
The flowers and branches are all throwing their shadows to the
east.

In a war of resistance where invading forces were far more powerful than his people, the Emperor could have such sorrowful feelings, much more in the campaigns to overcome threats of security caused by some smaller powers in the remote borderland. In a poem written in a campaign to put down havocs in Laos in the spring of Canh Dần (1290), the Emperor expressed his sorrows:

錦 帆 輕 趁 浪 華 開
蓬 底 厭 厭 首 不 抬
三 峽 暮 雲 無 雁 到
九 灘 明 月 有 龍 來
淒 涼 行 色 添 宮 夢
撩 亂 閑 愁 到 酒 杯
漢 武 翻 招 窮 黷 謗
男 兒 汲 汲 若 爲 哉

With brocaded sails the ship is riding the waves lightly;
In the bow I am too depressed to raise my head.
No wild geese comes in the evening clouds over the mountains;

There appears only a dragon in the moonlight on the falls.
How gloomy the journey is with frequent dreams of the Citadel.
There remain the glass of wine and my deep sorrow.
Were the Emperor Wu of Han ever blamed for his warlike actions,
There is, then, no need for hurry at the present time.

This is a war waged by the Emperor himself for the welfare of the people as is recorded in the *Complete History*: "Learning that the king himself is about to command the fighting expedition to Laos, the courtiers say, 'How can we mobilize the Army when the losses caused by the Yüan enemy have not yet been made up?' 'This is the most favorable time for mobilizing the Army. For, after the enemy's retreat, the three regions, thinking that our troops and horses and supplies are all lost, certainly disregard us. So, we must have our Great Army mobilized to show them our strength,' said the Emperor. The courtiers, however, all said, 'The people are all exhausted; why does His Majesty not take care of them but concern himself with [fighting only]?' So said the courtiers because they could not think so deeply as the sages."[4]

Thus, the fact that our Army marched into Laos under the Emperor's command was aimed at nothing but proving to them that our armed forces were still strong after many years of war and that they should not wreak havoc on our country's borderland. Indeed, less than four years later, i.e., in the eighth month of Giáp Ngọ (1294), having handed over the throne to Anh Tông, the Emperor himself marched an army into Laos once more together with the Generals Phạm Ngũ Lão, Trung Thành Vương. Accordingly, it is obvious that the threat of Laos on the frontier of

---

[4] Vol. 5, pp.58b5-59a1.

Đại Việt was truly existent, and such a military action performed by the Emperor was quite necessary for the country's security. In spite of this, the just-cited poem, which was written in the Laotian campaign of 1290 or 1294, explicitly revealed the author's strong dislike for war, that which is usually termed "destructive actions"; that is to say, war in essence is after all a manifestation of a leader's personal ambitions.

In his lifetime the Emperor Nhân Tông suffered two violent wars. So he could understand much more deeply than anyone that suffering would fall on both sides and that the usage of war against war was by all means a temporary solution. For that reason, it seems hard for him to conceal his dissatisfaction in such fighting expeditions. Indeed, all of this actually originated from his own view of the common characters and qualities of human beings. Although they were present on different front lines, the warriors of all ranks had the same sensations, reflections and expectations. For the past more than 500 years, few Vietnamese people have been able to suppress their emotions at the picture of the Emperor Nhân Tông's act of taking off his military robe to cover So-tu's corpse in the war of 1285.

It is from such strong hate for war that the Emperor mustered up all his strength to make a long-termed peace not only for his people but further for the neighboring ones, particularly the Chinese people. As soon as the image of fire and smoke of the 1288 war ceased arising in all the battlefields of the country, the Emperor, in his reception of a Chinese delegation coming by Kublai Khan's order to request the release of their generals and soldiers captured by our Army, expressed openly in his following lines

The peaceful atmosphere permeates all the quarters of earth,
The dust of war is all cleaned by water from the heavenly river

that he resolutely did his best to maintain the peace of Đại Việt. It may be said that this is a characteristic feature of his literary works, exposing all of his abiding aspiration for peace. It is rather surprising for us that a man who ever took part in fighting and gained glorious victories over the enemy as Nhân Tông was capable of demonstrating publicly his earnest wishes for life at peace. Undoubtedly, it once more proves that in his innermost the Emperor hardly regarded war as a ladder for him to mount to the peak of fame and glory. During his lifetime, even when he became a Buddhist monk, that is, the one who is generally considered to renounce the world for some peaceful deliverance of his own, the Emperor did not abandon his noble vow to work for the benefit of all sentient beings, for the welfare of his people and country.

Formerly, it has been generally believed by many people that after the Emperor Nhân Tông officially entered into monastic life it would be time for him to retreat from society, as what is falsely expressed in the following statement "the more [he] practiced [Buddhist teaching], the farther [he was separated] from social actualities, from the Buddha's ideal of saving the world." Yet it is factually in the period of his living as a Buddhist monk that the boundary of Đại Việt was extended more than 200 kilometers southward and the Viet-Cham peace was kept for dozens of years, laying the foundation for the common cause of advancing southward of the people.

Reading the two lines written by him

Following the fallen morning flowers, ideas of praise and blame perished,

Together with the cold night rains, desires for fame and wealth ended,

some people, who fail to put them on the logical grounds of Nhân Tông's thought, have hurried to comment superficially that they are "the lines of extreme pessimism," representing "the thought of absolute nihilism that originates from within Buddhism...within the regime of 'field-and-farm,' within the excessive prosperity of monasteries, and from all of its decadence." In such a comment, they have forgotten that the Emperor Nhân Tông is one of the "most celebrated authors" of Vietnamese literature in the Trần dynasty. And these outstanding authors "all exposed their firm confidence, their invincible spirit and their unshakeable volition through a series of long-standing verses." For whatever purposes such comments as just cited have been made, and in whatever degrees they have been used to distort the history of Vietnam in the past, the Emperor Nhân Tông's career, and the contributions of his own and of his reign to the Vietnamese people will never be denied. For they have actually constituted a period worthy of pride and gratitude in the history of the Vietnamese people.

Through the thought of Nhân Tông we have discovered his view of a type of 'one-way' time; that is to say, from his view a day that has passed away will never come back as in the words of Tuệ Trung Thượng Sỹ Trần Quốc Tung:

It is hard to recover our shadows
When the moon has set in the west.
Similarly, how can a river raise its waves again
When it has already flowed into the sea?

Therefore, in his own as well as others' lives in society time has become extremely precious. Human life is so short for some deed to be fulfilled:

Time passes by easily;
Man's lifetime does not remain.

For that reason, life becomes valuable. If one cannot find again a day that has already passed, one must devote one's whole time to affairs that are helpful to one's own and others' lives. In this connection, we can imagine how hurriedly and busily our people lived at that time. Indeed, they did live a busy and hurried life not because they wanted to enjoy as much as possible in return for their numerous losses in war but because they did not want to waste any moment in their efforts to rebuild their country and struggle for the protection of their country. It may be said that the people as a whole at the time were filled with wholesome emotions proceeding from their love of life, of their country, of their people. It was due to their optimistic views that they could conceive that time might be easily lost and life would pass day after day without returning, as what the Emperor Nhân Tông ever reminded them:

The cuckoos sing away in the bright moonlight;
Let not the spring pass wastefully.

For so long it has been generally thought that time is conceived in the East to be likened to a cycle; that is to say, such phenomena as prosperity and decadence or fortune and misfortune or wealth and poverty revolve one after another along a repeated circle just like the operation of four seasons year after year. Yet, in addition to this concept, there is another one, that is, the one-way time. Accordingly, a day that has passed will never return just as the sun once sets in the west, there will not be its own appearance in the sky of the same day. Our ancestors did have a concept of time rather similar to that of our modern age. It has sometimes been graphically described as the movement of a bicycle. Just like the one-way time, the bicycle always moves forward. But, in order to move forward, it must have its wheels. Similarly, the one-way time passes forward; but its passing must rest upon the cycles, that is, spring, summer, autumn, winter or prosperity and decadence, fortune and misfortune.

It is from such a concept of time that in war-time the people of Đại Việt were capable of gaining glorious achievements in many different battle-fields at Chương Dương, Hàm Tử, Tây Kết, Bạch Đằng. And within only a few years after war, they could rebuild a prosperous Đại Việt with fruitful rice-fields, vast mulberry-fields verdant all year round, great achievements in economy, handicraft, trade, and so on, which actually made the Yüan messenger Ch'ên-fu admire and respect. Indeed, the people of Đại Việt in both war and peace led their living according to what the Emperor Nhân Tông set forth in the "Worldly Life with Joy in the Way":

Making bridges and ferries, building temples and stūpas,
That is to cultivate the teaching on the ornamentation of form.

And

Faithfully serving one's lord, respectfully obeying one's father,
That is a Superior Man of loyalty and filial piety.

In reality, that our people could make enthusiastic efforts in fighting and building does not proceed from any aspiration for reputation and interest or praise and admiration, but from life itself. From their view life is not long; so they thought they had to live in such a manner as to be worth their short and precious time. The Emperor himself once formulated in the "Worldly Life with Joy in the Way" that "some desires for fame and affection are truly of ordinary people." Therefore, it is not surprising at all that, when living alone in a meditation room on the mountain, he had enough inspiration to write the poem:

Following the fallen morning flowers, ideas of praise and blame perished.
Together with the cold night rains, desires for fame and wealth ended.
The flowers are falling, the rain stopping, the mountain was serene.
The sound of a bird echoed and the spring was gone.

Though he got rid of ideas of fame, wealth, praise or blame, the author did not forget the spring. And then at the sound of a bird early in the morning when flowers had all fallen in the cold rain during the night he was surprised, being aware that the spring was gone. Time passes so fast. The previous year had recently left room for the new one; but, now, the spring in turn no longer existed. This concept of time took control of every thought and activity of the Emperor himself. In the "Worldly Life with Joy in the Way," he ever said:

Already for half a day I have let go of mind and body.

Yet, mundane affairs went on to emerge endlessly. Even when he was living in a secluded place where it is usually thought that there would never be any shadow of secular disturbance, worldly affairs did not cease occurring. The *Complete History* tells us that

"Nguyễn Quốc Phụ, who was working as a *nội thư chính chưởng*, was a close courtier of the Emperor Nhân Tông. In the years of Hưng Long (1293-1324), since the position of an executive official had not been occupied, the Emperor-Father (i.e., Trần Anh Tông) came to consult Nhân Tông at the Sùng Nghiêm temple. At the latter's suggestion that Quốc Phụ could undertake that position, the Emperor-Father said, 'if based upon his present position, it is possible; but, he is fond of drinking only.' Thereupon, Nhân Tông spoke nothing more. After all, [Quốc Phụ was] not appointed."[5] And as been said before, before his journey to Champa as a messenger in the 10th month of Kỷ Mão (1303), Đoàn Nhữ Hài also came to see Nhân Tông at this temple.

Such a life always fraught with work is obviously not spent for personal benefits, much less for some fame. Nothing could be considered to be of interest or fame when he himself was "wearing kṣaya, lying behind the paper curtain" and storing for himself nothing but "a pot of egg-fruit, a jar of soy." The idea of benefit has not been able to arise, much less that of fame; for, benefit and fame always follow each other. Nevertheless, such a view of conventional values does not imply an attitude of giving up all the responsibilities for life. The essential point is that the so-called secular achievements should not be aimed at as the only objective of life. The central objective that Nhân Tông's and the Đại Việt people's lives aimed at is to "let go of mind and body," and their "being calmed." If expressed in modern language, that is to pursue happiness. But, what happiness is must be answered by each individual. Whether Nhân Tông was settling on Mount Yên Tử as

---

[5] Vol. 6, p.37a5-9. [LMT]

a Buddhist monk or he was commanding a certain fighting in the battlefield in Tây Kết, he was undoubtedly the one who always lived in his state of being free of fetters and defilements. No one can bind us unless it is ourselves who are doing as such. No one can hinder us from leading a free life unless we ourselves refuse such a way of living. One must transform oneself and the world so as to have a life at peace and in freedom. This is the very message Nhân Tông's verses and writings convey to us today as well as many preceding generations:

Nobody ties you, why do you ask for liberation?

Once having no worldly thoughts, you don't need to search for the holy.

The gibbons are resting, the horses exhausted, men must be old.

There remains a meditation bed in a hermitage covered in cloud.

It is through the Emperor Nhân Tông's life that we may visualize how peacefully and pleasantly the whole people of Đại Việt lived and worked at the time. They earnestly worked for their living and fought for the protection of it. They did not seek after another world where they would be freed from passions and defilements of this world. Life is too short for them to form such deluded ideas in their mind. They had to make their great efforts to live and work in that short lifespan without wasting any moment. It may be said that it is the picture of the dishes of *cuốn* cakes that were prepared by the Emperor's order in a banquet for the Chinese messenger Chang Li-tao at the time the enemy had just been driven out of the country:

柘枝舞罷試春衫

況值今朝三月三

紅玉堆盤春菜餅
從來風俗舊安南

After the dance of "giá chi", let us try the robes of spring.
Particularly, today is the Thanh Minh festival.
The trays are full of "cuốn" cakes like rubies;
That is the ancient custom of the Vietnamese.

Or more simple, it is only the image of the remote mountains contemplated from the balcony of some pavilion in the evening:

楊柳花深鳥語遲
畫堂簷影暮雲飛
客來不問人間事
共倚欄杆看翠微

Deep in the blossoming willows the birds sang leisurely.
Beneath the eaves were floating the shadows of evening clouds.
Not concerned with worldly affairs,
The guest, leaning on the balcony, watched the verdant landscape lonely.

The Emperor Nhân Tông's poetry and writing are capable of representing "a skillful crystalization of philosophical senses and feelings for life and the world in an optimistic and generous spirit of a great personality as well as intrinsic inspiration and aspiration for freedom of an artist," but not to convey the "extremely pessimistic" ideas as some have imagined. Consequently, his position in the history of Vietnamese literature is very great. With the "Worldly Life with Joy in the Way" and the "Song of the Realization of the Way," he initiated a new period in the history of Vietnamese literature, where the national language played a major role. Furthermore, through his verses in Chinese and abstruse writings, he can provide us with new perceptions of human beings' eternal problems such as time and life.

Until now, we have just mentioned some Vietnamese writings and Chinese poems of Nhân Tông. There remain some of his Chinese writings that have not yet been published and satisfactorily studied. They are 22 letters written by Nhân Tông to Yüan emperors and officials in his political and diplomatic struggles against them for protecting the country's ownership and thereby gaining enough time to strengthen and develop his armed forces for the wars imposed by the enemy. Of these letters some are completely preserved but some remain only fragments. And the most considerable point is that they are all preserved in Chinese documents alone, that is, the *Yüan-shih*, the *T'ien-nan Hsin-chi*, the *Ch'ên Kang-chung shi-chi*, and the *Annan chi-lüeh*. None of them has been preserved in our country's historical documents; if any, they are merely some extracts from the works just cited.

Reading these letters, the first impression on the part of readers is that the Emperor Nhân Tông always held a consistent attitude toward the enemy. He bluntly rejected any ideas of surrendering to them and resolutely protected the country's ownership in spite of any requests made by them that he should open up a road for them to attack Champa or he himself had to go for audience at their court. Though Kublai Khan made use of various cunning measures, from the delicate diplomatic ones of promising noble titles to the Emperor to the cunning m0ilitary ones of ordering invasions carried out, he was finally defeated by the fighting strength of the Đại Việt people under the Emperor Nhân Tông's leadership.

In addition, the Emperor helped discover the hypocritical words that Kublai Khan ostensibly suggested. The latter, for instance, boasted that he had always welcomed those who came to his court for audience and treated them as his "children" whom he had the responsibility to "take care of". All the messengers sent by his order to our country always spoke of his tolerance so enormous as sky and sea. The most often phrase they liked to make use of is "universal humaneness," that is, his humane sympathy for all people. In face of such arguments, the Emperor Nhân Tông pointed out that had Kublai Khan truly possessed such an enormous amount of humanity, he should not have forced him to go for audience. What would happen if he had died en route for the Yüan court? We will see that these two reasons were frequently set forth by the Emperor for his refusal.

More than anyone else, the Emperor understood that presenting himself at the Yüan court for some audience would be to give up himself to the enemy, to hand over the national ownership to them. Therefore, he resolutely accepted no concessions in relation to the enemy's request. In effect, through his letters Kublai Khan might show some hope of overwhelming the Emperor's firm resolution. At the same time, however, he knew obviously that however persuasive those letters might be they could not change the Emperor's resolution. Consequently, following those letters he carried out the two consecutive invasions of our country with a staff of experienced generals and tens of thousands of troops and ships.

Equally impressive are the letters written by the Emperor to Yüan functionaries, particularly to the delegation headed by Liang-tseng to our country in 1293. These letters are of both tender and resolute style aimed at condemning Kublai Khan's hypocritical policy just mentioned and simultaneously pointing out his evil plot to invade our country behind his apparently righteous statements. On the other hand, these letters may reveal some contemptuous attitude of our court to the representatives of the so-called "Heavenly Court" and our challenges to their endurance. In the *Annan chi-shih* of *Ch'ên Kang-chung shih-chi*, Ch'ên-fu wrote down the fact that no sooner had his mission entered our country than they received the order of our court to follow the roads just opened up such that they all felt frightened: "Our messengers arrived in that country not by the former roads but by the new ones just opened up and winding very perilously right in the mountains. Their intention was to show us that the way to their country was far and dangerous."[6] In spite of this, they had to follow our court's indications without a word of protest.

Then, having reached the capital Thăng Long, they had to struggle many times for an entrance into the citadel through the Dương Minh Gate, that is, the South Gate of the citadel, instead of the Vân Hội Gate or the Nhật Tân Gate as our court proposed. In the words of the *Liang-tseng chuan* in the *Yüan Shih*: "In the 1st month of Chih Yüan 30 (1293) [our mission] arrived in Annan. That country [i.e., that capital] has three gates. The middle gate is called Dương Minh; the left is Nhật Tân and the right Vân Hội. Their officials received us outside the citadel and intended to lead us through the Nhật Tân gate. Very angrily, Tseng said, 'If the

---

[6] Vol. 2, p.34a3-4. [LMT]

decree were not received through the central gate, it would mean that I were indirectly causing the king's order to be disregarded,' and decided to go back to the House of Messengers. They then opened the Vân Hội gate for us to enter, which was again refused by Tseng. After all, they had to receive our decree through the Dương Minh gate. Tseng blamed Nhật Tôn not to go out to receive the decree."[7]

It may be said that it was a warning of our court to the mission from the Heavenly Court. The same warning was formerly given to Ch'ai-ch'ung by the Emperor Nhân Tông when he ordered a banquet in honor of the former held in a corridor. At that time Ch'ai Ch'ung also got angry and refused the invitation until the Emperor ordered the banquet to be moved to the TậpHiềnPalace, as in the words of the *Anna Chuan* in the *Yüan Shih*: "As usual, Nhật Huyên had the banquet held in the corridor. Ch'ung and his companions refused to come. After they returned to the House of Messengers, Phạm Minh Tự came with a letter of apology by Nhật Huyên's order, saying that the banquet was to be held at the Tập Hiển Palace."[8]

In 1291 Chang Li-tao's mission also underwent such a warning though they were later welcomed by the Emperor Nhân Tông as what was written down by the former in the *Chang-shang-shu hsin-lu* and later cited by the Vietnamese traitor Lê Sực in his *Annan chih-lüeh* 3, pp.45-47.

The 22 letters written by the Emperor Nhân Tông to the Yüan

---

[7] Vol. 178, p.1b3-6.
[8] Vol.209, p.4a11-12.

emperors and officials, therefore, should be read by all of us so as to see how hard and tactfully our court's struggles against the enemy on the diplomatic front occurred. They represent the firm resolution not only of the Emperor but also of our people as a whole to protect the country's ownership, to refuse any concessions to the enemy in any forms. Consequently, they may be considered to have initiated a style of literature employed as an effective device in our court's political and military struggles, which Nguyễn Trãi, in the name of Lê Lợi, would later represent in the *Quân Trung Từ Mệnh Tập*.

This style has its own characteristics; that is to say, the wording must be characterized by both flexible gracefulness and sharp resoluteness. It must consist of various arguments to overcome the enemy in the ideological aspect, attacking precisely and destroying completely any assumptions that have ever been considered by them to be eternal truths and supposedly never to be rejected. Indeed, whereas Kublai Khan argued that no one in the world could avoid death and that there would be no place where one would be immortal, the Emperor Nhân Tông pointed out to him that it was not important that one would die or not but that one's death would be beneficial or harmful to others. If Kublai Khan was always proud of his alleged tolerance, which was incessantly praised by his courtiers, the Emperor Nhân Tông put up the question as to why the former always forced him to go for audience. Although the Emperor, in response to Kublai Khan's reasoning that to come for audience would be fully rewarded and bestowed, stated that in addition to his desire of being fully rewarded he also wanted to see for himself the landscape of China, he was afraid that he would die on the way. And such a death would bring about nothing beneficial for himself as well as for Kublai Khan, let alone some possible hurts to the latter's "kind-heartedness".

Apart from the arguments for the purpose of overcoming the enemy's volition, these letters are aimed at condemning their crimes against the people of Đại Việt. In a letter sent to the Yüan emperor in 1291 and cited by Hsu Ming-shan in his *Tien-nan hsin-chi* of the *Shu-fu*, the Emperor Nhân Tông depicted Wu-ma-er's brutal actions of looting the people, burning their houses, destroying temples and pagodas: "In the winter of Chih-yüan 24 (1827), the Great Army came here, destroying and burning all pagodas and temples across our country, digging our ancestors' graves, killing our innocent countrymen, damaging the common people's properties--none of brutal destructive offenses were not committed by them (...). Taking control over the sea, Wu-ma-er ordered his troops to arrest all the inhabitants along the coast, among whom the old were killed, the young taken captives. The bodies of those who had been hanged, tied, cut, were scattered everywhere."[9] The letter may be regarded as the first conviction of war crimes committed by those warlike invaders who would have to be severely punished by our people.

The letters sent by the Emperor Nhân Tông to the Yüan emperors, therefore, occupy a definite position in the history of Vietnamese literature. Most particularly, they could initiate a style of literature that the *Quân Trung Từ Mệnh Tập* inherited later and brought into effect fully in the struggle against the enemy. This is a type of literature serving the strategy of "fighting combined with

---

[9] Vol.51, p.18b 6-7. [LMT]

negotiation." The weight of statements in the letters of negotiation is to be determined by some victory on the front. In other words, statements must be supported and represented by forceful actions. Accordingly it may be truly hard, particularly in the diplomatic relation between the two countries, for statements of negotiation, whatever righteous content they may have, to bring about some concrete results in the task of protecting a country's ownership unless they are somehow supported by and accompanied with certain military actions.

In spite of their such great value in various aspects, the role of those letters in the history of Vietnamese literature has not yet precisely evaluated, not to mention some distorted remarks as to them particularly in some textbooks of the History of Vietnamese Literature. For that reason, we insist once more that there should be a new manner of evaluating the Emperor Nhân Tông's diplomatic correspondence for the purpose of justifying and clarifying his own characteristic contributions to the history of our people's literature. This is also the reason for us to collect and publicize the whole correspondence sent by the Emperor Nhân Tông to the Yüan court. Until now they have not been sufficiently collected and published in Vietnamese literature, at least within the range of materials known hitherto.

Concerning the Chinese style of the letters themselves, it is interesting for us to discover that they are more or less influenced by the Vietnamese style, particularly as to some structures that have been detected in the *Collected Teachings of Six Pāramitās*. In the following letter numbered "the Fifth" by us, for instance, there is the sentence "不能身見末光然中心欣幸 (Though not able to see you personally, [I am] pleased in mind)" where the verbal structure of "中 心 欣 幸" (literally, "pleased in mind") is of special style. Such a structure in the Chinese language as "中 心 (in mind)" is found first to appear only in the *Ching shi* and then in Khương Tăng Hội's translation of the *Collected Teachings of Six Pāramitās*.[10] Yet, in the 13th century it is found again in a letter written by the Emperor Trần Thánh Tông to Kublai Khan in the spring of Chih Yüan 12 (1275), which was recorded in "Annan chuan" in the *Yüan Shih*,[11] that is, "中 心 喜 悦" (literally, "satisfied in mind"). This points out the influence of the *Collected Teachings of Six Pāramitās* on our country's literature in the 13th century. Besides, in Tuệ Trung Trần Quốc Tung's poetry the influence of this text may be clearly recognized, particularly in the "Vật Bất Năng Dung."[12]

Thus, through these diplomatic documents we further know the influence of Buddhist texts upon writings not only of the Emperor Nhân Tông but also of many other poets and writers in the Trần dynasty. Further, the images used by the Emperor in his letters reveal more or less his view in commenting on Kublai Khan's personality. Though he modestly addressed himself to be "bề tôi nhỏ bé" (i.e., a little subject) under the latter's command, the images that he depicted to praise Kublai Khan ironically are in essence only blames figuratively expressed. Many times Kublai Khan was mentioned by him in such phrases as "[your heart is as enormous as] mountain and sea, containing all the dirt" or "[your

---

[10] Lê Mạnh Thát, Lục Độ Tập Kinh Và Lịch Sử Khởi Nguyên Dân Tộc Ta, Tu Thư Đại Học Vạn Hạnh, 1972, p.264-271. [LMT]

[11] p.3b2-10.

[12] Lê Mạnh Thát, Tuệ Trung Thượng Sỹ Toàn Tập, manuscript, 1979. [LMT]

heart is of the same quantity as] sky and earth encompassing all the waste." It is evident that in his invasions of our country Kublai Khan's heart or mind was all the time filled with "so much dirt" literally and figuratively alike. Therefore, the Emperor Nhân Tông's diplomatic correspondence is worth reading and studying elaborately so that we can see the depth and majesty of a Vietnamese man who ever created a heroic age of our people. He represents a personality of invincible and deep tenderness, full of altruistic tolerance but, simultaneously, fraught with unshakeable resolution to smash the enemy's plots of invading the nation's ownership and the country's territory. It is for such a purpose that we have decided to publicize the whole collection of the Emperor Nhân Tông's diplomatic correspondence.

Trans. by **Đạo Sinh**

EMPEROR NHÂN TÔNG AND THE MAKING OF PEACE IN THE POSTWAR PERIOD

BY PROF. **LÊ MẠNH THÁT**

As our people were joyfully celebrating the victory in the capital of Thăng Long, Kublai Khan began to inflict severe punishments on the generals who had fortunately survived the fighting expedition. By his order, T'o-huan had to go into exile for life in Yangchou whereas Ao-lu-chih had to move to Kianghsi as in the words of *Yuan Shih* 117, p.5a1-2, and 131, p.7a9. On the part of Emperor Nhân Tông, as a precaution against some possible invasion by the Yuan Court in the coming years a diplomatic campaign was urgently carried out and, at the same time, some measures were taken for recuperating the country in the postwar period.

The emperor's initial measure was to grant an amnesty for prisoners throughout the country and give orders for complete exemptions from taxes of all kinds and civil services for the people in the areas heavily destroyed by war and partial exemptions for those in other areas. In *ĐVSKTT* 5, p.55a1-3, we read: "*In the summer, the 4th month, [of Mậu Tý, 1288] the Emperor-Father, who was then taking his imperial seat in the corridor of Imperial Guards' building (because the palace had been burned down by the enemy), issued the decree of 'nationwide exemption'. Those areas that had been heavily destroyed by war were completely exempted from taxes; the others were completely or partly exempted according to their different circumstances.*" Thus, it was quite natural that all efforts had to be mustered, after such a terrible war, to make up the losses caused by the enemy; and the exemption from, or reduction of, taxes and civil services was inevitably the first target to be focused on. For this purpose, the decree was issued shortly after Emperor Nhân Tông and his father returned to the imperial capital on the 27th of the third month of Mậu Tý (1288).

Apart from what concerns the issue of the emperor's general amnesty ordinance, *ĐVSKTT* 5, pp.55a3-b5, further tells us a story from which we can acquire some more knowledge of history, culture and society of our country in those days. It says, "*The King ordered the 'Office of Administration' to make good relations with the Academy. According to regulations, before announcing the King's decree the Academy had to transfer its manuscript to the Office of Administration in advance so that the latter could have enough time to practice reading it. For, in the course of announcing, a functionary of the Office of Administration had to expound both sound and meaning of each word of the decree to the public since the positions in this office were all held by eunuchs alone. At that time the relationship between Lê Tòng Giáo, the left-assistant [of the Office of Administration], and Đinh Củng Viên, the Decree-Scribe of the Academy, was not so good that the latter intentionally delayed the transfer of manuscript although the former had repeatedly asked for it and the date of issue was coming nearer. That day, it was just as the King was going out of the citadel that Củng Viên agreed to pass the manuscript to Tòng Giáo. Not understanding the sounds and meanings of words of the decree, the latter had to stand silent. By the King's order, the former had to dictate both sound and meaning to Tòng Giáo, at which the latter felt so much shame. The more loudly Củng Viên dictated the decree, the more softly Tòng Giáo repeated it. Consequently, everyone there could hear only the voice of the former. On his return to the Inner Palace, the King summoned Tòng Giáo, saying, 'Củng Viên is a man of letters whereas you are a middle-ranking official; why do you dislike each other so much? As an official in Thiên Trường where shrimps and yellow oranges abound, why haven't you thought of offering him some?' Since then, their relationship became more and more friendly."*

From the fact above, it may be assumed that in the Trần Dynasty, or rather, prior to the year 1288, there must have been the order that a king's decree should be announced in both Chinese and Vietnamese. In the words of *ĐVSKTT* the event above is referred to simply as an *old event*, which connotes that the announcement of decrees in those two languages had been applied long before. Yet, the book does not tell us when it began. Was it, then, possibly employed in the reign of Lý, or even earlier in the reigns of Đinh and Lê? The latter is a possibility. For most of the kings of Đinh and Lê were not so well learned [in Chinese] as those of Lý as is mentioned in *ĐVSKTT*. Further, the issue of a decree was aimed not only at a king but chiefly at his courtiers and the masses. In those dynasties and even in those that followed, the Chinese language was scarcely needed by most of officials and people of Đại Việt. If any, it was employed simply for signing papers of some kind.

In this connection, we may come to admit that in the history of our country the Vietnamese language had ever been, in some measure, an official administrative language even though all of historical documents concerning the matter in question, with the exceptions of "The Mourning Speech in Memory of Nguyễn Biểu" by Trần Trùng Quang, "The Oaths Taken by Lê Lợi and His Men at Lam Sơn", or Emperor Quang Trung's "Proclamation of Fighting against Ch'ing Invaders", and so on, were lost. Otherwise stated, it seems quite unreasonable to claim that the Vietnamese language might never have been employed in political life of Vietnam. On the contrary, it did play the role of an official language of the imperial court. There remains a single question as to whether this language was easy or difficult to read. In his *Chỉ Nam Ngọc Âm Giải Nghĩa*, Dhyāna Master Pháp Tính (1470-1550) tells us the fact that the script of our language employed in his time and earlier, that is, by the first half of the 15th century, was for the most part composed of "compound characters"[1]:

Formerly so many compound characters were created
That people of little education found it hard to read them.

---

[1] Viet. nôm xe chữ kép.

Pháp Tính therefore held that a new script of 'national speech', easy to read and write, should be invented for the sake of the masses:

Today simple characters should be introduced to people of little education
So that they can read and understand them easily.

Thus, the Vietnamese language did have its own official bearing under the reign of Emperor Nhân Tông. This is evidently proved by the fact that the very amnesty ordinance of the emperor had to be further announced in Vietnamese. The emperor himself, too, had writings in Vietnamese that have been completely preserved so far, such as *Cư Trần Lạc Đạo Phú* and *Đắc Thú Lâm Tuyền Thành Đạo Ca*. They are among the oldest writings extant in the history of literature of our country, let alone *Giáo Trò* of Từ Đạo Hạnh and a much older text entitled *Việt Ca* in *Thiết Uyển*.

The fact that the Vietnamese language was actually employed to announce imperial decrees is of great value in the social aspect. It reveals a historical fact that the king and the public had some desire to speak with each other in such an equal manner as those of one and the same great family, of the same national race. ĐVSKTT 5, p.61a4-8, gives a further detail in the Section "The Third Month of Nhâm Thìn (1292)": "*The King often went out. On the way, seeing servants of the nobles, he called them by name, asking 'Where are your masters?' and, simultaneously, forbade his escorts to drive them away. On his return to the palace, he called in his subjects, saying, 'In ordinary days, my courtiers are always found around me; but only those people, [that is, the nobles], present themselves when the country falls into misfortune.' Thus spoke the king since he had been deeply moved by their loyalty and assistance through his terrible times.*" In reality, it was this intimate and friendly relationship that worked effectively as a motive to establish the people's powerful solidarity, setting the premise for our glorious achievements in the two wars of defense under the leadership of the emperor himself.

It was not until the year that followed the issue of decrees with respect to the general amnesty and the exemptions of taxes and civil services, i.e., in the fourth month of Kỷ Sửu, that Emperor Nhân Tông gave orders for acknowledging the achievements of those who had devoted themselves to the recent resistant war. ĐVSKTT 5, pp.56b7-57a8, writes down the task of rewarding as follows: "*In the summer, the 4th month, having deliberated over the achievements [of our people] in [their efforts at] annihilating the Yuan enemy, [the King] conferred the title Đại Vương on Hưng Đạo Vương, Khai Quốc Công on Hưng Vũ Vương, Tiết Độ Sứ on Hưng Nhượng Vương. Those who had great merits were named after the 'National Surname'. Among them was Khắc Chung, who himself was appointed Đại Hành Khiển. Đỗ Hành was appointed to be 'official of internal attendance' only because he did not turn over Wu-ma-er, whom he had captured in fighting, to the Emperor but to the Emperor-Father. Hưng Trí Vương did not get any promotion because he had halted the Yuan captives who were on their way back to their country by the Emperor's order, according to which our officers were not permitted to hinder them. In addition, Lương Uất, the Chieftain of the Man minority group in Lạng Giang, was appointed to be Head of Camp Qui Hóa, and Hà Tất Năng to be Phục Hầu because they had commanded their men to fight against the enemy. Observing that some of his subjects showed seemingly unsatisfied with his decisions, the Emperor-Father said, "Tell me whether you are sure the Hồ enemy would no longer come and rob our country. If so, I would have no regret at all in giving you the highest titles. If not, what titles would be left for me to give you in case the enemy would come back and you would get more achievements? At this, everyone showed their satisfaction."*

Thus, the fact of rewarding those officials who had had achievements in the two wars took place rather excitingly. The noteworthy point here is that Đỗ Hành failed to get higher promotion as he broke the imperial order by not turning over Wu-ma-er to the Emperor but to the Emperor-Father Trần Thánh Tông. This indicates that it was none other than Emperor Nhân Tông who was the Supreme Leader of Đại Việt and made, for the most part, ultimate decisions during the war time.

From the account cited above, too, we may acquire a further detail that the situation of fighting between our troops and Yuan invaders in many different fronts had permanently been kept under observation by the emperor himself. The most typical fact is Hưng Trí Vương's failure to be promoted due to his halting Yuan troops on their return home without the emperor's order. No doubt, the heaviest responsibility for our struggle against Yuan invasion was then actually entrusted to the Emperor with the assistance of his father as an advisor and Trần Hưng Đạo as a direct commander. It is necessary to clarify this fact so that everyone can precisely recognize the crucial role of Emperor Nhân Tông in the two wars of 1285 and 1288, a role of which many people today do have so poor knowledge and thus false evaluation, let alone those in the former days when

"Civilization in East Asia has been so completely taken away by Heaven
That moral principles are being 'turned upside down' in society today."

Furthermore, such poor knowledge and false judgment may manifest themselves in terms of modest streets named after Emperor Nhân Tông in many different cities of our country today.

Following the rewarding just mentioned, by the fifth month, the emperor gave orders for further rewarding, which was aimed at *"conferring the additional title Liệt Hầu on Nguyễn Khoái and granting him a district (...) called Khoái Lộ"*, and for recording names, biographies and portraits of those who *"had pioneered in eliminating the enemy"* in *Trung Hưng Thực Lục.*

Parallel to this was *"the carrying-out of punishment on those who had surrendered to the enemy. Among them were functionaries, who would be punished according to their own faults. The soldiers and civilians who were not sentenced to death had to carry wood and rock for building palaces"* as in the words of ĐVSKTT 5, p.57a8-b1. In addition, Emperor Nhân Tông paid special attention to the two villages of Ba Điểm and Bàng Hà, since, according to ĐVSKTT 5, p.52b5-6, *"on the 30th (of the 12th month of Đinh Hợi, i.e., February 2n , 1288) when the Yuan Prince A-thai and Wu-ma-er, having gathered their 300,000 men in an attack on Vạn Kiếp, moved downstream eastward, the people in Ba Điểm and Bàng hà surrendered to them."* And the punishment implemented by the emperor's order is clearly described in ĐVSKTT 5, p.57b7-9, as *"punishing troops and common people of the two villages of Ba Điểm and Bàng hà to serve in Thang Mộc Army, where they would never have opportunity to be promoted officers but merely employed as servants for consecratory affairs."*

Also in relation to the emperor's measures of punishment, *ĐVSKTT* 5, pp.57b9-58a6, tells us a most remarkable fact that the Emperor-Father gave orders for burning all the papers concerning the officials who had given up to the enemy. It says, *"In the former penetration of Yuan invaders into our country, some of our nobles and officials had sought to surrender to them just in their encampment. After their withdrawal, our troops discovered a case [in their command post], in which were some papers [concerning the Vietnamese traitors] stored...The Emperor-Father ordered all the papers burned for the purpose of allaying the traitors. Only those who had fled to the enemy's country were delivered judgment by default. They were sentenced to death or exile, their properties confiscated and their national surname stripped. As for Trần Kiện and Tính Quốc's son, for instance, their surnames were changed into Mai; so were others such as Mai Long and his companions. Regarding [Trần] Ích Tắc, though a relative of the emperor's, he was still treated in the same manner as other traitors except that his surname was allowed to remain. Yet, he was simply called Ả Trần, which implies the one who was as cowardly as a woman. In contemporary accounts, they were all called Ả Trần, Mai Kiện, etc. Furthermore, Đặng Long, who was a low-ranking official but well versed in literature and very close to the king, was sentenced to death. Formerly he had ever been listed in the promotion and the king had intended to appoint him to the Academy but the King-*

Father did not agree. Unsatisfied [with the King-Father's decision,] he had, too, surrendered to the enemy. When the enemy were defeated, he was captured. To prevent some wrong-doing like this from being committed again among the officials, the emperor gave the order for him to be cut down."

The facts mentioned above point out not only the emperor's humane policy of allaying the people in their attempts to build the country in the postwar period but also his tolerance towards a minority of people who had unfortunately been driven into wrong-doings. Moreover, it was necessary to reorganize the machinery of administration that had been militarized during the war. According to *ĐVSKTT* 5, p.58a5, in the spring, the second month, of Canh Dần (1290), Emperor Nhân Tông *"appointed officials of literature to the Routes"* to implement the policy of ruling by law, laying a firm foundation for the people's living and production.

Simultaneously, he also carried out the inspection of those officials' tasks. *ĐVSKTT* 5, p.60b1-4, tells us the story of Phí Mạnh, who was struck with poles due to bribery but later became a very qualified official, in 1292: *"Shortly after being appointed An Phủ Sứ of Diễn Châu, Phí Mạnh began to show corruptive. The King sent for him and punished him with poles. Having been reinstated in his former office, however, he became so well known for his justice and purity. The inhabitants of Diễn Châu District all said, "An Phủ of Diễn Châu is as pure as water."* Emperor Nhân Tông also appointed such men of good achievements as Phùng Sỹ Chu to be Hành Khiển, Trần Thì Kiến to be An Phủ of Yên Khang, and so on. As a consequence, the State's machinery equipped with functionaries well versed in law and capable of stabilizing the people's living could gradually operate as effectively as before.

Thus, the reorganization of civil administration had been carried out rather systematically. Yet, it did not mean that there would be more officials to be appointed to central and local administrative positions. We have seen how strictly the task of rewarding those who had had great contributions in the two wars of 1285 and 1288 was restricted by the emperor to the point that some officials had asked for further rewarding and how tactfully the Emperor-Father set forth his own explanation, let alone the task of appointing officials and bestowing titles. And we will later see that when reading the register of officials appointed and titles bestowed in the reign of Trần Anh Tông, Emperor Nhân Tông had to utter, "*Why can such a small country as a 'palm' have so many officials appointed and titles bestowed?*", as in the words of ĐVSKTT 6, p.36a9. It was this very thought of Emperor Nhân Tông that gave rise to the concept "officials increasing, populace perishing" advanced later by Ngô Thời Nhiệm. It may be said that the status of a government as a service but not as a support for the authorities to exploit the masses was definitively conceived in our country long ago, undoubtedly in the days of Emperor Nhân Tông. Accordingly, though it was necessary for Emperor Nhân Tông to civilize the administrative machinery, he surely did not make it a cumbersome one to exploit 'blood and fat' of the masses.

Therefore, according to ĐVSKTT 5, pp.58b4, 59a5-60a7, 59b9-60a1, when, due to the unfavorable change of weather, "*drought lasted from the summer, the 6th month, to the winter, the 10th month, [of the year 1289],*" then "*the Tô Lịch River ran upstream (i.e., owing to heavy rains the water rose and flowed in the direction opposite to the regular movement of the river) in the summer, the 4th month, [of the year 1290],"* and *"many people died of famine on roads [in 1291],"* Emperor Nhân Tông urgently ordered *"the delivery of free rice to and exemption from poll-tax for the poor"*. It was thanks to such ingenious measures that on their arrival in 1293 Liang Seng and Trần Phu witnessed a rich and beautiful postwar Đại Việt with well-developed agriculture, prosperous commerce, and powerful industry.

Agriculturally, *"four crops of rice are gained a year; seedlings grow well even in cold winter"* and the fields of mulberry, banana, longan, litchi, jackfruit, coconut, etc., were verdant. Concerning commerce, *"every village has its own market, which is held every two days, with a large variety of goods. Every five miles is a three-apartmented house built, all sides of which are arranged with stands for displaying goods"*, *"nothing needs to be stored by the state, all depending on supplies from merchant ships."* And our people's business was carried on not only in the country but also in the neighboring countries: *"in Chinghua Prefecture, i.e., Huanchou in the T'ang Dynasty, over 200 miles far from the town of Giao Châu there come a great number of ships from the 'barbarian' countries. The business on ships is very busy."* To reach such a foreign trade Đại Việt had to develop handicraft and industry well apart from its prosperous agriculture.

For such prosperous agriculture and commerce to be achieved within just four years after war, our country must have developed industry in a parallel direction with handicraft. This development was aimed, in the first place, at rebuilding the postwar country in which numerous palaces, towns, temples, pagodas, homes, and so on, had been burned down by the enemy, and countless roads, bridges, and so on had been destroyed on account of strategic requirements of warfare. Despite such terrible aftermath of war Trần Phu, on his arrival in Thăng Long, could see four bridges around the imperial capital. In the words of his *An Nam Tức Sự*, "*there are no ramparts but very low earthen walls in Giao Châu. In the west is Hoa Phúc District, encircled by the river, in front of which are four bridges named Mạc Kiều, Tây Dương, Ma Tha, and Lão Biên for traffic into and out of [the district].*" A little far from the capital, still in the words of Trần Phu, that is, "*sixty miles far from the House of Messengers, is the An Hóa Bridge, a mile from which is the Thanh Hóa Bridge. On this bridge is a house of nineteen apartments.*"

Regarding the Thăng Long capital, when it was brought under T'o-huan's control in the war of 1285, the palaces therein were simply described, in *Yuan Shih* 209, p.7a12-13, as follows: "*the palace has five gates, above which is [a tablet] engraved 'Đại Hưng Gate'; on both sides are smaller gates. The central building named Thiên An Ngự Điện has nine apartments. Its south door is named Triều Thiên Pavilion.*" According to ĐVSKTT 5, p.55a2, the palace was completely burned down. In the words of *Chang Shang-shu Hsin Lu* cited by Lê Sực in *An Nam Chí Lược*3, p.46, however, on a mission to our country in 1291 Chang Li-tao claimed that the palaces that were then in such perfect condition could not have been burned down by T'o-huan. In reality, some of these might have been destroyed by T'o-huan's troops but they could have been rebuilt later by our court. Consequently, it was not surprising at all that when he arrived in 1293, Trần Phu had seen Đại Việt, particularly the Thăng Long capital, in such a greatly magnificent appearance.

Still in *An Nam Tức Sự*, Trần Phu described the residence of our emperor as follows: "*Its gate is called Dương Minh, above which is the pavilion Triều Thiên. The small gate on the left is called Nhật Tân, the small one on the right called Vân Hội. Inside is a large 'celestial well' about tens of feet deep. Behind it is a stair leading to the Tập Hiền Palace, above which is a large pavilion called Minh Linh. A corridor on the right leads to a large palace called Đức Huy, the left door of which is called Đồng Lạp, the right one called Kiều Ứng. The inscriptions on the tablets are all gilded.*"

For such bridges and palaces to be perfectly built, the industry of producing tiles and bricks must have been well developed. Trần Phu gave us a description of special tiles in our country at that time: "*the tile has the shape of a board, the upper half of which is square but the lower haft pointed, similar to the balance for weighing rice in the old days. Fixed to wooden rafters with bamboo nails, the tiles overlap one another from the lower ends of rafters on to the ridge of roof as scales of fish.*"

In addition to the production of tiles and bricks for construction, the Vietnamese ancestors could learn how to use boats as skillfully as the Hồ barbarians could ride on horses. Especially, in the time of Emperor Nhân Tông this skill was put to its best use in such naval battles as Vân Đồn, Vạn Kiếp, Bạch Đằng. And in the progress of trade with foreign countries at seaports, the industry of building ships received special attention from our court. Trần Phu ever mentioned the warships of Đại Việt as follows: "*Made of very thin boards, the ship is light and long. Its bows look like the wings of mandarin ducks; its sides curve rather highly and normally seat thirty oarsmen. When manned with a hundred oarsmen, it can move as fast as flying."*

Just as civil industry, military industry was well developed, too. In the defense of Thăng Long in 1285, as we have seen before, Đại Việt troops are said to have employed 'cannons'. Today, although we are not quite sure whether these cannons were designed to shoot stones or 'fire-balls', they were no doubt used by Đại Việt troops on the battlefields as is recorded in *Yuan Shih*. In addition, in the two wars of 1285 and 1288 some generals of the enemy asserted that many of their troops such as A-pa-chieh had been shot down with our poisoned arrows. Thus, even the manufacturing of bows, arrows, spears, scimitars, etc., was of special interest, too. In *An Nam Tức Sự*, Trần Phu gives us further information on another kind of weapons called 'water-bow', which is not mentioned in history books of Vietnam and China: *"water-bows, otherwise called 'xá sa', are designed to shoot out water by the force of compressed air. If being shot, the skin where the water touches will turn into a pink round swelling, which causes a fatal itch unless it is cut off."*

Further, in the economy under the reign of Emperor Nhân Tông not only weapons and materials of construction but such a variety of goods as cloth, ingredients, ornaments, and so on, were also produced. According to Trần Phu, for example, a kind of incense called *long nhụy*[2] *"is made from pollen of 'dragon-flowers' mixed with oil of gum penzoin, which is rolled into small sticks about one*

---

[2] Lit. 'dragon stamen'.

meter long. They are usually hung on the wall and can produce very sweet smell for more than a day when burning." As to cloth, various kinds were produced such as silk, satin, tulle, muslin, canvas, cotton cloth, paper cloth, etc. and they were of various colors; but, according to Trần Phu, the black was the most popular for the people.

In short, in spite of several famines caused by so many natural disasters as drought and rains lasting for months, the postwar economy of Đại Việt began to recover its strength by early 1293. Through tactful policies, Emperor Nhân Tông was capable of recovering an economy that had been destroyed by war and natural disasters so that the country could soon regain its beautiful appearance as what was described by Trần Phu in *An Nam Tức Sự*.

Parallel to the reconstruction of the country and the improvement of living conditions of the people, Emperor Nhân Tông took special care for spiritual life of the people. He attempted to preserve the sacred past, which his predecessors had sacrificed their lives to found, by conferring sacred titles upon those who had devoted themselves to the country, such as Phù Đổng Thiên Vương, Triệu Quang Phục, Lý Phật Tử, Phùng Hưng, Lý Thường Kiệt, and so on. With respect to the heroes who had sacrificed their lives in the two wars of defense in 1285 and 1288, Emperor Nhân Tông showed his gratitude by giving them noble posthumous titles.

The fact above was not found in *ĐVSKTT*, yet it was, fortunately, written down in *Việt Điện U Linh Tập*. In effect, the fact that the heroes and those who made great contributions to the country were granted noble titles had occurred long before the time of Emperor Nhân Tông. Emperor Lý Thái Tổ, for instance, did the same toward the young hero Phù Đổng Thiên Vương.[3] The task, however, had not been carried out so formally and systematically until Emperor Nhân Tông's time. For the first time in the history of Vietnam, a sacred shrine has been officially built for the genuine characters, whose careers and achievements for the sake of the country were recognized by the history, but not for some gods or saints either imported from abroad or invented by people in the country.

According to Lý Tế Xuyên's account in *Việt Điện U Linh Tập*, those who were conferred in the years of Trùng Hưng the First (1285) and the Second (1288) amount to 27, and this is not a small number. Further, from the records in relation to the task of conferring, we are aware that his *Việt Điện U Linh Tập* could be based on some documents concerning the saints, which had been submitted to Emperor Nhân Tông for consideration. It should be noticed that according to his preface to the work, Lý Tế Xuyên was ever entrusted with the task of commanding the transportation of the Chinese Buddhist Canon[4], a position that was more or less related to Buddhism. The fact that 27 heroes and heroines were sanctified and many gods of mountains, rivers and land officially enshrined points out that Emperor Nhân Tông had the intention of establishing a sacred and heroic past for our people, acknowledging these great characters brilliant examples for them to follow in their efforts to lead a living deserving what their ancestors have left just in their Fatherland. Hence, it may be said

---

[3] Lit. The Heavenly King of Phù Đổng Village.

[4] Original title: Thủ Đại Tạng Thư Văn Chính Chưởng Trung Phẩm Phụng Ngự An Tiêm Lộ Chuyển Vận Sứ.

that patriotism and heroism of the Vietnamese were cultivated at their best in the reign of Emperor Nhân Tông on the basis of the sacred past just mentioned. Furthermore, it may also be a great contribution by the emperor to our people's spiritual life.

Simultaneous with the measures taken to reestablish a prosperous postwar Đại Việt, materially and spiritually, Emperor Nhân Tông initiated a tactful diplomatic policy shortly after the enemy's defeated generals T'o-huan and Ao-lu-chih had run away beyond the frontier and had their troops encamped at Szŭming in Kwanghsi on the 18th, Nhâm Dần, of the third month of Mậu Tý. This policy was aimed at discouraging the enemy from carrying out their plot of invasion and, at the same time, keeping peace for the country. *Pen Chi of Yuan Shih* 15, p.3a9, tells us that on the same day (the 18th) Emperor Nhân Tông *"ordered his messengers to come for excuse and offer a golden human form in place of himself."* The fact is not recorded in our history books but it is mentioned in *An Nam Chí Lược* 14, p.140, with full details of each member of this mission. It says, *"In the spring of Chih-yuan, Mậu Tý (1288), Chên-nan-wang withdrew his Army. Thế Tử ordered Lý Tu and Đoàn Khả Dung to offer local gifts with his apology [for not coming]."* On recording the withdrawal of T'o-huan's Army in the spring and the mission of Lý Tu and Đoàn Khả Dung to the Yuan court, *An Nam Chí Lược* must have mentioned the date 'the third month', that is, the 18th day, Nhâm Dần, since at that time Emperor Nhân Tông and the court of Đại Việt sent no other mission than that just mentioned. This must have been a mission sent for investigating the enemy's situation after they had been swept out of our country.

In effect, just a month after his triumphant return to Thăng long, i.e., the 27th, Canh Thìn, of the fourth month of Mậu Tý, Emperor Nhân Tông ordered Trần Khắc Dụng to offer local gifts to the Yuan court as is recorded by *Pen Chi* of *Yuan Shih* 15, pp.3b13-4a1. This mission is not dealt with in *An Nam Chí Lược*, but Từ Minh Thiện's *Thiên Nam Hành Ký* in *Thuyết Phu* 51, pp.18b4-19b6, recorded a letter sent by Emperor Nhân Tông to Kublai Khan. From the letter, we know that the objective of Trần Khắc Dụng's mission was not merely to offer local gifts but mainly to carry out a diplomatic task, that is, managing to smash the enemy's plot of invasion.

In the letter mentioned above, Emperor Nhân Tông pointed out clearly the reason why the war had taken place and stated explicitly the responsibility of those who had waged it. He wrote, "*In Chih-yuan 23 (1286), P'ing-ch'ang A-li-hai-ya, due to his own desire for making merits in the border areas, disobeyed the Emperor's edict. As a consequence, the people of this small country had to suffer misfortunes. (...). In the winter of Chih-yuan 24 (1827), the Great Army came here, destroying and burning all pagodas and temples across our country, digging our ancestors' graves, killing our innocent countrymen, damaging the common people's properties— none of any brutal destructive offenses were not committed by them.(...). Taking control over the sea, Wu-ma-er ordered his troops to arrest all the inhabitants along the coast, among whom the old were killed, the young taken captives. The bodies of those who had been hanged, tied, cut, were scattered everywhere. The people were all compelled to face death; so there accrued the situation of beasts 'that were being chased against the wall'.*"

Thus, from Emperor Nhân Tông's standpoint, the two recent wars should be regarded as having been caused not by Kublai Khan himself but by his commanding officers on the borderland, who, in thus doing, attempted to make some merit of their own. Obviously, this was an ingenious diplomatic tactics aimed at maintaining Kublai Khan's honor in his unsuccessful plot to invade our country. Furthermore, the passage above indicates our people's state of seething with anger at the enemy's brutal crimes. It may be considered our emperor's official statement concerning not only Kublai Khan's military subjects, who had received his orders of implementing their genocide crime, but also his own brutal policy of waging wars. It may be said that this is one of the earliest documents condemning war crimes not only of our people but also of the world.

However, the more war and crimes were condemned, the more strongly our supreme leader's tolerance was made possible to manifest itself to the world. He was deeply aware that war could not be totally ended by means of war itself but necessarily by some other measure, that is, tolerance and humaneness. It should be kept in mind that it was one of the deepest impacts exerted by Buddhism upon everyday attitudes and behaviors not only of Emperor Nhân Tông but also of Đại Việt's highest-ranking generals such as Trần Hưng Đạo, Trần Quang Khải and common people. And this is verified through the letter in which Emperor Nhân Tông, following his condemnation of Yuan generals' savage crimes in the two recent wars, is said to have actively shown his humaneness by giving orders for the release of prisoners of war.

The letter dated 1288 of Emperor Nhân Tông reads, "*Since the people turned over Tich-le-co, who is reportedly a 'great king' and a noble relative of Your Majesty in the Great Nation, to me, I have treated him in the greatest respect. Whether this is true or not is naturally to be known by him. As for Wu-ma-er's cruel actions I dare not tell anything beyond what the great king has seen for himself. In my small country, the climate is originally unfavorable for health and hence a great deal of climatic diseases, so I fear that [he] might get sick if he would stay here long. Even though I have done my best to have him well cared for, I think it hard to avoid being falsely accused by those who have desire to make merits on the border. I, therefore, have had everything necessary for his journey sufficiently prepared, and given orders for accompanying him back to the Great Nation (...). Further, by my order, more than a thousand men of the Great Army are released, too. Later, if anyone is discovered, he will be allowed to return home."*

It is obvious that even though their action of waging war could be supposedly motivated by their own desire of making some merits, the Yuan generals and their officers' crimes were worth punishment. For they had not only made wars but also destroyed the peaceful existence of other communities, let alone their various cruel actions of looting, burning houses, killing people so savagely that "*the bodies of the dead were scattered everywhere.*" In face of such brutal actions, however, our people could show mercy to them, sparing their lives so that they could safely return to their homes. Suffice it to say unquestionably that the Vietnamese of that time seemed to possess some subtle and profound feeling for the sufferings of others. Indeed, few peoples in the world have had enough compassion and patience to compose such literary works expressing their genuine sympathy for their own enemy as a poem titled *Thương Kẻ Thù Bị Bắt*[5] by Trạng Nguyên Lý Tải Đạo, later Dhyāna Master Huyền Quang (1254-1334), of our country at that time:

In this letter written in blood my words are to be sent to you,
A lonely wild goose among the icy clouds over the frontier pass.
Who would feel their melancholy under the moon tonight?
Though far away in different places, we are surely of the same mind.

Thus, humaneness did manifest itself not only within the leaders of the nation but also in the minds of common people typified by Lý Tải Đạo. In 1288 when the war ended and the enemy's captives were being kept in our country, Lý Tải Đạo was probably just at the age of 34. As a man of a country in time of war, he could not fail to join the army in the two wars of defense in 1285 and 1286 and thus had seen for himself brutal actions the enemy caused to his country. Nonetheless, in face of their miserable situation of being homeless, he could not suppress his utterly spontaneous feeling for their sufferings. Never before in our history had our people's hatred for the enemy been so violent as that in the struggle against Yuan invaders, which was self-evident in terms of the two words "sát thát" engraved on the arm of each of our soldiers. Yet, never before had our people and soldiers' sympathy for the enemy been so highly cultivated that it was once expressed in verse as in the period of these two wars.

Indeed, the fact that Emperor Nhân Tông gave orders for the

---

[5] Lit. "The Pity on the Enemy Captured".

release of prisoners of war does not only verify his ingenious diplomatic policy but obviously shows our people's sympathy and pity for individual human beings in their suffering, regardless of whatsoever races or nationalities they were pertained to. It was the national tradition of humaneness that was, more than 100 years later, inherited and developed by Lê Lợi, a national hero of our country's, in his declaration of general release for more than 10,000 Ming troops captured by his army. Besides this, he also gave orders for rebuilding roads, bridges and providing boats, horses, supplies so that they could go back to their country safely. From such historical evidence, despite some description found on Li Tien-yu's tombstone of his *"having been shaved or given no food or unendingly insulted during his imprisonment"*, we are evidently convinced that, if any, it might be a single and peculiar reaction hardly controlled by our people in face of the unimaginably savage and barbarian action of digging the late Emperor Trần Thái Tông's grave by Wu-ma-er's war criminals.

Around six months after the sending of a mission headed by Trần Khắc Dụng, Emperor Nhân Tông ordered another mission headed by Đỗ Thiên Hứ,[6] as recorded in *ĐVSKTT* 5, p.56a4: *"In the winter, the 10th month, [the King] ordered Đỗ Thiên Hứ to go to the Yuan court. The latter was recommended by his brother Đỗ Khắc Chung, who was once successful in a mission to the Yuan."* This mission is not written down in *Yuan Shih* and *An Nam Chí Lược*. It must be said that the diplomatic acts above were aimed at allaying the situation when our country had just won the two wars in which the enemy's veteran and famous generals such as So-tu, Wu-ma-er,

---

[6] Khắc Chung's younger brother. [LMT]

P'an Chieh, T'ang-wu-tai, A-pa-chih, etc., were either eliminated or captured alive.

Subsequent to our three missions, on the 18th of the 11th month of Mậu Tý, Kublai Khan ordered a mission headed by Li Szŭ-yen to arrive in our country for the purpose of asking our emperor to go to the Yuan court for audience with the threat that they would launch another invasion unless the emperor accepted their request as is recorded in *Pen Chi* of *Yuan Shih* 15, p.7a5-6: "*On Kỷ Hợi (of the 11th month) Li Szŭ-yen was appointed Li-pu-shih-lang in a mission to Annan, in which he was assisted by Wan-nu, who was working as Ping-pu-lang-chung. They carried the decree that Trần Nhật Huyên would have to come for audience or he would be punished again [by our Yuan].*" Thus, this mission consisted of Li Szŭ-yen and Wan-nu but not Liu Ting-chih, who was recorded in other documents as being the head of the mission.

The first document in question is *An Nam Chí Lược* 3, p.45, where the name Liu Ting-chih was added: "*Chih-yuan the 26th (1288), (...) Liu Ting-chih, Li Szŭ-Yen, Wan-nu, accompanied by our (Annan's) messengers, that is the group of Nguyễn Nghĩa Toàn, were ordered to go to [our] country for issuing the [Yuan] king's decree.*" The second is *Annan Chuan* of *Yuan Shih* 209, p.10a7-8, where it runs, "*in the 11th month (of Chih-yuan 25, 1288), Luu Ting-chih, Li Szŭ-yen, Wan-nu were chosen to be messengers to Annan, carrying the decree that Trần Nhật Huyên would have to come for audience.*" The last is Từ Minh Thiện's *Thiên Nam Hành Ký* in *Thuyết Phu* 51, p.21a2, where not only Liu Ting-chih is named but also T'ang-wu-tai, Ko-san-la (Qasar), Yung-ko-la-tai (Onggiradai) and even Từ Minh Thiện himself as being Ts'an-i-chung-shu.

Obviously, this was an important mission entrusted with two great tasks, that is, requesting Emperor Nhân Tông to come for audience and give the order for the release of all Yuan prisoners, particularly Wu-ma-er. In addition, they also transmitted Kublai Khan's statement of the cause of the two wars. These requests were essentially aimed at responding to the three issues Emperor Nhân Tông had set forth in his letter carried to Kublai Khan by our messenger Trần Khắc Dụng. Reading the responses in his letter cited below, we can realize how consistently and difficultly our mission had fulfilled their diplomatic task in the Yuan court.

Concerning the cause of the war, Kublai Khan fixed all the responsibilities on Emperor Nhân Tông. His edict was completely written down by the traitor Lê Sực in his *An Nam Chí Lược* 2, p.36, and later copied by Từ Minh Thiện in *Thiên Nam Hành Ký* as follows: "*I am ruling ten thousand countries, where those who have talent and virtue are all employed by me. It is said that you are always subject to me but you have never come for audience. Though I have many times sent for you, you have refused on the pretext of sickness. When I ordered your uncle to conduct national affairs, you dared to kill him, explicitly protesting me. As far as A-li-hai-ya's attack on Champa is concerned, when he asked you to have the road opened up, bridges repaired, and grass and rice transported, you did not only break your word but also resisted my Army. In face of such actions, may the king's laws remain meaningful if I do not give the order for an attack on your country? Whether your people are eliminated and your country destroyed will all be caused by yourself.*"

Concerning the request for audience at his court, Kublai Khan set forth his persuasion accompanied with his threat: "*Why do you not come here to profess everything if you are truly loyal to me? Why have you always managed to escape on my generals' arrival but then sought to offer gifts in their retreat? In such a manner of respecting the superior, it is hard for you to conceal your disloyalty. What have you ever thought would be better: continuing to hide yourself in the mountains or at sea with constant anxiety of my Army's attack or coming for audience by my order to be granted wealth and honor on your return home? Of these two ways, which is good and which is bad? (...) If you have got ready to come here immediately as does a faithful subject, I will forgive all your faults, reinstating you in all of your former titles. If you go on to show your caution and hesitation, I can hardly forgive you. Rebuild your ramparts, sharpen your weapons at will to wait for my Army.*"

Concerning their request for releasing prisoners of war and Emperor Nhân Tông's polite treatment to Hsi-li-chi, Kublai Khan pointed out that "*the reason you have respectfully treated Hsi-li-chi and let him return is that you have clearly known him to be a relative of mine. Nonetheless, with such a fault he will have to go into exile. If you intend to belie your disloyalty in such ostensible actions, you had better release Wu-ma-er and So-tu's officers and troops to show your obeisance. By the time you receive this edict, Wu-ma-er's officers and troops must return together. If they need to be somehow treated, it will be my affair. Let them all return.*" That Kublai Khan mentioned directly the case of Wu-ma-er is obviously aimed at responding to Emperor Nhân Tông's accusation of his crimes. In reality, he was a notorious general for his cruelty who had commanded his troops to kill common people, burn their homes, rob their properties and dig their ancestors' graves in Thiên Trường as has been said before.

Despite their requests and threats mentioned above, Emperor Nhân Tông maintained his calmness in receiving the Yuan mission, as in the words of *Thiên Nam Hành Ký* of *Thuyết Phu* 41, pp.4b-5a: "*On the 28th of the 2nd month of Kỷ Sửu (Chih-yuan 26, 1289) [our mission] reached the citadel gate of that country. There we were received by Thế Tử's brother..., then rode on horses to the House of Messengers. On the 29th Thế Tử and the messengers met with each other. Earlier, he had entered through the buck door of the pavilion behind the House of Messengers, ordering the middle door to be opened for the messengers. He greeted them and wished, through them, the King longevity. On the 1st of the 3rd month, having had flags, yellow parasols, trumpets, drums arranged sufficiently, he received the edict into the citadel. At the door of the palace, he dismounted his horse and walked inside. That was the Tập Hiền Palace, where, after the ceremony of receiving the edict, he gave the order for a banquet to be held for the sake of our messengers for two days.*" In the section "Shih Chiao-chih" of his *Chue Kêng Lu* 4, Tao Tsung-i further mentioned that Emperor Nhân Tông ordered gold given to those messengers. And *An Nam Chí Lược* 17, p.158, adds that Li Szŭ-yen was, too, granted gold and silver.

Generally speaking, the mission was warmly received but Kublai Khan's requests were all rejected. The messengers went back with their empty hands: the emperor did not go for audience, Wu-ma-er could return to his family only in a pot.[7] His death is described in ĐVSKTT 5, p.56a6-8 as follows, *"In the spring, the 2nd month, of Kỷ Sửu (1289), Hoàng Tá Thốn was ordered to accompany Wu-ma-er back to his country. According to Hưng Đạo Vương's plot, only those troops who were good at swimming were chosen to be oarsmen. One night, they sought to sink the ship by breaking holes at the bottom. Wu-ma-er and his companions were all drowned."* In his letter sent to Kublai Khan, however, Emperor Nhân Tông told him about Wu-ma-er's death as follows, *"Wu-ma-er selected the date when he would go back. Since the way ran across Vạn Kiếp, he asked to meet Hưng Đạo [Vương] for preparation of luggage. During its course at night, the ship on which he was traveling was hit and soon filled with water. Due to his tall big body, it was impossible to rescue him. As a result, he was drowned. So were all the oarsmen of my small country. His wife and concubines and boy-servants were nearly drowned but we could rescue them because they were not so tall and big. I had them buried at the seashore, which Tien-shih-lang-chung saw for himself. If I had any impolite words, I were not able to deceive his wife and concubines who had been present there. I had enough gifts prepared for the journey of his wife and concubines and Shê-jen-lang-chung."*

Such was the death of Wu-ma-er on his way back home. No matter how he died, it is evidently true from the letter above that Emperor Nhân Tông promised to release more than 8,000 Yuan captives. Thus, within only more than half a year after Yuan troops had been swept out of our country, nearly 10,000 men of the enemy were set free by our court. It should be kept in mind that it

---

[7] It was used for containing his remains after cremation.

was the first time in our history when such a large number of enemies, who had owed blood to our people, were released. This fact has since then become a precedent that Lê Lợi, another national hero of ours, applied to his treatment of Wang Tung's defeated troops at Đông Quan. Indeed, it was Emperor Nhân Tông's humane and tolerant policy combined with the victories at Tây Kết, Bạch Đằng, where most of Yuan's veteran generals had been eliminated, that partly deterred Kublai Khan from carrying out his plot of invasion.

No doubt, whether Đại Việt would be retaliated upon must have been discussed by Kublai Khan and his close subjects such as Huan-chai (Oljäi) and Pu-hu-mu (Bigmiš), who all proposed a diplomatic solution, according to which Chang Li-tao would be appointed messenger to Đại Việt as is recorded in *Chang Li-tao Chuan* of *Yuan Shih* 167, pp.2a13-b2. On the side of Đại Việt, on the 25th of the fifth month of Canh Dần (1290), by Emperor Nhân Tông's order, Ngô Đình Giới went to Tatu to announce the Yuan court of the Emperor-Father Trần Thánh Tông's death. And in the ninth month of the year that followed, the mission headed by Nghiêm Trọng Duy and Trần Tử Trường was sent with the task of *"offering local gifts and an excuse for Emperor Nhân Tông's absence for audience"* as recorded in *Pen Chi* of *Yuan Shih* 16, p.11b8-9 and *An Nam Chí Lược* 14, p.140.

In the 10th month of the same year, Chang Li-tao came to our country with the same task as before, that is, seeking to persuade Emperor Nhân Tông to go for audience. During his stay in our country the former was always well treated *"with music played by a great band at the lower apartment and by a smaller band at the upper one, in both of which were served a variety of wine, rare fruits, meat, seafood at eight tables. Besides, areca-nuts and betels with lime were occasionally served, too. The King himself received them, reading his own poems to them. Li-tao also responded with his poems right at table."* Though having much experience in negotiating with our court, Li-tao did not fulfill his task this time. Emperor Nhân Tông maintained his refusal for any audience at the Yuan court, especially after his successful resistance against their invasions in the years 1285 and 1288.

In the sixth month of Nhâm Thìn (1292), Chang Li-tao went back to his country, accompanied by Nguyễn Đại Phạp and Hà Duy Nhan. According to *ĐVSKTT* 5, p.60a8-9, the latter went to explain the reason Emperor Nhân Tông could not go for audience, that is, he was going into mourning for his Emperor-Father's death. *ĐVSKTT* 5, pp.61a8-b4, further tells that when Nguyễn Đại Phạp reached the Hall of Ngohchou, he saw Trần Ích Tắc there but did not greet him. Thereby, the latter asked, *"Are you a scribe at Chiêu Đại Vương's?"* Đại Phạp answered, *"Everything in life constantly changes. Formerly I was a scribe at Chiêu Đại Vương's, but now I am a messenger. Similarly, you, Bình Chương, were formerly the son of a royal family, but now you have given up to the enemy."* Then *ĐVSKTT* concludes, *"Ích Tắc appeared to be shameful. Since then, on their arrivals that followed, our messengers could no longer see him at the Hall."*

Three months after Chang Li-tao's failure to persuade Emperor Nhân Tông to come for audience, i.e., the ninth month of Nhâm Thìn (1292), Liang Seng and Trần Phu came with a letter from Kublai Khan, in which the same request as before was set forth. In the words of *ĐVSKTT* 5, p.63a2-3, Emperor Nhân Tông refused it again on the pretext of sickness but he ordered Đào Tử Kỳ to go to the Yuan court with local offerings. On the Kỷ Tỵ of the seventh month of Chih-yuan 30 (1293) when Liang Seng's mission did not return yet, Kublai Khan hurried *"to order Liu Kuo-chieh to accompany Mieh-chi-li[8] (Ikirädai) in their army to attack Giao Chi"* as in the words of *Pen Chi* of *Yuan Shih* 17, p.11a5. In the meantime, having had Đào Tử Kỳ detained in Kiangling and Hukwang Annan-hsin-shêng founded, Khublai Khan ordered Liu-er-pu-tu to dispatch troops to Shêngkiang, preparing for a blow on Đại Việt. In the words of *Annan Chuan* of *Yuan Shih* 209, p.10b3-10, *"In [Chih-yuan] 30 (1292), after Liang Seng's return from a mission [in An Nam], Nhật Tôn ordered his subject Đào Tử Kỳ to come for offering. Knowing Nhật Tôn's refusal to come for audience, the subjects of [our] court discussed the plan of attacking Giao Chi, detaining Tử Kỳ in Kiangling. The [Yuan] King ordered Liu Kuo-chieh and Mieh-li-chi-tai[9] to go to Ngohchou to discuss the plan of attacking An Nam with Trần Ích Tắc. In the 8th month, Pu-hu-mu proposed founding Hukwang Annan-hsin-shêng entrusted with two 'seals', at disposal of which were 1,000 hundred-holded ships, 56,570 men, 35,000 piculs of rice, 20,000 piculs of horse-food, 210,000 'kilograms' of salt, 700,000 weapons of all kinds, allowances for officers, salaries for infantrymen and sailors each two coins. With a staff of eleven officers [Liu] Kuo-chieh ordered the advance, both by sea and by land. In addition, Ch'ê-li-man (Cäriman), Assistant-Messenger of Kianghsi Hsin-chü-mi-yuan, was appointed Yu-chêng*

---

[8] Mieh-chi-li-tai. [LMT]

[9] huongtichbooks.

of the fighting expedition; Ch'ên Yen, Chao Hsiu-chi, Yün Sung-lung, Chang Wen-hu, Ts'en Hsiung, all were also ordered to assist Ích Tắc in the army to Trường Sa."

An Nam Chí Lược 4, p.56, also gives the same account: *"In Chih-yuan of the year Quý Tỵ (1293) [by Thế Tử's order] Đào Tử Kỳ came for offering. Having refused the [Yuan] king's summon for audience for many times, he was detained in Kiangling. [The King gave orders] for Annan-hsin-sh'êng to be founded and Liu Kuo-chieh together with I-i-chi-ta to join the Army commanded by 'Great King' I-chi-li-tai (Ikirädai). That winter, the Army was encamped in Shêngkiang, waiting for the departure in the fall of the year that followed."* Nevertheless, it was while he was in Shêngkiang that Liu Kuo-chieh set to his challenge to our country by sending a letter to Emperor Nhân Tông with his complaints of the latter's aid to militiamen of Huang Sheng-hsü in Kwanghsi. The letter was originally copied in *An Nam Chí Lược* 5, pp.64-66.

On the Quý Dậu of the 1st month of the year that followed, however, Kublai Khan died and Yüan Ch'êng-tsu succeeded him. Đào Tử Kỳ was allowed to return home. As a consequence, their plan of invading our country was officially cancelled; and our people's struggle for peace may be considered to have ended in victory.

In the spring of Quý Tỵ, i.e., the ninth of the third month (1293), Emperor Nhân Tông officially transferred the supreme power to his son, Crown Prince Huyên, and ascended the 'throne' of Emperor-Father.

Translation by **Đạo Sinh**

EMPEROR TRẦN NHÂN TÔNG AND THE WAR OF DEFENSE IN 1285

BY PROF. **LÊ MẠNH THÁT**

As it has been said before, it was just in 1279 when Emperor Nhân Tông ascended the throne and the Sung Dynasty was exterminated in China that Kublai Khan gave orders for warships to be built in his plan of invading Đại Việt. His intention seemed to take advantage of the victory his well-trained troops had just gained as an impetus for their campaign to smash our people's fighting power. From his own experience in the war of 1258, however, Kublai Khan's preparation of tactics and strategy for this war showed to be much more elaborate. In addition to the north-eastern and south-western armies, he attempted to form the third one south of our country by ordering So Tu to occupy Champa in 1282. In reality, the war proceeded exactly in the strategy he had planned, yet the effect was not so satisfactory as he had expected.

Kublai Khan's Preparation for the War of 1285

Despite his failure to impose the puppet government headed by Trần Di Ái upon our country, Kublai Khan patiently expected a victory from the battlefield of Champa. Unfortunately, his expectation could not come true as it is noted in *Pen Chi* of *Yuan Shih*13, pp.2b2-3 and 2b9-11, that the defeated army of So Tu had to retreat from Champa and *"P'ing Chang A Li Hai Ya of Hu Kwang Hsin Shêng volunteered to reach the seashore to gather beaten troops [fleeing] from Champa."* Obviously, in the long-termed strategy of resistance by combining fighting with negotiation, the Cham people had sunk So Tu's troops in the 'swamp' of a guerilla warfare in their tropical country.

Having received only requests for reinforcement in stead of some expected victory, on the 28th, Đinh Sửu, of the 5th month of Chih Yuan 21 (1284) Kublai Khan stripped Wu Ma Er of his commanding seal due to his failure of supplying So Tu with reinforcements. Then, on the 12th, Mậu Tý, of the seventh month of the same year he ordered his son, T'o Huan, officially to command troops to attack Champa, as recorded in *Pen Chi* of *Yuan Shih* 13, p.4a8. Yet, it was merely a pretense of his since the objective of T'o Huan's invading troops was not Champa, but Đại Việt. Just on the same day, Mậu Tý, by order of Emperor Nhân Tông, the mission of Trung Lương Đại Phu Nguyễn Đạo Học submitted our local offerings to the Yuan king and thereby investigated their situation. Also it was the day when the Yuan king allowed our envoy, Lê Anh, to return home.

In the meantime, a powerful staff of their headquarters was formed by Kublai Khan's order. In addition to T'o Huan, most of veteran generals of Mongol armed forces, who had acquired military merit in annihilating the Sung, were gathered. Among them were A Li Hai Ya, who had gained victory in Hsiang Yang, Ngoh Chou, P'an Ch'êng, Shêng Kiang, Kiang Ling and many other battlefields in China, and Li Hêng, who had succeeded in the Yai Shan operation, bringing the Sung Dynasty to an end; and several generals and high-ranked officers who had ever cooperated with and received aid from A Li Hai Ya such as Ao Lu Chih, Cheng P'êng Fei, Wu Ma Er, So Tu, P'an Chieh, and so on. Otherwise stated, Kublai Khan had a powerful staff of most talented and veteran officers in his hands.

In the seventh month of Chih Yuan 21 (1284) when T'o Huan's troops were halted at Ching Hu Chan Ch'êng Hsin Shêng, Emperor Nhân Tông ordered the mission of Nguyễn Đạo Học to meet with him there. Thereafter, the latter ordered Ch'ü Lieh (Külä) and T'a Hai San Li (Taqai Sarïq) to accompany Nguyễn Đạo Học to our country with his letter, blaming and requesting our emperor to provide supplies for Yuan army and receive T'o Huan from the border into our country on their way to attack Champa. Just as T'o Huan moved his troops to Hsin Shan District of Hu Nan, Ch'ü Lieh and T'a Hai San Li left Đại Việt, accompanied by the mission of Trần Đức Quân and Trần Tự Tông who carried the emperor's letter of refusing T'o Huan's request for taking the route of our country: *"Whether by land or by water, traveling from my country to Champa is not convenient."* Upon receiving the letter, T'o Huan ordered Chao Tzŭ Ch'i to reply to Emperor Nhân Tông, requesting him to open the road and supply provisions. He was, too, informed at the same time that Trần Hưng Đạo had deployed troops to the border.

In *An Nan Chuan* of *Yuan Shih* 209, p.5b11, all of these facts are said to have occurred in the second month of Chih Yuan 22 (1285) since, according to *Pen Chi* of *Yuan Shih* 13 p.6a5, T'o Huan's troops marched into our country in the 12th month of Chih Yuan 21. It is more carefully recorded in *An Nam Chi Luoc* 4, p.53: *"On the 21st of the 12th month the army reached the borderland of An Nam."* This is quite in accordance with the account in *Ching Shih Ta Tien Tzŭ Lu* of *Yuan Wen Lei* 41, p.27a2-3: *"In the 10th month of [Chih Yuan] 21, [our] troops reached Yung Chou. The An Nam [king] ordered Hưng Đạo Vương to dispatch 20,000 men to their posts to halt [our] king's troops. In the 12th month, they were defeated at the frontier pass Khả Ly."*

Thus, it must be in the 10th month of Chih Yuan 21 (1284) that T'o Huan and his troops reached Yung Chou of Hu Nan. There, A Li Hai Ya ordered Chao Tzŭ Ch'i to write a letter, requesting our emperor to *"open the road and prepare supplies to receive Chên Nan Wang"*, as recorded in *An Nan Chuan* of *Yuan Shih* 209, p.6a5-6. Also in the words of *An Nan Chuan* of *Yuan Shih* 209, p.6a6-7, upon reaching Yung Chou of Kwang Hsi, T'o Huan learned that the Đại Việt General Điện Tiền Phạm Hải Nham had deployed troops at Khả Lan, Vi Đại Trợ. When the former's army reached Szu Ming of Kwang Chou, he sent a letter to Emperor Nhân Tông, repeating the same demands set forth in A Li Hai Ya's letter. Thereafter, he went on to move his troops into Lộc Châu of our country, that is, Lộc Bình District in what is now Lạng Sơn Province.

There, having heard that Emperor Nhân Tông had dispatched troops to the positions at the frontier passes Khâu Ôn and Khâu

Cấp Lãnh, T'o Huan divided his troops into two wings. According to *An Nam Chí Lược* 4 p.53, this took place on the 21st, Giáp Tý, of the 12th month of Giáp Thân (i.e. January 27th, 1285); the west wing commanded by Wan Hu Po Lo Ho Ta Er (Bolqadar)[1] and A Shên (Atsin) advanced down via Khâu Ôn whereas the east wing commanded by San Ta Er Tai (Tatartai) and Wan Hu Li Ping Hsien via Cấp Lãnh.

Even at that time, Emperor Nhân Tông kept on sending a letter to T'o Huan, carried by Thiện Trung Đại Phu Nguyễn Đức Dư and Triều Thỉnh Lang Nguyễn Văn Hàn, demanding his army's withdrawal with the emperor's reference to an edict issued by Kublai Khan in 1261: "*ordering our [Yuan] troops not to enter your [An Nam] territory,*" as recorded in *An Nan Chuan* of *Yuan Shih* 209, p.6a9-10. A Li Hai Ya detained Nguyễn Văn Hàn but allowed Nguyễn Đức Dư to return with A Li, who carried a letter from him replying to the emperor's request for their withdrawal: "*the reason we launch the campaign is [to punish] Champa, not An Nam.*" Nevertheless, A Li could not approach our court since on his arrival at Cấp Bảo District he encountered our troops commanded by Quản Quân Nguyễn Lộc, and then more troops deployed by Trần Hưng Đạo in Lý Village, Đoản District, and Vạn Kiếp. Being informed of this, A Li Hai Ya ordered I Jun to investigate the situation of our troops to prepare his attack. Shortly thereafter, he was reported by San Ta Er Tai, Liu Ping Hsien and Tsun Yu that they had encountered our troops' counterattacks at the frontier

---

[1] Author's note: transliterated in An Nam Chí Lược as Wan Hu Li Lo Ho Ta Er. [From here on, all the footnotes by the author are marked with LMT in brackets.]

pass Khả Ly. The fact above is taken from *An Nan Chuan* of *Yuan Shih* 209 p.6a3-b2.

The Battle of Nội Bàng

In this battle, Tsun Yu captured our two officers, Quản Quân Phụng Ngự Đỗ Vĩ and Đỗ Hựu, and had them killed later. Then he advanced to Động Bàng where Yuan troops had fought with our troops and killed our general Tần Sâm. Afterwards they moved to BiếnTrúVillage for a halt.

According to *ĐVSKTT*, on the 26th of the 12th month *"the enemy's forces attacked the frontier passes at Vĩnh Châu, Nội Bàng, Thiết Lược, and Chi Lăng."* Thus, after five days' advance from Lộc Châu, the west wing of Po Lo Ho Ta Er together with T'o Huan's great army completely broke through our line of defense, chiefly formed to protect Thăng Long, by crossing our frontier passes in the north down to our plains in the south. According to *An Nan Chuan* of *Yuan Shih* 209 p.6b5, to besiege and attack the frontier pass Nội Bàng, T'o Huan's troops were divided into six directions. In the words of *Pen Chi* of *Yuan Shih* 13, p.6a5-6: *"That month, Chên Nan Wang's troops marched into An Nan, killing [their] frontier troops and advancing in six directions. Hưng Đạo Vương of An Nam commanded his troops to counterattack."*

Accordingly, it may be said that this is a great battle, if not a strategically decisive battle. For, on our part, the troops commanded by Quốc Công Tiết Chế Trần Hưng Đạo had suffered a heavy loss with Đại Liêu Ban Đoàn Thai captured alive. Later, as it will be seen below, Emperor Nhân Tông ordered Trần Hưng Đạo to mobilize troops from other Routes, of which troops of princes and Trần Hưng Đạo's son mounted to nearly 200,000. Further, the fact that Trần Hưng Đạo had withdrawn his troops urgently and suddenly shows that the sudden defeat on the Noi Bang front seemed to be beyond his own planning.

In *ĐVSKTT* 5, p.45a4-b1, the withdrawal of our troops is described rather graphically with the detail of Tỳ Tướng Yết Kiêu's waiting for Trần Hưng Đạo at Bãi Tân: *"Earlier, Hưng Đạo Vương had two servants called Dã Tượng and Yết Kiêu, who were very well treated by him. When the Yuan troops came, Yết Kiêu posted boats at Bãi Tân whereas Dã Tượng followed Trần Hưng Đạo. When our troops were defeated, all boats were scattered. [Hưng Đạo] Vương was about to retreat along the way in the foothills when Dã Tượng said, 'if he does not see you yet, surely Yết Kiêu will not move his boats to anywhere else.' [Hưng Đạo] Vương followed him to Bãi Tân, where remained Yết Kiêu's boats alone. So pleased, Vương said, 'It is due to its six strong bones supporting wings that the Great Bird can fly high. Without them, it remains merely an ordinary bird.' After these words, he had his boats handled away from the enemy's pursuit. Reaching Vạn Kiếp, he deployed troops to defend Bắc Giang."* This shows clearly that the front of Nội Bàng was broken in an extremely unfavorable situation, even seemingly unexpected not only to the direct commander, Trần Hưng Đạo, but also to Emperor Nhân Tông, the leader and the commander-in-chief of our war of resistance at that time.

This situation may be seen through the fact that Emperor Nhân Tông, being informed of the fighting at Nội Bàng, gave up his breakfast, taking boat all day toward Hải Đông to confer with Trần

Hưng Đạo, as recorded in *ĐVSKTT*: "*Then the king was seated in a light boat, traveling to the Route of Hải Đông. It was, then, nearly at twilight but the king had not had his breakfast yet. A common soldier brought a meal with rice of bad quality for him. The king praised him to be loyal, giving him the title of 'superior rank' and the position of Tiểu Tư at Hữu Triều Môn commune in Bạch Đằng.*" Obviously, the fact that Emperor Nhân Tông gave up his breakfast to hurry to Hải Đông by boat shows that the front there played a very important role in the strategy of defense of the Trần Dynasty at that time.

It may be said that through the fact above Emperor Nhân Tông and Trần Hưng Đạo's primary plan of fighting seemed to dispatch troops of defense to the positions right on the frontier of our country, a plan quite in accordance with the tactics Lý Thường Kiệt had applied more than 200 years earlier. Indeed, the defeat on the Nội Bàng front required that Emperor Nhân Tông and Trần Hưng Đạo should have a new strategy in place of the old ones in facing the enemy. This must have been the reason why the emperor himself had to confer with Trần Hưng Đạo so urgently in Hải Đông.

What Emperor Nhân Tông and Trần Hưng Đạo discussed in this brief conference is not known today; yet, in the words of *ĐVSKTT* 5 pp.44b7-45a4, following their discussion "*Hưng Đạo Vương was ordered to mobilize troops and militiamen of the Routes in Hải Đông, selecting strong men as volunteers for crossing the sea down to the south. The situation of our army became rather favorable. Hearing of this, our troops gathered from everywhere. The king wrote a poem on his bows:*

The former event of Cối Kê you should remember;
In Hoan Ái remain one hundred thousand of troops.
Under Trần Hưng Đạo's command, Hưng Vũ Vương Nghiễn,
Minh Hiến Vương Uất, Hưng Nhượng Vương Tảng, Hưng Trí
Vương Hiện concentrated troops from Bằng Hà, Na Sầm, Trà
Hương, Yên Sinh, Long Nhã, totally 200.000 men, then moving to
Vạn Kiếp to fight against the Yuan army."

Thus, there really occurred some change in our army's strategic measures that would then be manifested in Emperor Nhân Tông's art of leading the war. Today, this measure is generally designated by military theorists as *"strategic withdrawal and strategic counterattack."* The urgent conference between Emperor Nhân Tông and Trần Hưng Đạo shortly after our defeat on the front of Nội Bàng points out some brilliant reflection in the military aspect not only of Trần Hưng Đạo but also of Emperor Nhân Tông, who was acting as the commander-in-chief of our armed forces at that time. That Emperor Nhân Tông suffered hunger all day to reach Trần Hưng Đạo's position for conference shows how perilous the situation of our country was then. Further, it points out how closely and seriously the emperor observed the situation of our army's fighting so as to resolve on the spot whatsoever problems created by complicated and dangerous changes in various situations. That he mobilized troops from the Routes, the princes and the nobles to Vạn Kiếp was a typical fact. The two lines of verse mentioned above indicated that Emperor Nhân Tông was unceasingly seeking to lend encouragement to Trần Hưng Đạo and other generals. *"The former event of Cối Kê"* refers to a historical fact in the old days when Kou Chien, head of the Yüeh state, was defeated and captured by Fou Ts'ai, head of the Wu state, but the former, having suffered a great deal of hardship and humility, eventually rose to gain a victory over the latter. It should be noticed that the defeat on the Nội Bàng front was such a great loss to our army that Emperor-Father Trần Thánh Tông ever asked Trần Quốc Tuấn, the general who was directly commanding our troops on the front, whether our army should surrender in such a situation; and the talented strategist replied: "*Your Majesty should first cut my head and then surrender*", as in the words of *ĐVSKTT* 6 p.11b. The figure '200,000 men', however, shows that the force of our army remained perfectly preserved. With such a strong army, in addition to his unceasing attempt to maintain the officers' morale in terms of "*the former event of Cối Kê*", Emperor Nhân Tông kept on encouraging them through his announcement that o100,000 men were being concentrated in Hoan Ái for reinforcement. Indeed, according to *An Nan Chuan* of *Yuan Shih* 209 p.6b6, after the battle of Nội Bàng the enemy admitted "*Hưng Đạo Vương was commanding more than 1000 warships deployed ten miles far from Vạn Kiếp.*"

The Battle of Vạn Kiếp

T'o Huan's attack on Nội Bàng on the 26th of the 12th month of Giáp Thìn, which is dated the 27th in *An Nam Chí Lược*, must have lasted for several days. Thus, the year of Giáp Thân was coming to an end; that is to say, the greatest festival of the year was waiting for the whole people of Đại Việt. Yet, all that they were preparing for the longest and most exiting holidays of the year was weapons, provisions and, above all, their unyielding spirit. The battle of Nội Bàng ended and Trần Hưng Đạo retreated into Vạn Kiếp, concentrating troops from the Routes to prepare for the coming battle. *ĐVSKTT* 5 p.45b2-3 says: "*On the 6th of the 1st month of Ất Dậu, i.e. the spring of Thiệu Bảo the Seventh (1285), Wu Ma Er of the Yuan army attacked Vạn Kiếp and Mount Phả Lại. Hưng Đạo Vương of An Nam, who was commanding troops of defense in Vạn Kiếp, fought against him. Wan Hu I Jun was killed at Lưu Thôn.*"

According to *An Nan Chuan* of *Yuan Shih* 209 p.6b6-7, T'o Huan had built factories for making warships and organized naval troops, who were commanded by Wu Ma Er to launch a major attack on Vạn Kiếp. On their way of advance, they picked Emperor Nhân Tông's two letters sent to T'o Huan and A Li Hai Ya with respect to his request that they should observe Kublai Khan's order issued in the year of Chung Tung 2 (1261) and that they had to withdraw their troops. Afterwards, A Li Hai Ya wrote a letter to Emperor Nhân Tông, requesting him to open the road for "*the troops of the [Yuan} court to fight Champa.*" The letter was carried to Vạn Kiếp by our detained messenger, Nguyễn Văn Hàn, who had just been released by the Yuan army.

Even at that moment A Li Hai Ya went on with his impudent words as recorded in *An Nan Chuan* of *Yuan Shih* 209, pp.6b11-7a3: "*Leading troops to fight Champa, the [Yuan] court has repeatedly sent letters to you, asking for opening the road and preparing supplies. It is sufficiently surprising that you have opposed the order from the court, letting Hưng Đạo Vương command troops to fight against and cause losses for our army. To let the people of An Nam suffer disasters, it is your country's fault. Now, the Great Army is crossing your country to fight Champa. His Majesty gives orders for you to think seriously. Your country has long been subject [to the imperial court]; you should think of His Majesty's great mercy to open the road immediately and advise the people to make their living as before. When our troops pass by, there will not be anything harmful. You should go out receiving Chên Nan Wang, discussing military affairs with him. Otherwise, the Great Army will be quartered and establish their bases in An Nam."*

On the part of Đại Việt, as has been mentioned above, Emperor Nhân Tông and Trần Hưng Đạo ordered troops from the Routes in the northeast such as Hải Đông, Vân Trà, Ba Điểm, and other places, Bàng Hà, Na Sầm, Trà Hương, Yên Sinh, Long Nhãn to be concentrated at Vạn Kiếp and Mount Phả Lại. According to Section "Sơn Xuyên" of *An Nam Chí Nguyên* 1 p.42, Mount Phả Lại is *"situated in Từ Sơn District, facing Bình Than, embraced on the left by the Như Nguyệt River and on the right by the Ô Cách. It is a magnificent landscape of the region."* Concerning Emperor Nhân Tông, he himself commanded the Thánh Dực army of more than 1000 men to help Trần Hưng Đạo counterattack, as recorded in *An Nan Chuan* of *Yuan Shih* 209, p.7a3-4.

Thus, according to *Pen chi* of *Yuan Shih*, by the festival of Ất Dậu New Year Wu Ma Er had ordered a decisive blow on our base in Vạn Kiếp, where a fierce battle occurred with the death of the Yuan General Wan Hu I Jun at Lưu Thôn. This is in accordance with an account in *An Nan Chuan* of *Yuan Shih* 209 p.6b5-6, where it says: *"Hưng Đạo Vương fled; [our] mandarins and men pursued him to Vạn kiếp, attacking and destroying [their hold at] the frontier pass."*

The Battle of Bình Than

According to *An Nam Chí Lược* 4 p.54, on the ninth, Nham Ngọ, of the first month, Emperor Nhân Tông *"commanded 100,000 troops in a great battle at Bài Than. Yuan Shuai Wu Ma Er, Na Hai (Naqai), and Tsun Lin Tê destroyed all the boats they had captured before.*" Concerning the same day *Pen Chi* of *Yuan Shih* 13 p.7a8-9 says: "*Wu Ma Er with his troops encountered Hưng Đạo Vương's troops of An Nam and defeated them*", without mentioning the place. Accordingly, in the fighting at Bài Than commanded by Emperor Nhân Tông there were surely 1,000 warships Trần Hưng Đạo had deployed about ten miles from Vạn Kiếp as recorded above by *Yuan Shih*.

Here, Bài Than is nothing other than Bình Than because in a passage on the Bình Than River *An Nam Chí Nguyên* 1, pp.46-47, says: "*[The river] named Bài Than or Bình Than is in Chí Linh District. It flows from Xương Giang to [its confluence with] the Thị Cầu River, where they incorporate into each other to flow between Mount Chí Linh and Mount Phả Lại, winding so vastly that it is hard to see its border. At the mouth of the Đỗ Mộ River, it is divided into two branches flowing into the sea.*" In this quotation, Bài Than is transliterated according to Manuscript B cited by Gaspardone in *Kao I* on page 47.[2]

The Battle of Thăng Long

Following the battles at Vạn Kiếp, Phả Lại and Bình Than, the enemy went on to attack Vũ Ninh and Đông Ngạn and then advanced down to Gia Lâm. Meanwhile, our troops were compelled to retreat into Thăng Long along the Thiên Đức River, where occurred some small combats. In the words of *ĐVSKTT* 5

---

[2] E. Gaspardone, Ngan-nan Tche Yuan, Hanoi: Imprimarie d'Extreme-Orient, 1932, p.47. [LMT]

p.45b3-5: "*On the 12th day the enemy attacked Gia Lâm, Vũ Ninh, Đông Ngạn. Seeing the two words 'sát thát'[3] inscribed on the arms of our troops they had captured, they got so angry that they killed a large number of them. Then they advanced into Đông Bộ Đầu and erected their big flag there. [Our] King wanted to be informed precisely of the enemy's situation but he did not yet know who could undertake it. Realizing his intention, Chi Hầu Cục Thủ Đỗ Khắc Chung stepped forward, saying: 'Though humble and untalented, I would like to go.' The King was very pleased, saying: 'No one dares to say that among the horses pulling carts of salt there would not be any swift and excellent ones.' Then Chung left, taking the letter with him.*"

In *Yuan Shih* 13 p.7a9, the day cited above is dated "*Ất Dậu, when An Nam Thế Tử Trần Nhật Huyên commanded more than 1000 warships to counterattack. On the day Bính Tuất, [our army] fought with [An Nam] troops and destroyed them totally. Nhật Huyên ran away. [Our army] marched into his citadel and then went out, quartered north of the Phú Lương River.*" In the words of *An Nam Chí Lược* 54: "*On the 13th day, Bính Tuất, Thế Tử held [the position on] the Lô River but soon left because it was broken. Chên Nan Wang's troops crossed the river, entering the citadel and holding a party there.*" The same is recorded in *Ching Shih Ta Tien Tzǔ Lu* in *Yuan Wen Lei* 41, p.27a4-56: "*Mandarins and troops reached the Phú Lương River. Nhật Huyên himself fought against them. Defeated, he left his citadel for the Thiên Trường Prefecture. Mandarins and troops entered the capital.*"

---

[3] 殺 韃 , killing the Tatars (韃 靼), a designation of the Mongols by the Vietnamese at that time.

In *An Nan Chuan* of *Yuan Shih* 209, p.7a4, the battle is very clearly described: *"Accompanied by the mandarins of Hsin Shêng, Chên Nan Wang himself reached Đông Ngạn to command troops to fight the [An Nam] troops. [We] killed a large number of men and captured twenty boats. Hưng Đạo Vương was defeated and ran away. Mandarins and troops built a bridge of connected rafts to land on the north bank of the Phú Lương River. There had existed their troops and boats and wood barriers along the river. Seeing [our] mandarins and troops, they fired cannons, shouted loudly and challenged to fight. In the afternoon, Nguyễn Phụng Ngự was ordered to carry a letter to Chên Nan Wang and the official of Hsin Shêng, asking for our great army's withdrawal. The official of Hsin Shêng wrote a letter of blame and then ordered troops to advance. Nhật Huyên fled out of the capital, but soon ordered Nguyễn Hiệu Nhuệ to come with his letter of excuse and some local gifts, asking for [our] withdrawal. The official of Hsin Shêng sent him a letter, persuading the [An Nan] army to surrender. Then he commanded troops to cross the river and halted near the An Nan capital. The following day, Chên Nan Wang entered their capital. The palaces were deserted; there remained some decrees and some letters from our Hsin Shêng, all being torn into pieces."*

From the account above, we may acquire some significant remarks. First, though it was a great battle on water in which was involved an army of more than 100,000 men, the battle of Bình Than in essence was really of a 'mobile warfare', that is, fighting for retreating and attracting the enemy into trap. Accordingly, when T'o Huan ordered his troops to connect rafts to make a bridge across the Thiện Đức River, now known as the Đuống River, on their way toward the Phú Lương River, i.e. the Red River, Emperor Nhân Tông once again ordered to *"fire cannons, shout loudly and challenge to fight"* when he was personally commanding troops in the battle of Thăng Long.

Secondly, though challenging the enemy to fight, Emperor Nhân Tông kept on establishing some corridor of relationship with the enemy for the purpose of carrying out his tactical intention and fathoming the enemy's situation. In *Yuan Shih*, the people having such names as Nguyễn Phụng Ngự and Nguyễn Hiệu Nhuệ are said to have carried Emperor Nhân Tông's letters to T'o Huan but in reality they are not found in our history books. Instead, in *ĐVSKTT* 5 only the name Đỗ Khắc Chung is mentioned.

Thirdly, the reason Emperor Nhân Tông could have such an active relationship with the enemy is that he had been capable of maintaining his entire armed forces after the battle of Bình Than. Thereafter, he concentrated all troops in Thăng long to prepare for a strategic retreat into Thiên Trường, where he could defend our people against the enemy's attack in three directions, that is, the armies commanded by T'o Huan and A Li Hai Ya in the north-east, by Na Su La Ting (Nasir ud Din) in the north-west, and particularly by So Tu in the south.

It was on the 14th of the first month of Ất Dậu (1285), when T'o Huan entered our citadel to hold a party with his staff and then retreated to halt north of the Red River, that *"So Tu, T'ang Wu Tai (Tangutai) ... moved their troops to join with Chên Nan Wang"*, as recorded in *Pen Chi* of *Yuan Shih* 13, p.7a10-11. T'ang Wu Tai was the general whom T'o Huan, when commanding troops to advance, ordered to go to Champa with the task of telling So Tu to retreat his troops for a concentration of fighting forces, as recorded in *An Nan Chuan* of *Yuan Shih* 209, p.5b12-13: *"ordering Tso Chêng T'ang Wu Tai to go to Champa by post-horses, informing So Tu of the date of concentrating all the armed forces."* In reality, as it will be seen later, So Tu's troops could not move to the position of concentration in time; and only the major army commanded by T'o Huan could gather in Thăng Long to suffer the thundering counteroffensives by the troops and militiamen of Đại Việt in the triumphant victories in Chương Dương, Tây Kết, Hàm Tử.

Before the above-mentioned victories of our country over the Yuan army, T'o Huan, in his headquarters in Thăng Long, on the one hand, *"ordered Wan Hu Li Ping Hsien and Liu Shih Ying to command troops to open a route from Yung P'ing into An Nam. Along the route within each 30 miles they set up a camp and within each 60 miles a station, where 300 men were regularly posted to hold and patrol. He also ordered Shih Ying to establish posts to handle camps and stations"*, as recorded in *An Nan Chuan* of *Yuan Shih* 209, p.7b7-9. It was one of their measures to secure the areas occupied by them but frequently harassed by our troops.

On the other hand, also in the words of *An Nan Chuan* of *Yuan Shih* 209 p.7b9-10, T'o Huan ordered *"Yu Chêng Kuan Ch'ê (Könčäk) to command Wan Hu Mang Ku Tai (Manquadai) and Po Lo Ho Ta Er by land and Li Tso Chêng to command Wu Ma Er Pa Tu (Omar ba'atur) by water"* to pursue our troops' withdrawal and and attack our positions along the Red River and the troops who were holding Thiên Trường south of Thăng Long. Thus, it was on the bank of Thiên Mạc that the first battle broke out.

The Battle of Đà Mạc

Đà Mạc or Thiên Mạc, which was later named Mạn Trù, is a bank of land along the Red River in what is now HưngYênProvince. *Khâm Định Việt Sử Thông Giám Cương Mục* 6 p.42a3-4 says: "*The Thiên Mạc River is the lower Phú Lương at Bank Mạn Trù in Đông Yên District of Hưng Yên Province.*" There, our army set up a stronghold commanded by Trần Bình Trọng. According to *An Nam Chí Lược* 4 p.54, "*On the 21st, Nhâm Thìn, [the Yuan troops] swept through the Thiên Hán frontier pass, cutting down General Bảo Nghĩa Hầu.*" In reality, the Nhâm Thìn day of the first month of Ất Dậu must be the 19th and not the 21st. Certainly the number 19 was mistaken for 21 because they are very easy to be falsely copied. Regarding the name Thiên Hán, obviously the character *Hán* (漢) is the mistaken form of the character *Mạc* (漠) because they are of rather similar forms.

In *An Nan Chuan* of *Yuan Shih* 209, p.7b10, the date of the battle is not mentioned but it has an account of the battle and the capture of Kiến Đức Hầu Trần Trọng by the Yuan army. In *Ching Shih Ta Tien Tzŭ Lu* of *Yuan Wen Lei* 41, p.27a6-7, the fact Trần Trọng was captured is, too, recorded but dated after the battles of A Lỗ and Thiên Trường and before Emperor Nhân Tông's retreat to the mouth of Giao Thủy. Among them, the information taken from *An Nam Chí Lược* is relatively correct because Lê Sực wrote down what he could more or less participate and know.

Trần Trọng, here, must be the national hero Trần Bình Trọng in *ĐVSKTT*. A single difference is that his title was Bảo Nghĩa Hầu instead of Kiến Đức Hầu as recorded in Chinese accounts. The title Kiến Đức Hầu might have been given to Trần Bình Trọng when he was alive whereas Bảo Nghĩa Hầu was his posthumous title, conferred on him to praise a general's bravery and consistency in the face of the enemy's persuasion, which is clearly discussed below in *ĐVSKTT*. That *An Nam Chí Lược* 4 p.54 has a different account concerning the fact above from that in *Yuan Shih* originates from the fact that Lê Sực, who was then working with Chương Hiến Hầu Trần Kiện in Vietnam when Trần Bình Trọng was killed and then given the title, could know very clearly the latter's change of title.

On the part of Yuan troops, their commander of this battle is nowhere mentioned. Yet, in Vietnamese history books a hero of ours in this battle was clearly recorded. In the words of *ĐVSKTT*: *"Bảo Nghĩa Vương Trần Bình Trọng (who, a descendant of Lê Đại Hành, was the later husband of Princess Thụy Bảo and whose father, an official under Thái Tông's reign, was given the 'national surname' Trần) died on behalf of his fighting against the enemy on the bank of Đà Mạc (namely, Thiên Mạc, present-day Mạn Trù). When captured, he refused eating. When asked by the enemy about our national affairs, he refused answering. Asked 'Would you like to work as a 'vương'[4] in the Northern Land?', he shouted loudly, 'I would rather become a demon in the Southern Country than a vương in the Northern Land.' Thereafter, he was killed."*

The fundamental difference is that in *ĐVSKTT* the battle of Đà Mạc and Trần Bình Trọng's heroic death are dated the second month of Ất Dậu, that is, after the surrenders of Chương Kiến Hầu Trần Kiện and Lê Sực, whereas according to Lê Sực himself it is the Nhâm Thìn day of the first month of Ất Dậu. In this case, Lê Sực's

---

[4] The highest of titles conferred on a subject of the Imperial Court.

information appears to be more reliable if it is based on the course of military situation at that time. Further, he was contemporary with Trần Bình Trọng and directly joined in some military activities at that time. Another reason is that it was not really necessary for him to change the date of the Yuan attack on our base at Đà Mạc.

Finally, as it has been said before, Trần Bình Trọng's death occurred a little before Lê Sực's surrender, approximately more or less than a month, surely had a great impact on the latter. Indeed, according to *Khâm Định Việt Sử Thông Giám Cương Mục* 7 p.36b2, on hearing of Trần Bình Trọng's death Emperor Nhân Tông cried so sorrowfully. This points out that the death of Trần Bình Trọng exerted a strong impact on the leading group of our country at that time. The title Bảo Nghĩa Hầu might have been conferred by Emperor Nhân Tông for the purpose of praising the unyielding spirit of a hero in a period when the emperor realized that there began to appear around him those who could not maintain some mutual affection between king and subjects, some loyalty to king and nation so that they might be ready to defect to the enemy at any time.

Moreover, concerning the battle of Đà Mạc what is mentioned in *ĐVSKTT* was chiefly cited from *Đại Việt Sử Ký Tục Biên* of Phan Phu Tiên, who could not have such favorable conditions as other historians when he was writing his own book. For that was the time when our country was dominated by the Ming for nearly 20 years and underwent many intense wars of liberation led by our patriots such as Trần Trùng Quang, Nguyễn Biểu, Phạm Ngọc, Lê Lợi. Most of historical materials, therefore, must have been confiscated or destroyed by the enemy, especially those recorded by Quốc Sử Quán of the Trần Dynasty, which we, today, cannot know exactly whether to have been hidden according to Hồ Quý Ly's plan or not. The most typical example is that the two wars of 1285 and 1288 were really the great wars of defense but they are described very plainly in *ĐVSKTT*, let alone some points to be found completely false. For that reason it might not be surprising for readers at all to face the above-mentioned differences.

In summary, the battle of Đà Mạc was not actually great. Yet, through it we can see not only the heroic, unyielding character of the commander Trần Bình Trọng but also our people's resolution of defeating the enemy in a most difficult period of our country. It was due to such courageous and strenuous people that the later victories in the battles of Hàm Tử, Chương Dương, Tây Kết, etc. could be gained.

The battle of A Lỗ

According to *An Nam Chí Lược* 4 p.54, subsequent to the battle of Đà Mạc, in which Kiến Đức Hầu Trần Trọng was captured, "*Thế Tử withdrew his troops to defend the frontier pass Hải Thị, ordering to set up poles for building a dam of defense on the west bank. Mandarins and troops stormed them with intersecting arrows shot from both above and below; they were broken down completely.*" *Ching Shih Ta Tien Tzǔ Luin Yuan Wen Lei* 41, p.27a6, says: "*[Our] Great Army pursued Nhật Huyên on the rivers of A Lỗ and Đức Cương.*" Based on these two reports, the names Hải Thị and A Lỗ obviously refer to the same place. Particularly in the words of *An Nan Chih Yuan* 1 p.47: "*The Hải Triều River in Khoái Châu is a tributary of the Hà Lỗ River; its upper stream is connected with the*

Ngọc Châu River." Here, Hà Lỗ is no doubt the A Lỗ River just mentioned in *Ching Shih Ta Tien Tzǔ Lu.* Concerning Khoái Châu, it was located in present-day Hưng Yên Province. And Đà Mạc, i.e. Thiên Mạc, is said in *Khâm Định Việt Sử Thông Giám Cương Mục* 6, p.42a3-4, to be situated on the lower Red River in HưngYênProvince. Thus, the two bases of Đà Mạc and A Lỗ were close to each other. This might be the group of bases established for defending Thiên Trường.

With the detail "*intersecting arrows shot from both above and below*", it is evident that the enemy's two-pronged attack, on land and on water, commanded by K'uan Ch'ê and Li Hêng was aimed at pursuing the great army of Emperor Nhân Tông and storming into our base at A Lỗ after occupying Đà Mạc. Once more, it was a battle that caused great loss for the enemy and drew them into the trap planned beforehand in our army's tactics.

The Battle of Đại Hoàng

According to *An Nam Chí Lược* 4 p.54, following their victory at A Lỗ, "*on the 3rd, Đinh Tỵ, of the 2nd month, Chên Nan Wang broke Thế Tử's troops on the Đại Hoàng River.*" It was the first time T'o Huan appeared in the area near Thiên Trường. The Đại Hoàng River, according to *An Nam Chí Nguyên* 1 p.42, is "*located in Lý Nhân Prefecture, where its upper stream is connected with the Lô River, its lower stream with the GiaoThủy or Phụng Hóa Prefecture.*" In *Khâm Định Việt Sử Thông Giám Cương Mục*, a note on "Hoàng Giang" says: "*The Hoàng River is in Nam Xương District, its upper stream connected with the Thiên Mạc River, its lower stream with the Giao Thủy River.*" Thus, due to its connection with Thiên Mạc, Đại Hoàng or Hoàng Giang is one in a series of positions south of Thăng Long established to defend Thiên Trường.

The battle that occurred there must have been extremely intense; for T'o Huan himself moved his great army down from Thăng Long to pursue our troops, who had also been concentrated at Đại Hoàng and commanded not only by Emperor Nhân Tông but also by other generals such as Trần Hưng Đạo, Trần Quang Khải. On the part of our army, however, it was not really a counteroffensive but an enemy-exhausting combat for the purpose of keeping our troops' withdrawal safe.

The Military Situation in Thăng Long after Our Army's Withdrawal

The battles of A Lỗ and Đại Hoàng are not mentioned in *ĐVSKTT*, but concerning the battle of Đà Mạc *ĐVSKTT* 5 p.47a5-6 says: "*The enemy's forces were so violent that the two kings[5] had to retreat into Tam Trĩ Nguyên in a small ship, ordering to drive it to Ngọc Sơn to deceive the enemy.*" In reality, our troops in that situation were not so demoralized and the two kings not so isolated that they had to have such seemingly frightened actions. *Yuan Shih* 13 p.8b8-10 says: "*On the Bính Tý day of the 3rd month, Hu Nan Chan Ch'êng Hsin Shêng requested for more men. Then, Trần Nhật Huyên had fled to Thiên Trường and Trường Yên, ordering his troops to be concentrated again. Hưng Đạo Vương gathered more than one thousand warships at Vạn Kiếp whereas Nguyễn Lộc's troops were deployed at Vĩnh Bình. In the meantime, due to the long march of fighting for a long time, our mandarins and troops, who*

---

[5] Emperor Nhân Tông and his Emperor-father Thánh Tông.

were like being "loosely hung" between them, had to ask for more men since the troops of So Tu and T'ang Wu Tai could not come in time. The reinforcement, by order of King, had to move by land since it would not be safe to move by water."

Accordingly, after Emperor Nhân Tông withdrew from Thăng Long and ordered troops to be concentrated at Thiên Trường and Trường Yên, the enemy fell into a very difficult situation. They themselves professed that they were being loosely hung in a thick net with which the troops of Đại Việt would cover them at any time. In fact, the Đại Việt army was developing their strategy of besieging and destroying these far-marching troops from three directions. The north wing was commanded by General Nguyễn Lộc and had great contributions to a battle that could break the hearts of those who were attempting to 'rob' and 'sell' our country as it will be seen below. The east wing was composed of warships deployed by Trần Hưng Đạo himself at Vạn Kiếp to stop the enemy's eastward retreat. The third wing, consisting of the entire armed forces, was concentrated at Thiên Trường and Trường Yên, now known as Nam Định and Ninh Bình respectively, and commanded directly by Emperor Nhân Tông and his emperor-father Thánh Tông together with two famous generals, Trần Quang Khải and Trần Nhật Duật. It was the major front with complicated occurrences on our part as well as on the enemy's.

Trần Kiện, Trần Tú Viên, and Trần Văn Lộng Surrendering

On the enemy's part, So Tu was urgently withdrawing his troops from Champa to the north by the order of T'o Huan transmitted by T'ang Wu Tai. On their way of retreat, there would be fierce combats with our troops as it will be seen below. On our part, subsequent to the battles and then withdrawals from Thăng Long and other bases at Đà Mạc, A Lỗ and Đại Hoàng, some of the political and military leaders of Đại Việt at that time began to show extremely puzzled, seemingly losing their confidence in the nation's potential strength and the brilliant leadership of Emperor Nhân Tông together with Emperor-Father Thánh Tông and such generals as Trần Hưng Đạo, Trần Quang Khải. Among those who sought to connect with the enemy for their surrender, the earliest traitor was Trần Kiện with his accomplices. *ĐVSKTT* 5 p.46b5-7 says: "*On the 1st, Giáp Thìn, of the 2nd month [of Ất Dậu], Tính Quốc Đại Vương Quốc Khang's elder son, Chương Hiến Hầu named Kiệt, and Lê Sực took their families to surrender the Yuan army. By So Tu's order, they were brought to Yen Ching. At Camp Ma Lục, they were stopped and attacked by Nguyễn Thế Lộc and Nguyễn Lĩnh, the natives of Lạng Giang. Kiện was shot dead by a servant of Hưng Đạo Vương's, Nguyễn Địa Lô. Lê Sực escaped in the night, having Kiện's corpse carried on a horse. After riding about ten miles, he reached Khâu Ôn and had Kiện buried there.*"

The fact is more clearly described in *An Nam Chí Lược* 4, p.54: "*Thế Tử ordered his younger brother, Chiêu Văn Vương Trần Duật and Trịnh Đình Toàn to command troops in Nghệ An. Being defeated, they all ran away. In such an urgent situation, Thế Tử ordered his brother's son, Chương Hiến Hầu Trần Kiện, to command the battlefield in Thanh Hóa. After long resistance, due to their weakness and lack of reinforcement, Chương Hiến and Sực surrendered.*" Also in *An Nam Chí Lược* 13, pp.131-132: "*That winter (1284), Chên Nan Wang's great army marched into the [An Nam] country, defeating Thế Tử. Yu Chêng So Tu, advancing from*

Champa, attacked them in the rear. Extremely puzzled, Thế Tử had no other way than calling for Trần Kiện and dispatching troops to him to fight against So Tu. Seeing that the troops were weak and there were no reinforcement, and further, without any information of whether Thế Tử was alive or not, Kiện sent for Sực, saying, "Due to Thế Tử's refusal of attending the audience, the war broke out. In the face of danger, he is still not awakened. He would be pleased to see our country lost and our houses broken, wouldn't he?" In the 1st month of the year that followed (1285), Kiện together with Sực's group of about some ten thousand people surrendered, handing in their weapons to Chên Nan Wang."

Thus, Trần Kiện's surrender was a very complicated event. For it was the first time when a descendant of the royal family, who was in charge of a great army on an important front in Thanh Hóa, surrendered the enemy. If it was not promptly resolved, such a fact might have a highly perilous impact, causing the collapse of the south front. As soon as he retreated from Thăng long, Emperor Nhân Tông realized the importance of this front. Right after the 15th of the first month of Ất Dậu (1285), therefore, he urgently ordered Chiêu Văn Vương Trần Nhật Duật to hold it.

According to *An Nam Chí Lược* 4 p.54 and *Ching Shih Ta Tien Tzŭ Lu* of *Yuan Wen Lei* 41 p.27a5-6, by the end of the first month *"Ta Wang Chiao Ch'i, Yu Chêng So Tu, Tso Chêng T'ang Wu Tai, and Shan Chêng Hei Ti, who just retreated from Champa, penetrated into Bố Chính Prefecture."* Thereafter, So Tu went on to advance to Nghệ An. Trần Nhật Duật's troops had to retreat because he could not resist them. *ĐVSKTT* 5 p.46b4-5, therefore, says: *"On the 26th, Hưng Đạo Vương asked [the King] for allowing*

Thượng Tướng Thái Sư Trần Quang Khải to halt Yuan Shuai So Tu in Nghệ An." It points out that shortly after Trần Nhật Duật urgently reported to our supreme headquarters on his failure to resist the enemy's forces, Emperor Nhân Tông appointed Trần Quang Khải to assist him. It was in this period that Trần Kiện was given the command of troops in Thanh Hóa, where "*Kiện led Sực's group of ten thousand men with weapons to surrender Chên Nan Wang*" according to *An Nam Chí Lược* 13 p.132.

The Battle of Phú Tân

Also in *An Nam Chí Lược* 4, p.54, on the day that followed, i.e. the second, Ất Tỵ, of the second month of Ất Dậu (1285), "*Chiao Ch'i commanded the cavalry to cross the gate of Vệ Bố, liquidating troops of the Trần family and killing some of their officers, that is, Đinh Xa and Nguyễn Tất Thống.*" Then, also according to *An Nam Chí Lược* 3 p.54, on the third day when T'o Huan was attacking our base at Đại Hoàng and Emperor Nhân Tông was retreating into Thiên Trường, Trần Tú Viên and Trần Văn Lộng surrendered to the Yuan. Four days later, that is, the sixth of the second month, as recorded in *An Nam Chí Lược* 4, p.54: "*on the 6th day, Kỷ Dậu, Chiao Ch'i led Chang Hsien to attack the troops of Thế Tử's brother Trần Khải at the Phú Tân ferry, cutting off a thousand [men's] heads. [Other troops in] Thanh Hóa, Nghệ An surrendered.*" This was the time when So Tu's troops could be united with T'o Huan's as in the words of *An Nan Chuan* of *Yuan Shih* 209 p.7b4-7: "*T'ang Wu Tai together with So Tu's troops from Champa met with [T'o Huan's] great army. Since they marched into Đại Việt, they fought in seven battles, great and small, occupying more than two thousand miles of land, four palaces of the [An Nam] king. Earlier they had defeated the troops of Chiêu Minh Vương. Chiêu Hiếu Vương and Đại Liêu Hộ were killed. Chiêu Minh Vương ran away, having no courage to appear again. In addition, they captured Trần Thượng Thư, and the son-in-law of Lương Phụng Ngự of Giao Chỉ together with Triệu Mạnh Tín, Diệp Lang Tướng and more than four hundred descendants of the Sung family-in-exile in Nghệ An, Diễn Châu, Thanh Hóa, Trường Yên.*"

Accordingly, Trần Kiện had led Chiao Ch'i to attack the Phú Tân base commanded by Thượng Tướng Trần Quang Khải with his son, Văn Túc Vương Đạo Tải, and his nephew, Tả Thiên Vương Đức Việp. Before Trần Quang Khải retreated from the base, Chiêu Hiếu Vương and Đại Liêu Hộ were killed.

Thus, the fact that Trần Kiện surrendered to the enemy had a great impact on our army. On the southern front such famous generals as Trần Quang Khải, Trần Nhật Duật gradually withdrew from Thanh Hóa and Nghệ Tĩnh toward Thiên Trường. After the battle of Đại Hoàng on the third of the second month of Ất Dậu (1285) and the battle of Phú Tân on the sixth, Emperor Nhân Tông together with Trần Hưng Đạo and Trần Quang Khải launched a strategic withdrawal. Before his declaration of this withdrawal as a postponement of military actions, Emperor Nhân Tông ordered Trung Hiếu Hầu Trần Dương and Nguyễn Nhuệ to negotiate with T'o Huan and, at the same time, ordered his servant, Đào Kiên, to offer Princess An Tư to Chên Nan Wang for the purpose of *"relieving the country's disaster."* Thereby, T'o Huan ordered Ch'ien Hu Ai to persuade Emperor Nhân Tông to attend the negotiation but the latter refused, as recorded in *An Nam Chí Lược* 4, p.54. In *ĐVSKTT* 5, p.47a1, the fact of offering Princess An Tư is mentioned but dated before the battle of Đà Mạc.

The Strategic Retreat into Thanh Hóa

Thus, after the battles of Đại Hoàng and Phú Tân the major armed forces of Đại Việt, besides the units posted in regional stations, were first concentrated in Thiên Trường and then withdrawn strategically at the river-mouth of Giao Thủy, as recorded in *An Nan Chuan* of *Yuan Shih* 209 p.7b10-11. Also it is said in *Yuan Shih* that the Yuan did not know where our army moved. Then on page 7b11-12, it says: "*Some of Tông's relatives such as Văn Nghĩa Hầu with his father Vũ Đạo Hầu, his son Minh Trí Hầu and Seng Shan Chêng, a mandarin of the Sung-in-exile, Tô Thiếu Bảo's son named Tô Bảo Chương, and Trần Thượng Thư's son named Trần Đình Tôn all surrendered.*" Thus, the fact that Văn Nghĩa Hầu, i.e. Trần Tú Viên, defected to the enemy occurred on the third of the third month of Ất Dậu (1285) as recorded above by *An Nam Chí Lược* 4 p.54.

According to *Yuan Shih* 209 pp.7b13-8a3, it was these traitors that supplied information for T'o Huan: "*Reaching the An Bang estuary, Nhật Huyên gave up his ship, oars, armor, and cane to race into the mountains. Mandarins and troops captured ten thousand ships, the good ones of which were used, the remaining burned. Then, after three days' pursuit on land, our army captured alive some men, saying that the emperor-father [i.e. Thánh Tông] and Thế Tử had only four ships left, Hưng Đạo Vương and his son three ships, Thái Sư [Trần Nhật Duật] eighty ships, all moved to Thanh Hóa. Wu Ma Er Pa Tu commanded 1300 men and 60 ships to help So Tu pursue Thái Sư's troops.*" Thus, this is obviously a withdrawal on a grand scale, a strategic one carried out by Emperor Nhân

Tông, his emperor-father, Trần Hưng Đạo and Trần Quang Khải.

When did the withdrawal take place then? *An Nam Chí Lược* 4 p.54 says: *"On the 9th, Nhâm Ngọ, of the 3rd month, on a sea patrol with naval troops in Tam Trĩ, Chiao Ch'i and T'ang Wu Tai nearly captured Thế Tử."* In the words of ĐVSKTT 5 p.47a5-6, however, the withdrawal of Đại Việt troops into Tam Trĩ (i.e. the Ba Chẽ Mountains in Quảng Ninh) took place toward the end of the second month. Also according to ĐVSKTT 5 p.47b4-5, on the first, Giáp Tuất, of the third month *"the two kings left their ships and walked to Thủy Chú. There, they took ships along the Nam Triệu River (i.e. Thủy Đường District), then crossed the Đại Bàng sea to Thanh Hóa."* Thus, the withdrawal certainly occurred before the ninth of the third month (or rather, the 10th day, Nhâm Ngọ) and after the battle of Phú Tân on the sixth of the same month.

Obviously, this strategic withdrawal was planned to avoid the two-pronged thrust by T'o Huan's troops from the north and by So Tu's troops which were penetrating into Thiên Trường and Trường Yên from the south. Thus, the great armies of T'o Huan and So Tu had been concentrated in the plains of north Vietnam whereas our major forces were quartered south of Thanh Hóa, where Emperor Nhân Tông, Emperor-Father Thánh Tông and generals Trần Hưng Đạo, Trần Quang Khải, Trần Nhật Duật, and so on would launch a decisive counterattack to liberate the Thăng Long capital and the whole country from the enemy's occupation.

Trần Ích Tắc Surrendering to the Yuan

According to *An Nam Chí Lược* 4 p.54, within the first ten days of the third month of Ất Dậu when Emperor Nhân Tông and his headquarters were carrying on the strategic withdrawal mentioned above, "*Chiêu Quốc Vương Trần Ích Tắc and his group surrendered to the Yuan on the 15th, Mậu Tý.*" In ĐVSKTT 5 p.47b5-7, the fact is dated later than the first of the third month: "*Chiêu Quốc Vương Ích Tắc together with Phạm Cự Địa, Lê Diễn, Trịnh Long led their families to surrender to the Yuan.*" Later, Trần Ích Tắc had to suffer the tragic fate of a traitor, living hopelessly and, eventually, ending his life in foreign soil, leaving a dirty name in our history books forever. Meanwhile, our war of defense was reaching the decisive moments and a glorious conclusion was waiting for well-known and unknown heroes who were sacrificing themselves for their beloved Fatherland.

Đại Việt Army's Counteroffensives: the Victory at A Lỗ

After his strategic retreat into Thanh Hóa, Emperor Nhân Tông must have assembled all the troops to prepare for a great counterattack. In Chinese historical accounts nothing is written about the remaining 20 days of the same month, except that the traitors, Chương Hiến Hầu, Minh Thành Hầu, Nghĩa Quốc Hầu, etc. had been taken to China. *ĐVSKTT* 5 p.48a7-8 mentions a remark by Emperor Nhân Tông on So Tu's troops: "*Having moved so far for years, the enemy must be exhausted; further, it is so hard for them to transport supplies for miles. In our plan of taking advantage of 'relief' to fight against 'anxiety', if we can demoralize them in advance, we can surely liquidate them.*" Emperor Nhân Tông's remark might have been set forth in a summit of military strategists in Thanh Hóa at that time. In any case, it was the precious time for our army to prepare urgently for the counterattack.

Concerning our counterattack, *An Nam Chí Lược* 4 p.54 records only one sentence: "*In the summer, i.e. the 4th month, due to [our troops'] negligence, An Nam [troops] reoccupied La Thành.*" It is also generally mentioned in *An Nan Chuan* of *Yuan Shih* 209 p.8a7-9: "*The generals were called to discuss the Giao's counteroffensives. Although our mandarins and troops had defeated them many times, they collected more and more troops. Outrunning their supplies, mandarins and troops suffered hardships, many of them being killed in fighting. Troops and horses of the Mongols could not perform their talent, too. Therefore, they had to give up the [An Nam] capital, crossing the river toward the north side to discuss the plan of withdrawal.*"

In the words of *Ching Shih Ta Tien Tzŭ Lu* in *Yuan Wen Lei* 41, p.27a8-9: "*In the 4th month, all of Giao Chi troops pushed on. Their [general] Hưng Đạo Vương attacked Wan Hu Liu Shih Ying at A Lỗ, Trung Thành Vương attacked Ch'ien Hu Ma Jung in Giang Khẩu. They were killed and retreated. Then, their army and naval forces besieged [our] command post thickly. A great number of them were killed, but their reinforcements became more and more crowded. Though having attempted to fight intensely all day, mandarins and troops, due to lack of weapons, had to give up their capital, crossing the river....*"

It is then evidently clear that in the fourth month the first attack of our army commanded by Trần Hưng Đạo was focused on the base of A Lỗ, which our troops had left behind on the line of defense at Thiên Trường. The counterattack was successful and the enemy's general, Liu Shih Ying, had to abandon the base. It may be said that this was the first victory of Đại Việt's army and people after a series of battles at A Lỗ, Đại Hoàng and Phú Tân in our tactics of retreating and discouraging the enemy simultaneously. It is surprising enough that the victory has not been recorded in our history books.

The First Battle of Tây Kết and the Victory at Hàm Tử

According to ĐVSKTT 5 p.48a8-b6, "*In the summer, the 4th month, our King ordered Chiêu Thành Vương (unnamed), Hoài Văn Hầu Quốc Toản, General Nguyễn Khoái to lead troops to stop the enemy in Tây Kết. The court's army fought with the Yuan troops in Hàm Tử Quan. All the troops were concentrated there. In Chiêu Văn Vương Nhật Duật's army were some Sung men dressed in Sung clothes, using bows and arrows. The emperor-father fearing that they might be mistaken for the enemy's troops ordered a servant to tell our troops that 'They are the Mongol troops of Chiêu Văn [Vương]. Be careful [not to mistake them for the enemy].' For the Sung men and the Yuan troops had rather similar speech and clothes. Seeing them, the Yuan were frightened, saying, 'They are assisted by the Sung men' and then ran away toward the north. Earlier, when the Sung was exterminated [in China], some Sung men turned to our court. They were received into Trần Nhật Duật's army, in which Chao Chung was appointed to be an officer. Therefore, Nhật Duật was the general who gained most merit in our people's victory over the Yuan enemy.*"

Thus, subsequent to the victory at A Lỗ, under the command of Chiêu Thành Vương, Hoài Văn Hầu Quốc Toản, Nguyễn Khoái and Trần Nhật Duật our troops proceeded to penetrate into Tây Kết and Hàm Tử Quan in the fourth month. These bases were established close to each other in the area of Châu Giang District of present-day Hưng Yên Province; particularly, if Tây Kết was the opposite village of Đông Kết in Đông Bình commune of Châu Giang District, the former was obviously situated right in the middle of the Đà Mạc base ever commanded by the national hero Trần Bình Trọng. For the Đông Kết village is now only three kilometers far from the Red River, that is, Bank Đà Mạc.

Accordingly, the counterattack in the fourth month of Ất Dậu (1285) was aimed at reoccupying the military bases that were first founded by our army and then occupied by the enemy two months earlier, and using them as strong-points for liberating the Thăng Long capital.

The Victory at Chương Dương

Like the battle of Hàm Tử, that of Chương Dương is not mentioned in Chinese history books as it was a great loss for the Yuan. In *ĐVSKTT* 5, p.47b, it is described as follows: "*On the 3rd of the 5th month, the two kings were launching a violent thrust on the enemy in Trường Yên, cutting off a lot of their heads and ears. On the 7th, [they were] informed that So Tu moved his troops there from Thanh Hóa. On the 10th, a man of ours escaping from the enemy's camp ran to the Imperial Park, reporting that Generals Trần Quang Khải, Trần Quốc Toản, Trần Thông, Nguyễn Khả Lạp and his brother, Nguyễn Truyền were commanding troops from the Routes to fight the enemy in the palaces. The enemy was completely defeated; T'o Huan and A Lo crossed the Lô River.*"

Thus, according to *ĐVSKTT* it is not until the 10th of the fifth month of Ất Dậu (1285) that Emperor Nhân Tông and his father, who were commanding the attack on Trường Yên, were informed of the victory at Chương Dương by a soldier of ours escaping from the enemy's hands. The situation of war might have been very urgent at that time. For Chương Dương was a base on the front line not very far from the Thăng Long Capital, i.e. Chương Dương Commune of Thường Tín District in present-day Hà Tây Province. Being a line of defending their command post in Thăng Long, it might be the concentrating place of a geat number of enemy's troops. After occupying Chương Dương, therefore, our troops proceeded to drive the enemy toward their headquarters in Thăng Long, where a fierce battle, as it will be seen, occurred with great losses for both sides.

As has been mentioned above, Emperor Nhân Tông was informed of the victory at Chương Dương on the 10th of the fifth month. Nevertheless, it might have come earlier in the fourth month since in both *An Nam Chí Lược* 4, p.54 and *Ching Shih Ta Tien Tzŭ Lu* of *Yuan Wen Lei* 41 p.27a8-9 it is said that our troops attacked and reoccupied Thăng Long in that month. The significance of this victory was appreciated and it made a strong impression on our military strategists, just as what the talented general, Trần Quang Khải, remarked later:

Taking away the enemy's spears in Chương Dương,
Capturing the Hồ[6] troops in Hàm Tử.

The Liberation of Thăng Long

Today, Chương Dương commune is located on the Red River, approximately 20 kilometers south of Hà Nội Capital. So was it in the old days. After forcing the enemy to retreat out of Chương

---

[6] Denoting to the invaders from the north.

Dương, therefore, our troops resolved to pursue them, developing our victory into a campaign to liberate the Thăng Long capital, which had been occupied three months earlier. Such a historical fact, however, was not described in detail in *ĐVSKTT*. The authors of *Khâm Định Việt Sử Thông Giám Cương Mục* (7 p.41a5-6) showed regretful that such a great fact had not been clearly recorded: "*the victory over the enemy in Chương Dương to retake the imperial capital was the greatest military success at that time. [Unfortunately,] the earlier history books did not record it clearly.*"

By synthesizing various historical materials, particularly those of the Chinese source, however, we can know that it was a great battle in which both sides suffered great losses. On the part of our army, besides the south army commanded by Emperor Nhân Tông and his father advancing from Thanh Hóa to liberate Trường Yên and Thiên Trường, which were being occupied by Chiao Ch'i and T'ang Wu Tai respectively, our major armed forces were totally concentrated near the Thăng Long capital and then divided into two wings. The first wing commanded by the generals Trần Quang Khải, Trần Quốc Toản, Trần Thông, Nguyễn Khắc Lạp and Nguyễn Truyển was urgently pursuing the enemy on their way toward Thăng Long. The second wing was commanded by Hưng Đạo Vương Trần Quốc Tuấn and his elder brother, Hưng Ninh Vương Trần Quốc Tung, i.e. Tuệ Trung Thượng Sỹ. The latter wing is not often mentioned in our history books and by researchers today. In *An Nan Chuan* of *Yuan Shih* 209, p.8a7-10, however, it is very clearly recorded: "*Our generals were assembled to discuss the Giaos' counteroffensive. Although they were defeated many times, they gathered more and more troops. Without sufficient supplies, mandarins and troops suffered hardships and many of them were killed. Troops and horses of the Mongols could not manifest their talent, too. Eventually, they had to abandon the [An Nam] capital, crossing the river toward the north side to discuss the plan of retreat into Szu Ming. Chên Nan Wang agreed to withdraw troops. That day, Liu Shih Ying fought fiercely with more than twenty thousand men of Hưng Đạo Vương and Hưng Ninh Vương."*

Obviously, it was when the enemy decided to withdraw from Thăng Long that the brothers, Trần Quốc Tuấn and Trần Quốc Tung, commanded more than 20,000 men to fight with the enemy's general Liu Shih Ying, who had been driven out of the base of A Lỗ by Trần Hưng Đạo in the first victory of our general counteroffensive. At that time, Liu Shih Ying was appointed by T'o Huan to defend the rear of their withdrawal so that their troops could have time to retreat out of Thăng Long safely.

In reality, the liberation of Thăng Long was a great campaign. The descriptions in *Ching Shih Ta Tien Tzŭ Lu* in *Yuan Wen Lei* 41 p.27a9-b1 are quite in accordance with what the enemy's leaders discussed before withdrawing out of Thăng Long: *"In their attack on Ch'ien Hu Ma Jung at Giang Khẩu, Trung Thành Vương's troops were partly killed and retreated. Yet, their army and naval forces proceeded to besiege [our] command post thickly. Many of them were killed, but their reinforcements became more and more crowded. Though having attempted to fight extremely hard all day, mandarins and troops, due to lack of weapons, had to retreat out of their citadel to make camps beyond the river; thereafter, they were ordered to withdraw."*

Thus, the campaign to liberate Thăng Long in which our major forces were mostly mobilized and commanded by such most gifted generals as Trần Hưng Đạo, Trần Quốc Tung, Trần Quang Khải, and so on proceeded so fiercely and gloriously. With our thrusts from many different directions, the enemy was surrounded by many rings of our troops in some battles we can know today such as the battle of Giang Khẩu, i.e. Hàng Buồm Street in present-day Hà Nội, where Trung Thành Vương defeated Ch'ien Hu Ma Jung; particularly the fierce battle of Trần Hưng Đạo and Trần Quốc Tung's troops with Liu Shih Ying's.

As has been said above, the campaign must have started in the fourth month of Ất Dậu (1285). According to *An Nam Chí Lược* 4 p.54, however, up to the fifth of the fifth month Chiao Ch'i's troops had fought with our troops in the capital before they crossed the river to meet with T'o Huan and finally withdrew with him on the sixth of the fifth month: "*The 5th, Đinh Sửu, of the 5th month Chiao Ch'i and Wan Hu set up an ambush in the citadel to shoot arrows [at the An Nam troops]. The following day, they withdrew across the Lô River.*" Chiao Ch'i might be the commander of troops who had occupied Trường Yên and Thiên Trường and had then been driven away by Emperor Nhân Tông on the third of the fifth month as recorded in *ĐVSKTT*. Thereafter, they retreated into Thăng Long in the hope of uniting with T'o Huan's troops to launch another attack. On their arrival at Thăng Long, however, T'o Huan had ordered an entire retreat and they moved north with him after setting up some ambush and shooting inside the citadel as recorded by Lê Sực.

Thus, from the start of our besieging the enemy to their withdrawal out of the capital the campaign of liberating Thăng

Long lasted for at least several weeks. It was a prolonged battle since T'o Huan had attempted to hold to our capital whereas our army resolved to drive them out. Therefore, exactly as recorded in *ĐVSKTT*, Emperor Nhân Tông had not been reported on this victory until the 10th of the fifth month.

The Battle of Như Nguyệt and General Trần Quốc Toản's Sacrifice

Having withdrawn out of Thăng Long on the sixth of the fifth month, T'o Huan's troops moved toward the Như Nguyệt River, where a battle was taking place, as recorded in Chinese history books, and a Vietnamese commander sacrificed himself, that is, Hoài Văn Hầu Trần Quốc Toản. In the words of *An Nan Chuan* of *Yuan Shih* 209 p.8a10: "*Mandarins and troops reached the Như Nguyệt River when Hoài Văn Hầu, by order of Nhật Huyên, came fighting.*" *Ching Shih Ta Tien Tzŭ Lu* of *Yuan Wen Lei* 41 p.27b1-2 says: "*On [our army's] arrival at the Như Nguyệt River, Hoài Văn Hầu, pursuing [us] by order of Nhật Huyên, was killed.*"

The battle is not mentioned in our history books. However, in an account of the military conference at Bình Than in the 10th month of Nhâm Ngọ (1282), where Hoài Văn Hầu Trần Quốc Toản, due to his young age, was not allowed to attend, *ĐVSKTT* says: "*So shameful and angry that he was unaware of having squashed an orange in his hand. On his return home, he mobilized his servants and relatives, more than 1000 in number, had weapons made and fighting boats built, writing six words 'destroying strong enemy for king's sake' on a large flag. Later, in the face of the enemy, he himself was always the spearhead of our army's advance. Seeing him, no one of the enemy dared to fight against. At his death, King showed extremely regretful, writing a verse of mourning and conferring the posthumous title 'Vương' in memory of him.*" Thus, although it does not record the battle of Như Nguyệt, *ĐVSKTT* indirectly mentions the heroic sacrifice of Hoài Văn Hầu in this battle through its account of his death and Emperor Nhân Tông's regret.

The Victory at Tây Kết: Cutting Off So Tu's Head

According to *ĐVSKTT* 5 p.47a, while our troops were pursuing the enemy, they were informed on the seventh of the fifth month of Ất Dậu (1285) that "*So Tu moved his troops from Thanh Hóa (...). On the 17th day, So Tu and Wu Ma Er launched an attack [on our troops] on the Thiên Mạc River from the sea, intending to gather their troops in the capital to assist each other (...). On the 20th day, the two kings deployed troops at the ferry Đại Mang. A Yuan officer, Chang Hsien, surrendered. The same day, our troops defeated the enemy at Tây Kết, cutting off So Tu's head and killing many of his troops. At midnight, Wu Ma Er fled across the estuary of Thanh Hóa. The two kings could not pursue him but captured more than 50,000 of his troops. With only one big ship, Wu Ma Er fled to the sea (...). Seeing So Tu's head, the King said pitifully, 'As being servants, let us do like this.' Then, taking off his robe, with which he ordered his officials to cover So Tu's head before burial. But later, by his secret order, the head was soaked in oil [and hanged up publicly] as a punishment because So Tu, on the pretext of taking the route, had invaded our country for three years.*"

That was the process of the battle of Tây Kết and So Tu's death according to *ĐVSKTT*. In Chinese historical materials the event above is rather differently recorded, let alone some contradictions among them. *Pen Chi* of *Yuan Shih* 13 p.9b10-11, for instance, says: *"Trần Nhật Huyên fled to the port. Chên Nan Wang ordered Li Hêng to pursue him, [but he was] defeated. Due to unfavorable weather and then epidemics, [our] troops wanted to retreat into Szu Ming in the north. [Chên Nan Wang] ordered So Tu to move troops back to Ô Lý. The An Nan [troops] pursued [our troops]. So Tu fought but was killed."* Thus, obviously So Tu had been ordered by T'o Huan to move his troops down to the south, in Ô Lý and Việt Lý of Champa, i.e, the present-day provinces of Quảng Trị and Thừa Thiên.

Nevertheless, *So Tu Chuan* of *Yuan Shih* 129 p.7b9-10 says: *"T'o Huan ordered So Tu to halt his troops in Thiên Trường, approximately more than 200 miles from the headquarters, to seek supplies. Suddenly the king issued the order of withdrawal. T'o Huan withdrew his troops, informing So Tu of nothing. Later, the latter was told by Giao Chỉ [people] but he did not believe. When he reached the headquarters, they were empty. Giao Chỉ [troops] stopped him on the Càn Mặn River. So Tu fought against them but was killed."* Accordingly, So Tu had not been ordered to deploy his troops in Ô Lý and Việt Lý but in Thiên Trường so that he could not learn of T'o Huan's withdrawal until he reached Thăng Long.

In the meantime, *An Nam Chí Lược* 4 p.54 affirms: *"Having then learned of the great army's withdrawal, So Tu led his troops northward from Thanh Hóa. On their way they fought with An Nam [troops] day and night. At Bái Khanh, Li Chiao Chang, a general under So Tu's command, turned on the army. So Tu's horse fell into water and he died. Wu Ma Er and Wan Hu Liu K'uei fled to the sea in their light boats. Following them was Hsiao Li, who, without any hope to escape, intended to cut his own throat. Seeing this, the Trần king ordered his rescue."*

Thus, *So Tu Chuan* and *An Nam Chí Lược* agree on the fact that So Tu moved his troops from Thanh Hóa to the plains of north Vietnam but they have different accounts of the subsequent events. The Càn Mãn River, where So Tu is said to have been killed in *So Tu Chuan* cited above, is identified, in Section "Sơn Xuyên" of *Đại Nam Nhất Thống Chí*, with the ThịCầuRiver. Is it then true that So Tu was killed in the battle of Như Nguyệt?

The answer may be found in *An Nam Chí Lược* and *ĐVSKTT*. The former says that when So Tu's troops reached Bái Khanh, one of his officers, Li Chiao Chang, betrayed them. Chang guided Đại Việt troops to fight So Tu and they cut off his head when he fell into the river with his horse. Meanwhile, the latter says that Emperor Nhân Tông and his father reached Đại Mang Bộ when an officer of the Yuan army, Chang Hsien, surrendered. Thus, Li Chiao Chang is none other than Chang Hsien; and Đại Mang Bộ is Bái Khanh. It was on the day of Chang Hsien's surrender that the Đại Việt army under the command of Emperor Nhân Tông and the emperor-father won the battle, cutting off So Tu's head and driving Wu Ma Er and Liu K'uei to the sea. Thus the southern wing of the Yuan army was completely annihilated.

The Victory at Vạn Kiếp

At the same time of our army's crucial victory in the south, the campaign of pursuing the enemy's forces in the north was urgently carried on by Trần Hưng Đạo. After their defeat on the NhưNguyệtRiver, T'o Huan's troops moved down to Vạn Kiếp, where they encountered Trần Hưng Đạo's troops. According to

ĐVSKTT 5 p.47b, "On the 20th day (...) Hưng Đạo Vương fought with T'o Huan and Li Hêng in Vạn Kiếp. The enemy was defeated and many of them were drowned. Li Hêng ordered troops to protect T'o Huan in their withdrawal to Szu Ming. Li Hêng was killed with one of our troops' poisoned arrows piercing his left knee. Hiding T'o Huan among bronze furniture, Pi Chiang Li Kuan gathered the remaining fifty thousand men and fled to the north. Hưng Đạo Vương pursued them to Szu Ming, using poisoned arrows to kill Li Kuan. The Yuan troops broke completely."

All the Chinese historical materials do not mention the battle of Vạn Kiếp, but they have accounts of the battle on the SáchRiver. *An Nan Chuan* of *Yuan Shih* 209 p.8a10-12 says: *"Reaching the Sách River, [our army] made a floating bridge to cross the river (...) Our troops were getting ready to cross the river when their troops in ambush rushed out from the forests. Mandarins and troops, most of whom were drowned, had to fight their way out of the land of Giao Chỉ. The troops of T'ang Wu Tai had to use post-horses to report the news [to the court]."* It is similarly recorded in *Ching Shih Ta Tien Tzu Lu* in *Yuan Wen Lei* 41 p.27b2: *"On the Sách River, their troops lying in ambush rushed out. Mandarin and troops competed with each other [to cross the river]. The floating bridge broke down and most of them were drowned."* In *An Nam Chí Lược* 4, p.54, it is somewhat different: *"An Nam troops advanced toward the Nam Sách River. Yu Chêng Li Hêng fought against them in the rear, cutting down Trần Thiệu, a strong officer of Hưng Đạo Vương."*

The SáchRiver mentioned in *Yuan Shih* and *Ching Shih Ta Tien Tzŭ Lu* is called the Nam Sách in *An Nam Chí Lược*. According to *Khâm Định Việt Sử Thông Giám Cương Mục Tiền Biên* 5 p.22a3, it

is "*in Nam Sách Prefecture of present-day Hải Dương Province.*"
Naturally, the battle of the Sách River might not occur in Nam
Sách Prefecture, which was then not on the way of T'o Huan
withdrawal. The Sách River must be close to Vạn Kiếp, where the
battle occurred between Trần Hưng Đạo's and T'o Huan's troops
as recorded in *ĐVSKTT*. The Sách River, therefore, must be the
Thương River; and thus the battle of the Sách River mentioned in
Chinese historical documents is the battle of Vạn Kiếp in *ĐVSKTT*.
It was an abrupt ambush that made T'o Huan's great army tread on
each other to flee and many of them were killed when the floating
bridge broke down.

According to *Pen Chi* of *Yuan Shih* 13 p.9b11-12, the reason T'o
Huan could flee to Szu Ming was due to Li Hêng's attempt to fight
fiercely with Trần Hưng Đạo: "*(On the Mậu Tuất day of the 5th
month...) Hêng fought in the rear to protect Chên Nan Wang. A
poisoned arrow pierced his left knee. Due to the effect of poison, he
died in Szu Ming.*" In order to cross the border, however, T'o
Huan's defeated troops had to face another ambush in Vĩnh Bình,
which was recorded only on the tombstone of Li Hêng and cited by
Yao Sui (1238-1313) in *Mu An Chi* 12 p.8b5: "*The enemy closed the
frontier pass in Vĩnh Bình, using poisoned arrows to hurt him on the
knee. He attempted to fight his way across the border. When
reaching Szu Ming, he died because of the effect of poison.*" This
battle is not mentioned in *Li Hêng Chuan* of *Yuan Shih* 129 p.9a12-
11b5: "*The 'barbarian' troops pursued, storming [our] army's rear.
Wang (i.e. T'o Huan) changed his order at once, posting Li Hêng to
the rear to secure our army's withdrawal. Hêng was pierced with a
poisoned arrow on the knee. A soldier had to carry him to Szu Ming,*

where he died due to the poison. He was then at the age fifty."

The Victory at Phù Ninh

While Trần Hưng Đạo pursued T'o Huan's troops in the north-east, Trần Nhật Duật drove Na Su La Ting's troops on their way back to Yun Nan. The latter troops are not mentioned in *Pen Chi* and *An Nan Chuan* of *Yuan Shih* to be among T'o Huan's invading armed forces in our country. They are merely recorded in *Na Su La Ting Chuan Fu* of *Yuan Shih* 125, p.3b, where the date of Chih Yuan 22 (1285) is mistaken for Chih Yuan 32 (1295). It says: *"In Chih Yuan 22, Na Su La Ting commanded 1000 troops of Ho La Chang[7] and Mongols, following Crown Prince T'o Huan to march into Giao Chỉ. Due to his merit, he was awarded 2000 coins of silver."*

In our history books Na Su La Ting's troops, too, were not mentioned until Chiêu Văn Vương Trần Nhật Duật's death in 1330. In an account of Trần Nhật Duật's participation in the anti-Ming war of 1285, ĐVSKTT 7 p.3a7-b3 says: *"Toward the end of Thiệu Bảo, he was defending Camp Thu Vật in Tuyên Quang. When the Yuan enemy had just come [to our country], Chiêu Quốc reported [to the king]: 'Chiêu Văn in Tuyên Quang might have called the Yuan enemy in.' (He said so because Nhật Duật liked making friends with Sung people.) When Tuyên Quang was lost, Nhật Duật withdrew downstream. The enemy pursued him along the river banks but he attempted to halt them. Seeing that they moved so slowly, he said to our troops: 'Generally the pursuing troops move very quickly, but in this case the enemy is moving very*

---

[7] Qarajang, that is Wu Tuan troops of Yun Nan. [LMT]

slowly. I think that there may be other troops standing ahead.' Then he sent a man to watch, who reported later that a troop of the enemy was posted on the lower river. He ordered his troops to flee from the river."

Thus, when Na Su La Ting moved his troops along the Red River, from Yun Nan down to Thăng Long, Trần Nhật Duật's troops stopped them and then withdrew by the end of Thiệu Bảo, i.e. the years 1284-1285. Therefore, when T'o Huan held a conference of his staff in Thăng Long and made a decision of withdrawal, Na Su La Ting must have been appointed to withdraw the north-western wing toward Yun Nan. And on their way of withdrawal, they encountered our troops' violent attack commanded by Hà Đặc and Hà Chương.

In an account of the movement of T'o Huan and Wu Ma Er's troops from the sea to attack our base at Thiên Mạc on the 17th of the fifth month of Ất Dậu (1285), ĐVSKTT p.47 says: *"When the enemy reached Phù Ninh District, the official of the district, Hà Đặc, commanded his men to defend Trĩ Sơn against them. The enemy's troops were encamped at the cave Cự Đà. Đặc ordered his men to make human forms of bamboo clad in genuine clothes, which were repeatedly moved out of and into the district at night [to deceive the enemy into thinking that there existed a great number of our resistant troops]. Moreover, he had holes drilled on the big trees, in which arrows were fixed through to deceive the enemy into thinking that our men were so strong that they could shoot through big trees with arrows. Accordingly, the enemy was frightened of fighting with us. Immediately, our troops rushed out to liquidate them. At A Lạp, Đặc had a floating bridge built for the troops to cross the river. In this pursuit he was killed. His brother, Chương, was captured but then escaped with some flags and uniforms taken from the enemy's troops, which he submitted to the king and suggested that, with those flags and uniforms, our troops could disguise themselves as the enemy's troops to penetrate into their camps. Due to that plan, our army could annihilate the enemy."*

The fact of our army's fight against Na Su La Ting has usually been misunderstood since, in *ĐVSKTT*, it is recorded in a mixed account of Wu Ma Er and So Tu's attack on our army's position at Thiên Mạc. Recognizing this confusion, the author of *Khâm Định Việt Sử Thông Giám Cương Mục 7* p.41b1-3 says: *"So Tu advanced from the sea to attack Thiên Mạc whereas his patrol moved to the district of Phù Ninh, where it would take them about three or four days to move from the former position. Naturally, this was not the case but some mistake alone. Let us study it later."* In reality, there is not any false account in *ĐVSKTT*. Yet, it is due to its combination of the two facts mentioned above in the same context that some confusion might be made by the reader. Phù Ninh was a district in what is now Phú Thọ Province. As regards the cave Cự Đà, it is not found today but Tử Đà Commune, which is said in Hà Đặc's posthumous record to be his native village, is located in Phù Ninh District. Similarly, the position named A Lạp is not found today but it is recorded in *Đồng Khánh Địa Dư Chí* that the communes An Lạp and Đức Lạp were situated in Lập Thạch District of Sơn Tây Province. Thus, it may be possible that Cự Đà is another name of Tử Đà and A Lạp of An Lạp. Hence, the battles in which Hà Đặc and Hà Chương were involved might occur along the Red River in present-day PhúThọProvince.

The Triumphant March into Thăng Long

After driving the enemy out of the country in the glorious battles of Vạn Kiếp, Phù Ninh, Emperor Nhân Tông, his emperor-father and generals Hưng Đạo Vương Trần Quốc Tuấn, Chiêu Minh Vương Trần Quang Khải, Hưng Ninh Vương Trần Quốc Tung, and so on, triumphantly marched into Thăng Long Capital amid the cheers of 10,000 troops and people of Thăng long, who had completely broken down the plan of occupying and dominating our people by the northern invaders. In the name of one of the outstanding generals who had commanded the campaign to liberate Thăng Long, Thượng Tướng Thái Sư Trần Quang Khải, the direct administrator of the civil government of the nation, wrote a poem, praising our people's war of resistance and appeal to the whole people's efforts of establishing an eternal peace for the Fatherland and the coming generations:

Stripping the enemy of spears in Chương Dương,
Capturing the Hồ troops in Hàm Tử,
Make great efforts to establish
An eternal peace for our beloved country.

*Translation by **Đạo Sinh***

EMPEROR TRẦN NHÂN TÔNG AND THE WAR OF DEFENSE IN 1288

BY PROF. **LÊ MẠNH THÁT**

On the sixth of the sixth month of Ất Dậu (1285) Emperor Nhân Tông returned to the imperial capital of Thăng Long in triumph. Less than two months later, the 20th of the seventh month, having gathered all reports on the preceding war, Kublai Khan ordered Ch'ü Mi Yuan to send reinforcements to T'o-huan and A-li-hai-ya in their second campaign to invade Đại Việt. According to *Pen Chi* of *Yuan Shih* 13, p.10a13-14, *"on the Kên-yin day [of the 7th month of Chih Yuan 22], reporting that the entire army that would be commanded by T'o-huan to attack Giao Chỉ had been rather worn out with the long fighting expedition, Ch'ü Mi Yuan proposed selecting 1,000 Mongols from the three Wan Hu of Ao-lu-chih (Ayuruyă), 4,000 Hans and recruits from the three Hsin Yuan in Kianghuai, Kianghsi, and Chinghu, who would all be put under the command of an experienced general assisted by T'o-huan and A-li-hai-ya. The [Yuan] King agreed, intending to appoint T'ang-wu-tai to be Tso Chêng Ching Hu Hsin Shêng; but the latter asked to be discharged from the army for retirement. The King decreed his approval and ordered T'o-huan and A-li-hai-ya to deal with military affairs themselves ."*

Then, on the Canh Dần of the ninth month, Kublai Khan proceeded to give orders for another enlistment of recruits. *Pen Chi* of *Yuan Shih* 13, p.11a8-10, says: *"Among the troops that had fought in Giao Chỉ, with the exceptions of 100 Mongols and 400 Hans serving as the Guards of Chên Nan Wang T'o-huan, the rest were allowed to retire. On the other hand, Hsin Ch'ü Mi Yuan in Kianghuai received orders to command all Mongol troops encamped in Kianghsi."* Still in the words of *Pen Chi* of *Yuan Shih* 13, p.11a12-13, in the 10th month Kublai Khan ordered Ho-san-er Hai-ya (Qasar Qaya), who had ever been appointed Chief- and Vice-Daruyaci (Ta-lu-hua-chih) in our country between 1273 and 1275, to investigate the situation of our country. In the same month, Ch'ü Mi Yuan proposed sending troops to Tanchou, who would be commanded by generals appointed by T'o-huan and A-li-hai-ya, as in the words of *An Nan Chuan* of *Yuan Shih* 209, p.8a12-13.

Also in *An Nan Chuan* of *Yuan Shih* 209, p.8a13-b3, in the first month of the year that followed (1286), Kublai Khan called a meeting with the ranking mandarins to discuss the plan of invading Đại Việt, which is clearly mentioned in *Pen Chi* of *Yuan Shih* 14, p.1b1-2: *"summoning A-li-hai-ya to discuss the campaign to attack An Nam."* This conference is definitely said in *Pen Chi* to have been held on the Tân Mão, i.e., the 24th of the first month of Bính Tuất (1286).

On the seventh of the second month, Kublai Khan appointed "*A-li-hai-ya to his former position, that is, Tso Chêng Hsiang of An Nam Hsin Chung Shu Shêng, Ao-lu-chih to be P'ing Chang Chêng Shih Tu Yuan Shuai, Wu-ma-er, Mieh-li-mi-shih (Yiymiš)[1], A-li Kuei-shun (Ariq Qusun), P'an Chieh to be all Ts'an Chih Chêng Shih. Then he ordered a messenger to tell Prince Chê-hsien Tieh-mu-er (Äsän Tämür) to mobilize approximately one to three thousand men of Ho-la-chang, whose registration would later be fully submitted, and dispatch them to A-li-hai-ya's expeditionary force,*" as recorded in *Pen Chi* of *Yuan Shih* 14, p.1b8-10. Furthermore, on the 20th of the second month, Kublai Khan ordered "*Hukwang Hsin Shêng to build 300 ships for attacking Giao Chỉ, which would be assembled in Ch'inchou and Lienchou in the 8th month. The day that followed, he ordered Ching Hu Chanch'êng Hsin Shêng to command 30,000 troops of the three Hsin Shêng in Kiangchê, Hukwang and Kianghsi to penetrate into Giao Chỉ. P'ing Chang Ao-lu-chih of Ching Hu Hsin Shêng asked to discuss the campaign to attack Giao Chỉ with the King. The latter ordered him to go to the imperial capital on post-horses.*"

On the 21st of the second month, Kublai Khan officially bestowed the title 'King of An Nam' on Trần Ích Tắc, giving him a seal and a 'tally', and appointed Trần Tú Viên to be Fu I Kung, as in the words of *Yuan Shih* 14, p.2a11, and 209, p.8b2-3. *An Nam Chí Lược* 13, p.132, mentions a further detail that Kublai Khan also

---

[1] Correct transliteration: Mieh-hei-mi-shih. [LMT]

appointed such Vietnamese traitors as Bá Ý, the eldest son of Ích Tắc, to be An Fu Shih of T'okiang Route, Lại Ích Khuy to be An Fu Shih of Nant'sêkiang Route, Trần Văn Lộng to be Hsuan Fu Shih of Kueihuakiang Route, and so on. In effect, Kublai Khan's intention was to impose a puppet government on our people when T'o-huan could bring the entire country under their control.

According to *An Nam Chuan* of *Yuan Shih* 209, p.8a13-b2, also in the second month, Kublai Khan sent a letter to our court, accusing our emperor of having killed his uncle Trần Di Ái, of having not received Ta Lu Hua Chih Pu-yen Tieh-mu-er (Buyan Tämür) and, at the same time, advising our people to make their living as usual when his troops would come to punish our emperor.

Thus, in the first two months of Bính Tuất (1286) Kublai Khan and his court urgently prepared tactics, men, weapons and supplies for their campaign to invade our country. On the fourth of the fourth month, to increase and boost productivity of Mongol troops who were working in their plantations, Kublai Khan ordered tax exemptions in those plantations which had contributed men to the fighting expedition, as in the words of *Pen Chi* of *Yuan Shih* 14, p.3a1-2. Twelve days later, i.e., the 16th of the fourth month, Na-su-la-ting received *"orders to lead 1,000 Mongol and Ho-la-chang troops together with experienced officers to assist Prince T'o-huan in Giao Chỉ."*

Also in the fourth month, when Ao-lu-chih was discussing the plan of invading Đại Việt with Kublai Khan in Tatu, the latter attempted to lend encouragement to him: *"Earlier, by virtue of their loyalty to the imperial house, Mu-hua-li (Muqali) and his companions have maintained their reputation [as outstanding men] so far. Accordingly, you should try your best so that you may, too, become as prominent as they,*" as in the words of *Ao-lu-chih Chuan* of *Yuan Shih* 131, p.17a2. Simultaneously, to show his concern Kublai Khan appointed Ao-lu-chih's son, T'o-huan Pu-hua (Toyan Buqa), to the position of Wan Hu. According to *Hukwang Hsin Shêng Tso Chêng Hsiang Shên Tao Bei* in *Yuan Wen Lei* 82, p.24b2, the reason Ao-lu-chih received so much attention was that A-li-hai-ya, after the long fighting expedition in Đại Việt, showed to be so seriously deteriorated that he finally died on the 25th of the fifth month of Bính Tuất (1286).

On the 16th of the sixth month, Kublai Khan sent a messenger, Yeh-ma-la-tan[2] (Iramadan), to our country. Two days later, i.e., on the Đinh Sửu, Hsien-kê (Sängä) of Hukwang Hsin Shêng, however, made a complaint of having to mobilize his 28,700 men to Shêngkiang, now known as Kwanghsi, where they would join the expeditionary forces. For, according to *Pen Chi* of *Yuan Shih* 14, p.4a6-8, apart from the number of well-trained troops that had been mobilized before, the rest, approximately 17,800 men, were not strong enough to serve in his army. The fact is more clearly described in *An Nan Chuan* of *Yuan Shih* 209, p.8b10-12.

According to Hsien-kê, it was quite true in the report of Hunan Hsin Shêng that people and troops had to suffer too much hardship caused by their incessant invasions of Japan and Champa. Further, a punishment on Giao Chỉ was not worthwhile when it was giving its offerings as usual. If the court intended to attack Giao Chỉ, it should wait for a favorable occasion. This was Hsien-

---

[2] Correct transliteration: Yeh-la-ma-tan. [L.M.T.]

kê's own view as was reported by Ch'u Mi Yuan. In addition, according to *Liu Hsuan Chuan* of *Yuan Shih* 168, p.8a1-10, Li Pu Shang Shu Liu Hsuan also set forth, right in the court, the same reasons for postponing the campaign to fight Đại Việt.

Under the pressure of these suggestions Kublai Khan reluctantly agreed, decreeing that the armed forces' advance should be postponed. Trần Ích Tắc lonely returned to Ngohchou, the headquarters of T'o-huan, as recorded in *An Nan Chuan* of *Yuan Shih* 209, p.9a1. Kublai Khan, however, never gave up his intention of invading Đại Việt. Five months later, on the Ất Mão of the 10th month, he gave orders for a supply of 4,000 horses for T'o-huan, and, on the Kỷ Tỵ of the 11th month, Cheng Chiao Chih Hsin Shêng, i.e., the office in charge of the campaign to attack Đại Việt, to be formed with A-pa-chih (Abači) as Yu Chêng, as in the words of *Pen Chi* of *Yuan Shih* 14, pp.5b12-13, 6a6-7. Together with the formation of Cheng Chiao Chih Hsin Shêng, on the Bính Thìn of the 12th month, by order of Kublai Khan, money was again bestowed on Trần Ích Tắc, of whom the former continued to make use as a card of his.

By the first month of Đinh Hợi (1287), Kublai Khan earnestly carried out further preparations for his plan of invasion. First, on the Đinh Hợi, he ordered 1,000 men of Hsinfu to follow A-pa-chih to An Nam. Then, on the Tân Mão he gave orders for mobilization of 5,000 ships and about 70.000 men, both Mongols and Hans, of the three Hsin-shêng in Kianghuai, Kianghsi and Hukwang, 6,000 men of Yunnan, and 15,000 Li men of the four districts along the coast. At the same time, Chang Wen Hu, Fei Kung Ch'ên and T'ao Ta Ming received orders to transport 17,000 piculs of supplies by sea. To formalize and thereby lay much more emphasis on the nerve center of his apparatus of war, he decreed that Cheng Chiao Chih Hsin Shêng should be renamed Cheng Chiao Chih Hsin Shang Shu Shêng, in which Ao-lu-chih was appointed to be Ping ChangChêng Shih, Wu-ma-er and P'an Chieh to be Ts'an Chih Chêng Shih, and T'o-huan to be Chieh Chih.

Thus, the machinery of Yuan invaders got ready to start its operation under the command of T'o-huan and Ao-lu-chih, who had more than 90,000 men in their hands. In addition, *An Nam Chí Lược* 4, p.55, mentions the presence of men called 'Troops of Caves' from minority groups in Kwanghsi. In *Hsi-tu-er Chuan* of *Yuan Shih* 133, p.9b, it is noted that these troops, included in T'o-huan's Great Army, were put under the direct command of Hsi-tu-er (Šiktur) in their penetration into Giao Chỉ in the seventh month of Chih Yuan 24 (1287). Thus, in this invasion T'o-huan mobilized more than 100,000 men, carefully organized into infantry, navy and convoys of supplies.

Preparations on the Đại Việt Side

According to *ĐVSKTT* 5, p.50b1-2, on the sixth of the sixth month of Ất Dậu (1285) having just returned to Thăng Long in triumph, Emperor Nhân Tông "*ordered Trung Phẩm Phụng Ngự Đặng Du Chi to take a group of thirty Chams, headed by Bà-lậu-kê-na-liên, back to their country. They had been captured by our troops while they were serving in So-tu's army.*" This was obviously taken as a step in his diplomatic policy, aiming at establishing and stabilizing the friendly relations between our country and the neighboring one in the south, which had been preserved by Emperor Nhân Tông for ten years since his enthronement. It was due to such a long and consistent strategy of diplomacy that Đại Việt could reap the best fruit that the country's boundary was extended for more than 200 kilometers to the south when the two districts of Ô Mã and Việt Lý officially became an inseparable part of the fatherland in 1306.

Also in the words of *ĐVSKTT* 5, p.50b3-4, his next step was to reward those who had much contribution to the country and punish those who had surrendered to the enemy. It says: "*In the fall, the 8th month, [the King] ordered Tả Bộc Xạ Khương Cương Giới to bestow various titles on the subjects who had merits and punish those who surrendered to the enemy.*" Thus, even the task of rewarding or punishing some of imperial officials and troops had to be postponed for a long time. For it might have taken some time for the court to collect sufficient evidence for proper judgment of the cases in question.

Of such great merits as those made by Hưng Đạo Vương Trần Quốc Tuấn, Chiêu Minh Vương Trần Quang Khải, Hưng Ninh Vương Trần Quốc Tung, Điện Tiền Phạm Ngũ Lão, and so on, it was naturally rather easy for the court to have proper appreciation. Yet, it would be extremely complicated in regard to people of low ranks in different places throughout the country. An inscription in relation to the Hưng Phúc temple discovered in Thanh Hóa reveals the fact that Lê Công Mạnh together with his brothers and relatives and other villagers of An Duyên fought courageously against So-tu's troops at the Cổ Bút ferry:

"*Around the year of Thiệu Bảo, the 'barbarian' enemy came down to the south again. Commanded by Yu Hsiang So-tu, they moved from the sea toward Cổ Khê along the route across the An Duyên village. In order to cut off their retreat, he (Lê Công Mạnh) commanded the villagers to fight them at the ferry of Cổ Bút. Yet, it was owing to a traitor in the village, who had surrendered to the enemy and then shown them the way to his (Mạnh's) home, that his house was destroyed and thus his task of building the temple was cancelled. After the enemy had been withdrawn [out of our country] and the King had returned to the imperial capital, he reported the fact to the King. The King issued a decree of investigating the fact, then ordering the compensation of local products of the village for his losses for the purpose of praising his own merits and encouraging loyal and diligent men."*

This is only one example of a man whose efforts to fight the enemy were actually made but not mentioned in historical books. Nevertheless, it is thanks to his merit of building temples recorded in an inscription at the Hưng Phúc temple that we can know something of how the imperial court rewarded those who had contributions, great or small, to the war of defense in 1285.

Concerning those who had been killed in the war and their families as well, we have today nothing other than some little information on a few outstanding figures. With respect to the death of the national hero Trần Bình Trọng, for instance, Emperor Nhân Tông himself is said to have wept mournfully and pitifully as in the words of *Khâm Định Việt Sử Thông Giám Cương Mục* 7, p.37a2. And at the death of the hero Trần Quốc Toản in the battle of Như Nguyệt, the Emperor wrote a verse, showing his extreme regret for a brave and heroic subject of his.

As for traitors, they must have been put on trial with sufficient proof. However, it was nearly a month later, i.e., in the ninth month when his era name was changed into Trùng Hưng, that Emperor Nhân Tông could give the order for the general release of prisoners throughout the country. Although prisoners, particularly those who had been charged with betrayal in the eighth month, were not all set free on this occasion, most of them must have received some favor from the emperor. For these were the indispensable steps to recover the people's morale, lend more encouragement to those who had devoted themselves to the previous war and, at the same time, wipe out some feeling of sinfulness within traitors who had given in to the enemy's power.

Next, Emperor Nhân Tông carried out a thorough investigation of population to estimate the people's force, preparing for his confrontation with the inevitable danger of a war caused by the enemy. In *ĐVSKTT* 5, p.48b, we read: "*In the winter, the 10th month, [the King] issued an decree of examining family registers across the country. His subjects attempted to dissuade him, saying that it was not a necessary task while the people were enduring so much hardship [caused by the recent war of resistance]. 'It is now most suitable for completing family registers so that the enemy cannot see the losses of our people,' said he. All the subjects appreciated his idea.*" It was true that his plan had not been approved of by the subjects at the beginning. Yet, having understood its aim and implications, they all agreed with him. Indeed, to cope with the urgent preparation for the coming war, the court had to contrive to control immediately the country's potential power.

Thus, about six months after the enemy had been completely driven out of the country Emperor Nhân Tông and his court implemented several domestic and diplomatic measures for the purpose of stabilizing and boosting the people's fighting strength. The following year, when the people of Đại Việt were joyfully holding the New Year Festival of Bính Tuất—the traditional one that they had given up in the previous year (Ất Dậu) due to their struggle against T'o-huan's invading army, the first action that Emperor Nhân Tông performed was *"to release the Yuan troops to their country in the spring, the 1st month,"* as recorded in ĐVSKTT 5, p.50b9. These troops had been captured by our army in different campaigns, particularly the campaign of Tây Kết commanded by the emperor himself, in which more than 50,000 troops of the enemy were taken captives. Obviously, this action pointed out, on the one hand, the humane policy and life-loving nature of a government of which the king, his subjects, and highest-ranking generals were all Buddhist laymen. It was, on the other hand, the manifestation of a tactful diplomatic policy in an attempt to avoid war and, at the same time, to take advantage of any possible opportunity to achieve a long peace for the country. In effect, his decision to release prisoners of war facilitated partly the diplomatic relation between our country and the Yuan. According to ĐVSKTT 5, p.51a1, *"in the 2nd month, the Yuan ordered Hop-tan-er Hai-ya (Qasar Qaya) to come to our country."* Although the Yuan mission arrived in our country with some intention of investigating our situation—a task that they had been appointed to fulfill earlier in the 10th month of the preceding year, they must have managed to ask our court for the release of their men in spite of the fact that Emperor Nhân Tông had done so in the first month. Whether it had taken place earlier or later, the act of releasing prisoners of war by our court undoubtedly exerted some remarkable political impact on the enemy.

As far as the Yuan court's activities in preparation for their invasion of our country were concerned, the leader of Đại Việt rapidly collected every report on them. ĐVSKTT 5, p.51a1-5 says: *"In the 3rd month the Yuan king ordered Shang Shu T'ing Ao-lu-chih, Ping Chang Shih Wu-ma-er, General Chang Wen Hu to mobilize 500,000 troops, and Hukwang to build 300 ships. All of them would gather in the districts of Ch'in and Lien in the 8th month. In addition, he gave the order for troops of the three Hsin Shêng in Kiangchê, Hukwang and Kianghsi to penetrate into the South on the pretext of escorting the traitor Trần Ích Tắc, who would be the king of An Nam, back to our country."* Thus, the information on Kublai Khan's preparations was promptly collected by Emperor Nhân Tông and his court.

In face of the danger of the coming war Đại Việt, of course, could not maintain a wait-and-see attitude. The first step Emperor Nhân Tông had to take urgently was *"to order, in the 6th month, princes and nobles to recruit new men and manage their own armies seriously,"* as in the words of ĐVSKTT 5, p.51a5-6. Also according to ĐVSKTT 5, p.51a6-b2, in a conference of the highest-ranking officials Emperor Nhân Tông asked Trần Hưng Đạo, *"'What is the enemy's situation in this year like?' 'When the Yuan invasion occurred last year, some of our people surrendered to the enemy since they did not know anything about military affairs due to their living in peace for a long time. It was, however, thanks to our ancestors' mystic forces and Your Majesty's heroic character that Hồ barbarians were eventually wiped out. Now that our troops have been accustomed to fighting and their troops are afraid of moving far, we can defeat them if they enter our country again. Further, the Yuan troops have been so badly demoralized by the defeat of Hêng and Kuan that they cannot have enough courage to fight. In my opinion, we can surely defeat them,' [answered Trần Hưng Đạo].*"

No doubt, Hưng Đạo Vương's remark about the prospect of a victory by our army over the enemy's forces in their coming invasion indicated a firm belief in the fighting strength and morale of Đại Việt's people and in the brilliant leadership of the Trần emperors, including Emperor Nhân Tông. Once more, Emperor Nhân Tông *"ordered Hưng Đạo Vương to urge princes and nobles to mobilize troops and make weapons and ships. By the 10th month, [he gave orders for] the troops, who had been mobilized, to be concentrated and trained,"* as recorded in *ĐVSKTT* 5, p.51b1-3. Thus, with unshaken confidence in a final victory our people were, too, urgently preparing men, materials, means and various things for facing the ghostly shadow of war that was to be cast over the country.

At the beginning of the year Đinh Hợi (1287) the confidence became stronger and stronger. According to *ĐVSKTT* 5, p.52a2-3, *"in the 2nd month (...) an official proposed recruiting strong men to strengthen our armed forces; yet, Hưng Đạo Vương refuted him with the reason that 'What we need is not quantity but quality. What was Bồ Kiên able to achieve even though one million men were gathered?'"* Accordingly, not only did he refuse to coerce people into joining the army but Emperor Nhân Tông also gave the order for *'general release of prisoners throughout the country'* in accordance with his policy of relieving the people's minds. The great release, which took place not more than half a year later than the previous one, must have occurred so urgently as to exhibit not only the humane nature of his regime but also his sense of responsibility for the whole people. That is to say, if a countryman committed some offense, not only he but also the government, or rather, its supreme leader would be responsible for his wrong-doing.

Before the war of 1285 broke out, the people of Đại Việt under the reign of Emperor Nhân Tông had been instructed as follows: *"Generally, when the invading enemy come in whatsoever districts of the country, the people there must try their best to fight them. If the enemy are too strong for them to resist, they are allowed to flee to the mountains or marshes but they must not surrender,"* as recorded in *An Nan Chuan* of *Yuan Shih* 209, p.7b1-2. In spite of this, there were some who had given in to the enemy's force. In the first place, the responsibility for such a betrayal, of course, belonged to those who had committed it. Nevertheless, just as his grandfather, Trần Thái Tông, had treated Hoàng Cự Đà in the war of defense in 1258, so Emperor Nhân Tông realized his responsibility for the surrender of some members of imperial family and common people during the Yuan invasion in 1285. It was surely because of this kind of feeling that the Emperor gave orders for the two consecutive releases of prisoners within a period of not more than a few months.

By the fourth month, Emperor Nhân Tông appointed his younger brother Tá Thiên Đại Vương Đức Việp to the position of Tướng Quốc, who conducted the final parade. Simultaneously, he gave the order for the fulfillment of trials left unfinished and issued some edicts concerning civil services. These tasks were urgently implemented during the last days of peace in a country where everybody was getting ready for an approaching war from beyond the northern border.

The Beginning of War: the Battle of Mộc Hoàn

According to *ĐVSKTT* 5, p.52a6-8, "*On the 14th (of the 11th month of Đinh Hợi, 1287) Trịnh Xiển submitted a report on the attack on Phú Lương by the Yuan Prince A-thai*". In effect, this was the attack on Mộc Hoàn by Ai-lu (Aruq), as described in *Pen Chi* of *Yuan Shih* 14, p.11a3-5: "*On the Nhâm Thìn of the 11th month (...) Ai-lu, Yu Chêng of Yunnan Province, had his troops encamped at Mộc Ngột in Giao Chỉ. The Giao Chỉ General Chiêu Văn Vương commanded 40,000 troops to defend there. Ai-lu launched an attack, capturing their officers Lê Thạch and Hà Anh.*"

This was the opening battle between our troops and Ai-lu's Northwest Army from Yunnan. Ai-lu was an eminent general of the Yuan. *Ai-lu Chuan* in *Yuan Shih* 122, p.8b3-5, says: "*(In Chih Yuan 24) Chên Nan Wang launched an attack on Giao Chỉ, ordering Ai-lu to deploy 6,000 men from Lolo to Giao Chỉ. The Giao Chỉ General Chiêu Văn Vương commanded 40,000 men to defend Mộc Ngột. Ai-lu defeated them, capturing their generals Lê Thạch and Hà Anh. After eighteen combats, great and small, during three months, [his troops] reached the enemy's capital, where they were joined by other troops and went on to fight with them more than twenty times, most of which were our attacks.*"

According to *Pen Chi* of *Yuan Shih* 15, p.3a5, in the year that followed, that is, on the Quý Mùi of the fouth month of Chih Yuan 25 (1288), when reporting the battle to Kublai Khan, Ai-lu said, "*Since leaving Chung-ch'ing for Giao Chỉ via Lolo, Paii, [our army] fought thirty-eight times, cutting off countless heads of the enemy's troops. The officers who had merits amounted to 474, including Tu Yuan Shuai."*

Accordingly, it was a great battle. Though only 6,000 men of the enemy were deployed, they were surely joined by many talented commanders, one of whom was Mang-ku-tai (Mangqudai). He was such an experienced general, who had spent numerous battles with a lot of achievements, that he was dealt with in an entire 'chuan' of *Yuan Shih* 149, p.13a6-7, where were mentioned not only Mang-ku-tai but also other generals such as Prince A-tai (Atai), who has just been referred to above by *ĐVSKTT*. The account of him says, *"Following Prince A-tai to enter Giao Chỉ, [Mang-ku-tai] fought with Chiêu Văn Vương of Giao Chỉ on the Bạch Hạc River, capturing 87 warships."*

Besides, in *An Nam Chí Lược* 4, p.54, we read, *"From Yunnan Yu Chêng Ai-lu's Army advanced to the Tam Đại Giang, fighting with the king's younger brother, Trần Duật, and capturing Hà Anh and Lê Thạch."* Tam Đại Giang literally means the 'three large rivers', which obviously indicates the confluence of the rivers Đà, Lô and Hồng in Việt Trì. It was in this place that *"the Ming troops occupied the river-bank of Mộc Hoàn in Việt Trì"* and *"[our troops] launched a thrust on Hồ troops in Mộc Hoàn District"* before reoccupying the town of Đa Bang more than 100 years later, as recorded in *ĐVSKTT* 8, p.53b2-7. Thus, the stronghold of Mộc Ngột mentioned in Chinese historical accounts must undoubtedly be Mộc Hoàn recorded in *ĐVSKTT*. According to *Đồng Khánh Địa Dư Chí*, the name Mộc Hoàn remained until the end of the 19th century. So Mộc Ngột was nothing other than Mộc Hoàn. Another proof is that the word *hoàn* (桓) is rather similar to *ngột* (朷).

The battle of Mộc Hoàn points out that Kublai Khan, in this invasion, paid much attention to the Yunnan Army through his reinforcement of it with 6,000 men and some experienced officers, who had been entrusted with some important tasks. Obviously, this reinforcement reflected his concern about the absence of an army to the south of our country. It was because of this absence that the Yunnan Army was strengthened; and the Commanding General Ai-lu was ordered to undertake the command of the South Army, which So-tu had attempted to fulfil at the risk of his life before. Indeed, the enemy's violent blow at the stronghold of Mộc Hoàn, one of our important positions in the line of defense in Phú Lương, showed partly Kublai Khan's strategy.

In the meantime, the Trần house carried out a quite different strategy from that of the previous war. Regarding the first battle mentioned above, Trần Hưng Đạo affirmed, in his reply to a question of Emperor Nhân Tông's, that *"this year it's easy to defeat the enemy"*, as in the words of *ĐVSKTT* 5, p.52a6-8. Indeed, in many different fronts our strategy of fighting combined with retreat was brought into action for the purpose of weakening the enemy's forces and maintaining ours. It was owing to this strategy that we had succeeded in attracting the enemy to places where we could launch our decisive counteroffensives to eliminate them. Therefore, although our army had endured the loss of generals Lê Thạch and Hà Anh and some warships in the battle of Phú Lương, General Trần Nhật Duật excellently achieved the task of maintaining his army in a strategic retreat.

The Advance of T'o-huan's Army

While Ai-lu's Army was advancing toward the Phú Lương pass in the northwest, another army commanded by T'o-huan and Ao-lu-chih departed from their base in Ngohchou on the third of ninth month of Đinh Hợi (1287). By the 28th of the 10th month, the latter reached Laihsin District in Kwanghsi. There, T'o-huan ordered the separation of infantrymen from naval troops. Under the command of T'o-huan, Ao-lu-chih and A-pa-chih, accompanied by the Vietnamese traitors Trần Ích Tắc, etc., the first wing marched to Szuming on the 13th of the 11th month. The second wing commanded by Wu-ma-er and P'an Chieh proceeded with their march toward Ch'inchou.

The dates cited above are, for the most part, derived from *An Nam Chí Lược* 4, p.55, and they may be verified by other sources such as *Lai-a-pa-chih Chuan* and *An Nan Chuan* of *Yuan Shih* 129, p.2a2-4 and 209, p.9a8 respectively. Similarly, *P'an Chieh Chuan* of *Yuan Shih* 166, p.10a10-11, says: "*In the next penetration into Giao Chỉ in the year [of Chih Yuan] 24 (1287), [P'an Chieh was] appointed Hsin Chung Shu Shêng Ts'an Chih Chêng Shih. The advance then took three directions: Prince Chên Nan Wang and Yu Chêng Cheng P'êng Fei's troops were divided into two wings, one entering Vĩnh Bình, the other the frontier pass of Nữ Nhi; whereas [P'an] Chieh and Wu-ma-er commanded their naval troops' advance by sea.*" The above account proves that Lê Sực wrote down the process of the enemy's advance in which he himself participated—an account that he employed to write partly his *An Nam Chí Lược* after he had fled to China again together with the Chinese defeated troops. The account was, therefore, of rather high accuracy in relation to the enemy's operation.

The Naval Battles

Thus, owing to the absence of an army to the south of our country in this invasion, Kublai Khan decided to strengthen the Northwest Army commanded by Ai-lu and organize a navy that was put under the command of Ao-lu-chih's two assistants, that is, Wu-ma-er and P'an Chieh. According to *An Nam Chí Lược* 4, p.55, the division of troops occurred on the 28th of the 10th month of Đinh Hợi (1285); and, in addition to 18,000 men commanded by Wu-ma-er and P'an Chieh, there were also some more 10,000 men and 500 warships and 70 supply ships commanded by Wu Wei, Chang Yü, and Liu K'uei.

On the 11th of the 11th month the naval troops crossed the Vạn Ninh Estuary in what is now Móng Cái. But they were later halted by General Nhân Đức Hầu Trần Lang in an ambush at Lãng Sơn, which was aimed at cutting off the enemy's rear as recorded in *An Nam Chí Lược* 4, p.55. Being aware of this, the enemy at once besieged the mountain on the very night and launched an attack on our troops right at daybreak. According to their account, the loss of our troops amounted to several hundred men and some dozen ships. Taking advantage of this, Wu-ma-er's troops pushed forward without any care of their supply ships in the rear, which were eventually trapped in our troops' ambush.

In the words of *An Nan Chuan* of *Yuan Shih* 209, p.9a11-12: "*Troops commanded by Wu-ma-er and P'an Chieh advanced by sea toward the An Bang Estuary via the 'double gate' at Mount Ngọc*[3]. *More than 400 warships of Giao Chỉ had been deployed at the*

---

[3] "Mount Ngọc Vương" in the original. It may be a mistake. [LMT]

estuary. [Our] troops stroke them, cutting off more than 4,000 heads, capturing more than one hundred men and one hundred ships, forcing Giao Chỉ [men] to race away." So is it described in *P'an Chieh Chuan* of *Yuan Shih* 166, p.19a11-13, *"Together with naval troops, Chieh and Wu-ma-er advanced by sea. Encountering the enemy's ships at the An Bang Estuary, Tiep ordered a violent thrust, cutting off more than 4,000 heads, capturing alive more than one hundred men, taking more than one hundred ships and dozens of weapons."* Similarly, the inscription on Li Tien Yu's tombstone, which was composed by Tsu Tien Chüeh and cited in *Hsü Ch'i Wen Kao* 18, says, *"Encountering Giao [Chỉ] men at An bang, [our troops] cut off more than 2,000 heads, capturing more than 60 warships."* According to *Pen Chi* of *Yuan Shih* 14, p.11b1-2, however, the battle might not occur until the Tân Sửu of the 11th month of Đinh Hợi (1287), that is, four days later than that in *An Nam Chí Lược*: *"On the Tân Sửu, Wu-ma-er, P'an Chieh and Cheng P'êng Fei's men entered Giao Chỉ. Wherever they came, they gained control."*

Regarding this battle, *ĐVSKTT* 5, p.52b-3 says, *"On the 28th Nhân Đức Hầu Toàn commanded naval troops in a battle in the lagoon of Đa Mỗ. The enemy's troops were drowned a lot. [Our army] captured forty men, some ships, horses and weapons, all submitted [to the king]."* Thus, it is clearly evident that the naval battle of Đa Mỗ commanded by Nhân Đức Hầu Toàn was also the battle of Lạng Sơn or that of An Bang mentioned in *An Nam Chí Lược*. The single difference is that it is dated the 11th day in *An Nam Chí Lược*, the 15th in *Yuan Shih* and the 28th in *ĐVSKTT*. These different dates may proceed from either mistaken information or some false recording in accounts. The most remarkable point is that both sides claimed victory in this battle.

According to *Lai-a-pa-chih Chuan* of *Yuan Shih* 129, p.2a, shortly after the encounters of our troops with Ao-lo's Northwest Army and naval troops commanded by Wu-ma-er and P'an Chieh, T'o-huan's Army reached Szuming from Laihsin together with 1,000 men commanded by A-pa-chih as spearheads. Upon reaching there, T'o-huan's troops were divided into two wings to advance into our country: one commanded by Cheng P'êng Fei and the other by Ao-lu-chih, which was reinforced with 10,000 men directed by A-pa-chih as spearheads.

This fact is more clearly recorded in *An Nan Chuan* of *Yuan Shih* 209, p.9a8-11: "*In the 11th month, Chên Nan Wang reached Szuming, leaving 2,500 men there to keep supplies under the command of Wan Hu Hsia Chih. And by his order, Cheng P'êng Fei and Po-lo-ho-ta-er (Bolqadar) commanded approximately ten thousand Hans to move along the west road via Vĩnh Bình; Ao-lu-chih commanded ten thousand men to follow Chên Nan Wang along the east road via the Nữ Nhi frontier pass, and A-pa-chih commanded ten thousand men as spearheads.*" According to *Pen Chi* of *Yuan Shih* 14, p.11b1, three days later, i.e., on the Tân Sửu, it was reported that Cheng P'êng Fei had won a battle whereas *An Nan Chuan* of *Yuan Shih* 209, p.9a12-13, further says that "*on their way across the three frontier passes of Lão Thử, Hãm Nê and Tư Trúc, Cheng P'êng Fei and Po-lo-ho-ta-er won seventeen fights.*"

T'o-huan's Army Marching into Đại Việt

According to *Pen Chi* of *Yuan Shih* 14, p.11b2-3, five days later, i.e., the 20th of the 11th month, T'o-huan's Great Army reached Giới Hà and encountered our army's resistance. By the 24th of the 11th month his army reached Lộc Châu, where he ordered the division of his troops as recorded in *An Nam Chí Lược* 5, p.55: *"[the army commanded by] Yu Chêng Cheng P'êng Fei and Po-lo-ho-ta-er advanced across the Chi Lang Pass; the Great Army together with A-pa-chih's spearhead troops across the Khả Ly Pass."* In the words of *ĐVSKTT* 5, pp.52a8-b1, there occurred a combat on the same day: *"On the 24th, the King ordered the troops that were being posted inside the citadel to defend the Lãnh Kinh Pass. Hưng Đức Hầu Quán commanded troops to shoot poisoned arrows. A large number of the enemy being killed and wounded, they retreated and halted at the Vũ Cao Pass."*

Accordingly, in the invasion of our country this time, T'o-huan ordered his army's advances along the roads of the former invasion, that is, the west and the east ones. The west wing advanced across the passes of Lão Thử (Chi Lăng), Hãm Nê and Tư Trúc, i.e., on present-day National Route 1, toward Thăng Long. The east wing advanced from Lộc Châu, now known as Ô Bình, via the passes of Khả Ly and Nữ Nhi toward Vạn Kiếp. Thus, their advance followed the road across the present-day Sơn Động District; and the first troops of ours they encountered were commanded by Hưng Đức Hầu Quán. This is the battle of Lãnh Kinh described in *Pen Chi of Yuan Shih* as *"Giao Chỉ troops had been deployed for defense"*.

The Battle of Vạn Kiếp

Following the battle of Lãnh Kinh, not any more remarkable one was mentioned in both Vietnamese and Chinese history books.

Even the West Army of the enemy, which is said to have been involved in 17 combats, is nowhere recorded. Regarding the East Army commanded by T'o-huan and Ao-lu-chih, it is said to have moved easily as if it had not encountered any resistance at all. Only one small battle is said to have occurred at Vạn Kiếp on the Giáp Dần of the 11th month according to *Pen Chi* of *Yuan Shih* 14, p.11b8, where Wu-ma-er's army is said to have joined T'o-huan's.

Liu Yüan Chuan of *Yuan Shih* 152, p.4b10-11, says, "In (Chih Yuan) 24, [Liu] Yüan joined the Giao Chỉ-invading army. Chên Nan Wang T'o-huan ordered him to command ten thousand men of army and navy to strike [Giao Chỉ's troops] on the Vạn Kiếp River. Capturing sixteen men, he proceeded to attack the town of Linh Sơn, liquidating mostly the enemy's resistance." Further, *Hsi-tu-er Chuan* of *Yuan Shih* 133, p.9b6, says that Hsi-tu-er, by order of A-pa-chih, occupied the town of Nhất Tự, capturing seven warships.

According to *An Nam Chí Lược* 4, p.55, by the third of the 12th month, T'o-huan reached Tứ Thập Nguyên where, being reported that Chang Wen Hu's ships of supplies had been sunk, he "*ordered Wu-ma-er to rob An Nam's supplies, and A-li and Liu Kiang to build wooden forts on Mounts Phổ Lại and Chí Linh to store supplies.*" This fact, however, is recorded in *Pen Chi* and *An Nan Chuan* of *Yuan Shih* 14, p.12a1-2 and 209, p.9a13-b1, to have occurred on the 15th of the 12th month. On the one hand, it says, "*On the Quý Dậu Chên Nan Wang's troops, posted at Mao La Port, attacked and destroyed Camp Phù Sơn.*" On the other hand, *An Nan Chuan* says, "*in the 12th month while Chên Nan Wang's troops were halted at Mao La Port, Hưng Đạo Vương of Giao Chỉ fled. [The former launched] an attack on Camp Phù Sơn and destroyed it. In the meantime, he also ordered Cheng P'êng Fei and A-li to command twenty thousand men to hold Vạn Kiếp and mend wooden barriers on Mounts Phổ Lại and Chí Linh."*

Thus, it is obvious that T'o-huan's Great Army reached Vạn Kiếp rather easily. The strategy of our army, however, was then that the more deeply the enemy could be attracted to move into our land, the more easily our counterattacks were launched to destroy them. Consequently, in their intensely sweeping blow with an army of more than 20,000 men, they could capture alive merely 16 of our troops. Nevertheless, it is, too, obvious that after reaching Vạn Kiếp and joined by Cheng P'êng Fei and Wu-ma-er, T'o-huan was informed that Chang Wen Hu's convoy of supply ships failed to arrive. Also it was just in this period that Emperor Nhân Tông ordered Nguyễn Thức to deploy the Thánh Dực Army to Hưng Đạo Vương's position to defend the Đại Than Estuary, as recorded in *ĐVSKTT* 5, p.52b3-4.

The Enemy's Control over Thăng Long

According to *An Nam Chí Lược* 4, p.55, on the 23rd of the 12th month, by T'o-huan's order naval troops commanded by Wu-ma-er and infantry troops commanded by A-pa-chih started advancing toward Thăng Long. When P'an Chieh's naval troops reached Bắc Giang, they were stopped by our troops. *ĐVSKTT* 5, p.52b3-4, writes down General Nguyễn Thức's victory over the enemy at Đại Than: *"On the 16th of the 12th month , the King ordered Nguyễn Thức to dispatch the Thánh Dực Army to Hưng Đạo Vương's position to defend the Đại Than Estuary. By the 26th day [our army] faced the enemy's troops and defeated them."* In spite of this victory, our army kept to the strategy of retreat. Accordingly, as in the words of *Pen Chi* of *Yuan Shih* 14, p.12a4, by the 29th of the 12th of Đinh Hợi, "*Chên Nan Wang commanded his troops to cross the Phú Lương River and then deployed them near the Giao Chỉ stronghold. The troops in charge of the stronghold were defeated; Nhật Huyên and his children raced to their position at Cảm Nam.*"

When T'o-huan's army reached Thăng Long, the Vietnamese traitors such as Lê Sực, Nguyễn Lĩnh, Lê Án, etc., who had been halted in Szuming by T'o-huan's order, thought that they could safely come to Thăng Long under the escort of 5,000 men commanded by Shêng Tu Shih Hou Shih Ta, a Wan Hu Hou (name unknown) and Ch'ien Hu Chiao. Yet, on their arrival at the Nội Bàng frontier pass by the 28th of the 12th month, they were swept out by our troops, only about sixty of them able to flee on horses. Later, when writing *An Nam Chí Lược* 19, p.181, Lê Sực expressed his feeling at that time as follows: "*In such a perilous situation, I found myself on the verge of death. Racing some hundred miles a day, I could, at last, reach the district at dawn. Not until my sight of the gate [of the district], [it occurred to me that] I could welcome the Festival of Mậu Tý New Year.*"

The Enemy's Pursuit

Having taken the control of Thăng Long, the enemy discussed how to pursue Emperor Nhân Tông and our army as before. According to *Lai-a-pa-chih Chuan* of *Yuan Shih* 129, p.2a5-7, their spearhead general A-pa-chih remarked, "*That the enemy have left their base for the mountains and the sea is aimed at waiting for another occasion to counterattack us when we have been exhausted. Our generals and troops, who come mostly from the north, would be gradually weakened due to deteriorating weather conditions in the transition period between the spring and summer. In such a situation we cannot go on with our occupation unless the enemy are all captured. Therefore, the most relevant measure for us at present is to dispatch our troops everywhere, persuading those who are willing to surrender, prohibiting our men from looting, and, most particularly, urgently seeking to capture Nhật Huyên."*

To carry out this plan T'o-huan ordered A-pa-chih to attack our base at Hàm Tử on the 29th of the 12th month of Đinh Hợi, as in the words of *An Nam Chí Lược* 4, p.56: *"On the 29th, Kỷ Dậu, (Chên Nan) Wang advanced west across the Lô River whereas A-pa-chih moved along the east bank to attack the Hàm Tử frontier pass. Thế Tử had to withdraw his troops into the pass of Hải Thị but they were defeated by the Great Army."* On the other hand, T'o-huan together with Wu-ma-er launched an attack on our stronghold at Cảm Nam as recorded in *An Nan Chuan* of *Yuan Shih* 209, p.9b3. From there, after our troops' retreat as in the words of *An Nam Chí Lược* 4, p.56, they went on to strike our base at Hải Thị. Hải Thị undoubtedly refers to our base at A Lo, a reach of the Hải Triều River, where Trần Hưng Đạo destroyed, for the first time, Liu Shih Ying's men at their posts three years earlier. Following their attacks on Cảm Nam and Hải Thị, T'o-huan pursued our army toward Thiên Trường and even close to the Thiên Trường Estuary. Thereafter, nothing is written down as to where our Emperor and army moved.

It was in his pursuit of Đại Việt army early in the spring of the year Mậu Tý that Wu-ma-er, despite his failure in the preceding invasion, assumed that he could bring Đại Việt under his control this time. This may be seen in his statement that whatever Emperor

Nhân Tông could do, *"fleeing to the Heaven or on the ground, hiding in the mountains or diving in the sea, he would be ready to pursue him,"* as is recorded in the fourth letter dated Chih Yuan 25 (1288) of Emperor Nhân Tông cited by Hsü Ming Shan in *Tien Nan Hsin Chi* of *Shu Fu* 51, p.19a1-3. Nevertheless, according to *Pen Chi* and *An Nan Chuan* of *Yuan Shih* 15, p.1a5 and 209, p.9b4 respectively, however aggressive they showed in such a statement, Wu-ma-er and even T'o-huan did not know where Emperor Nhân Tông and the total armed forces of Đại Việt had retreated.

Angrily agitated by their failure to pursue Emperor Nhân Tông and our armies, T'o-huan and Wu-ma-er turned to their mopping-up operations in Thiên Trường, i.e., present-day Nam Định. Regarding the havoc caused by the enemy in this area, Emperor Nhân Tông himself accused them of their crimes in his letter sent to Kublai Khan in the fourth month of Chih Yuan 25 (1288), cited by Hsü Ming Shan in *Tien Nan Hsin Chi* of *Shu Fu* 51, pp.18b12-19a1: *"None of any brutal destructive offenses were not committed by them, destroying and burning all pagodas and temples across our country, digging our ancestors' tombs, killing our innocent countrymen, damaging the common people's properties."* And Chang Li Tao, on his return home after a mission in our country, mentioned in one of his records that Emperor Nhân Tông had directly told him about their destruction in a reception banquet at Thăng Long, as in the words of *An Nam Chí Lược* 3, p.46: *" 'Last year, the Great Army came here, destroying and burning houses, digging [our] ancestors' tombs—bones scattered everywhere...' The king did not yet finish his words when his subjects all wept."*

By the fourth of the first month of Mậu Tý (1288), having failed to pursue Emperor Nhân Tông and the army of Đại Việt, T'o-huan commanded his troops to move back to Thăng Long. There, on the one hand, he ordered Ao-lu-chih and A-pa-chih to seek supplies; on the other hand, he ordered Wu-ma-er to lead naval troops to receive Chang Wen Hu's supply ships via the Đại Bàng Estuary, as in the words of *Pen Chi* and *An Nan Chuan* of *Yuan Shih* 15, p.1a6-7 and 209, p.9b4-6 respectively. Chang Wen Hu's supply ships, which had been earlier attacked by our naval troops under the command of Nhân Đức Hầu Trần Lang at Đa Mỗ by the 28th of the 11th month, were finally destroyed totally by General Nhân Huệ Vương Trần Khánh Dư's naval troops at Vân Đồn and then at Lục Thủy, i.e., the Lục Estuary in what is now Hòn Gai.

The Victory at Vân Đồn

In *An Nan Chuan* of *Yuan Shih* 209, pp.9b13-10a3, we read, "*By the 12th month of the previous year (1287), [our] ships of supplies commanded by Chang Wen Hu reached Đồn Sơn when they encountered thirty ships of Giao Chỉ. In this battle, the enemy's troops killed and captured were of the same number. Then our ships went on to move toward the Lục Thủy Sea where the enemy's ships were increasingly massed. Seeing that our troops could not fight against them and our ships were too heavily loaded to move fast, Chang Wen Hu gave the order for loads of rice to be thrown into the sea before traveling to Quỳnh Châu. Fei Kung Ch'ên's supply ships, which had been halted at Huệ Châu in the 11th month since they could not advance against strong wind, also floated to Quỳnh Châu and joined Chang Wen Hu's convoy. Hsü Ch'ing's supply ships, which floated to Champa, were, too, united to them at Quỳnh Châu. Generally speaking, for our part 220 men were killed, and 11 ships with more than 14,300 piculs of rice lost.*" According to *An Nam Chí Lược* 4, p.56, Chang Wen Hu fled to Ch'inchou in a small boat after his ships of supplies had been besieged by our troops, but this might be falsely recorded.

In *ĐVSKTT* 5, pp.52b6-53a7, we read: "*When Yuan naval troops were about to attack Vân Đồn, Hưng Đạo Vương put all military actions at this position under the command of Nhân Huệ Vương Khánh Dư. The latter, however, lost the defense. Being informed of this, the Emperor-Father sent a messenger to the frontier, by his order that Khánh Dư would be tied and brought to the capital. Khánh Dư said to the messenger, 'In terms of military regulations, I am hardly to be forgiven. Yet, I think it not too late for me to be given a delay of about several days to acquire some merit before returning to the capital for punishment.' The messenger accepted his request. Knowing that the enemy's ships of supplies often moved in the rear of their troops, Khánh Dư collected his men and waited for them. Shortly thereafter, they passed by as he had expected. He ordered a sudden thrust on them, capturing a large number of the enemy's men, weapons, and supplies. When he was informed of this, the Emperor-Father decreed to forgive him, saying, 'The Yuan troops' operation depends crucially on weapons and supplies, which have just been captured by our army. They could, however, go on with their actions unless they would be informed of this loss.' Therefore, he gave orders for the release of the Yuan captives so that they could report everything fully to their commanders on their return to their command post.*"

Thus, our victory at Vân Đồn was decisive and well known. Even the enemy admitted that it was a great loss for them, as in the remark of *ĐVSKTT* 5, p.53a6-7: "*In that year the people did not fall into so much misfortune as in the previous year. It was partly due to Khánh Dư's efforts.*" As we have seen above, before our victory at Vân Đồn, Đại Việt's naval troops had fought unceasingly from the 12th of the 11th month to the end of the 12th month of the year Đinh Hợi. During this period, the Đại Việt Generals Nhân Đức Hầu Trần Toàn and Nhân Huệ Vương Khánh Dư must have been defeated by the Yuan invaders. General Trần Khánh Dư himself, as in the words of *ĐVSKTT*, was nearly tied and brought to Thăng Long by order of the Emperor-Father because of his failure to defend the position. Nevertheless, this talented and unyielding general had succeeded in sinking the enemy's convoy of supplies for only a few days. It points out not only our troops and people's resolution to fight and defeat the enemy at that time but also the Đại Việt supreme commanding officers' attempts to observe closely the military situation in many different fronts in order to make appropriate decisions in the most crucial moments.

The Battle of Đại Bàng

Thus, the convoy of supplies commanded by Chang Wen Hu was totally beaten down; and the enemy captives, who were then returned to their command post by Emperor-Father Trần Thánh Tông, must have informed T'o-huan of this. However, it seemed that the latter had showed so stubbornly suspicious that he ordered Wu-ma-er to receive their supply ships via the Đại Bàng Estuary where our ships, but not Chang Wen Hu's, were waiting for him. *ĐVSKTT* 5, p.51a1-3, says, "*On the 8th [of the 1st month of Mậu Tý, 1288] our troops faced the enemy's ships on the sea of Đại Bàng, capturing 300 their scout ships and [cutting off] ten men's heads.*

Most of Yuan men were drowned." According to *Khâm Định Việt Sử Thông Giám Cương Mục 7*, p.38a4-5, the Đại Bàng Estuary "*is located at the local community of Đại Bàng in Nghi Dương District of present-day Hải Phòng Province*". Thus, the Đại Bàng Estuary is the mouth of the Văn Úc River in what is now Hải Phòng City.

After the battle of Đại Bàng, Wu-ma-er led his troops toward Tháp Sơn, that is, present-day Đồ Sơn in the north. There again he met our naval troops with more than 1,000 ships waiting for him, as recorded in *A Nan Chuan* of *Yuan Shih 209*, p.9b8-9: "*From the Đại Bàng Estuary Wu-ma-er advanced to Tháp Sơn where he met more than a thousand ships of the enemy and defeated them.*" According to the inscription on Li Tien Yu's tombstone cited by Tsu Tien Chüeh in *Hsü Ch'i Wen Kao 18*, the battle of Tháp Sơn was commanded by Emperor Nhân Tông: "*in the spring of the year that followed, [our] troops reached the sea of Tháp Sơn, defeating Thế Tử.*"

Hsi-tu-er Chuan of *Yuan Shih 133*, p.9b6-8, mentions Hsi-tu-er's fight with Hưng Đạo Vương's troops: "*In the spring, the 1st month, of the year that followed (1288) our great army launched an attack on Hưng Đạo Vương's command post, fighting with Giao men in Tháp Sơn. Taking away a scimitar from the enemy's troops, [Hsi-tu-er] advanced to kill them. Being shot with an arrow on the right arm, his wound bled as much as a handful of blood. Wiping off the blood, he shot down more than twenty Giao men, and then urged his men to defeat them.*"

Thus, Tháp Sơn was an important position of Đại Việt's naval troops, where were concentrated a large number of our men and ships together with such supreme commanders as Emperor Nhân

Tông and General Trần Hưng Đạo by the spring of Mậu Tý (1288). It was in this position that Wu-ma-er and Hsi-tu-er launched their attacks and were more or less defeated by our men, particularly Hsi-tu-er who had been shot with an arrow, losing *"a handful of blood"*.

T'o-huan's Retreat into Vạn Kiếp

According to *An Nan Chuan* of *Yuan Shih* 209, p.9b8-9, having not met Chang Wen Hu's convoy of supply ships on his arrival at the An Bang Estuary, now known as Nam Triệu, Wu-ma-er decided to move his troops back to Vạn Kiếp via the Bạch Đằng River, where Yên Hưng, one of our bases that had been founded close to the river, became the first target of their attack. *ĐVSKTT* 5, p.54a3, says, *"On the 19th of the 2nd month of Mậu Tý (1288), Wu-ma-er launched a blow on Camp Yên Hưng."* In effect, according to the strategy generally designed by our army at the time this was only one in a series of battles aimed at weakening the enemy's strength. In the meantime, the enemy, too, did not intend to pursue our troops since they were on their way to retreat.

Regarding the armies commanded by A-pa-chih and Ao-lu-chih, who had received orders to *"seek supplies in the mountains"*, they launched some attacks on our positions at Kẻ Trầm, Kẻ Lê, Ma Sơn, and Ngụy Trai. In the words of *An Nan Chuan* of *Yuan Shih* 209, p.9b5-6, they cut off over 10,000 of our men's heads; whereas Tich-tu-er's Army moved to Tháp Sơn and then followed A-pa-chih to Thăng Long. There, on the Đinh Tỵ of the 12th month *"Chên Nan Wang deployed his troops back to Vạn Kiếp"* as recorded in *Pen Chi* of *Yuan Shih* 15, p.2a1-2. This event is dated the third month in *An Nan Chuan* of *Yuan Shih* 209, p.9b6-8, which further says, "*The bridgehead troops commanded by A-pa-chih gained the frontier pass, built a floating bridge, destroyed the Tam Giang Estuary, breached thirty-two posts, cut off tens of thousands of heads, captured 200 ships and more than 113,000 piculs of rice.*"

Thus, in contrast to their easy penetration into Thăng Long some months earlier, the retreat of the enemy's troops into Vạn Kiếp was full of difficulty and hardship. From the An Bang Estuary Wu-ma-er also moved his troops towards Vạn Kiếp as we have seen above. After wooden barriers had already been made around the Phả Lại and Chí Linh Mountains, T'o-huan's troops were posted there together with more than 40,000 *piculs* of rice, which had been collected by Wu-ma-er and A-pa-chih as recorded in *An Nan Chuan* of *Yuan Shih* 209, p.9b9-10. *An Nam Chí Lược* 4, p.56, gives further information on the situation above: "*In the 2nd month, Thế Tử ordered his cousin, Hưng Ninh Vương Trần Tung, to go to our camp for some negotiations about their surrender, which was ostensibly set forth for the purpose of weakening our troops' morale; yet, by night their spearhead troops were ordered to attack our position. Being extremely angry, Chên Nan Wang was about to order Wan Hu Chieh Chên to burn the stronghold but then gave up this intention due to his officers' advice.*"

Lai-a-pa-chih in *Yuan Shih* 129, p.2a7-10, writes down the same fact but mentions nothing of who came to negotiate with them about our emeperor's pretense of surrendering: "*Then, Nhat Huyen ordered his messengers to enter into many negotiations with us about his surrender. To delay our army's actions, he gave orders for wealth to be given to our troops. Our generals all believed in his words, having the stronghold rebuilt for a plan of long settlement. Waiting for such a long time, our supplies were running out but Nhat Huyen did not come. Not only did he refuse to come but also ordered his troops to be deployed at Truc Dong and the An Bang Estuary."*

Thus, since their retreat into Vạn Kiếp the enemy had fallen into an extremely puzzling state, which was worsened when Tuệ Trung Trần Quốc Tung, a hero in our earlier campaign to liberate Thăng Long, undertook the task of enhancing their stress through his ostensible negotiations with them so that T'o-huan once had the idea of burning the very stronghold that was protecting his army. Eventually, it was in such a puzzling state that a military conference was held among the defeated army.

According to *An Nam Chí Lược* 4, p.56, Chia Jo Yü, an excellent expert in archery, set forth his suggestion that *"What our army can do now is to retreat, not to hold [the position]."* Lai A-pa-chih Chuan of *Yuan Shih* says, *"Then, most of our officers and troops were so badly tormented by epidemics that they could not advance any more. Further, minority groups rose against us; the frontier gates under our control gradually fell into the enemy's hands again. Accordingly, our army decided to withdraw."* Finally, the enemy had made up a decision of retreat as recorded in *An Nan Chuan* of *Yuan Shih* 209, p.9b10-11: *"Therefore, the generals said, 'we can hardly bring all the ramparts and moats in Giao Chỉ under our control; nor can we occupy their stores of rice. In addition, Chang Wen Hu's supply ships have failed to arrive whereas the weather is getting hotter and hotter. If rice ran out, our men would be so exhausted that they could not stand long. To protect our court from being humiliated, we should retreat to maintain our forces.' Chên Nan Wang agreed."*

The Victory at Bạch Đằng

Thus, the invaders finally decided to retreat. But how could they carry out their retreat?

According to *An Nam Chí Lược* 4, p.56, at the military conference mentioned above the enemy's naval officers said, *"Our convoys of supply ships had been twice besieged. So it would be the best way for us to move by land instead of by water."* The suggestion would have been accepted by T'o-huan if his staff had not shown their disagreement. At last, as in the words of *An Nan Chuan* of *Yuan Shih* 209, p.9b11-12, their troops were divided into two wings. The first naval wing commanded by Wu-ma-er and P'an Chieh advanced forwards, whereas the second wing that was composed of infantrymen was commanded by Cheng P'êng Fei and T'a-chu (Taču) to escort the first one. This event is dated the Nhâm Ngọ, i.e., the 27th of the second month of Mậu Tý, in *Pen Chi* of *Yuan Shih* 5, p.2b4.

According to *An Nam Chí Lược* 4, p.56, the second wing encountered a great deal of difficulties: *"On the 3rd of the 3rd month of Đinh Hợi, Yu Chêng Cheng P'êng Fei and T'ien Shêng Ta-mu*[4]*, who were commanding cavalry to lead naval troops across the 'market' of Đông Hồ*[5]*, could not cross the river because the enemy, who were waiting there to launch a blow on [our] troops, had destroyed all the bridges. Having asked the captured elders of the*

---

[4] correct transliteration: Ta-shu. [LMT]
[5] correct transliteration: Đông Triều. [LMT]

village about the way, Cheng Yu Chêng had ordered his troops to move overnight to catch the Great Army." Obviously, the task of escorting the naval troops, which was entrusted to Cheng P'êng Fei and T'a-chu by T'o-huan, failed due to our troops' destruction of all the bridges. And they attempted to withdraw by land together with T'o-huan's army in the hope that it would be much safer.

Regarding the naval troops commanded by Wu-ma-er and P'an Chieh, they could not move quickly on their way toward the sea because of our troops' everyday harassment. *Chang Yü Chuan* of *Yuan Shih* 166, p.9a3-4, says, "*In [Chih Yuan] 25 (1288), our troops were withdrawn. An Nan troops launched violent attacks [on them] all day.*" According to *An Nam Chí Lược* 4, p.56, by the seventh day, Tân Mão, Wu-ma-er's naval troops reached Trúc Động, where our troops stroke them but the enemy's General Liu K'uei counterattacked and captured 20 ships of ours. Trúc Động was an important base of our army, where A-pa-chih, particularly Wu-ma-er, had had a fighting with us a month earlier, as in the words of *Lai A-pa-chih Chuan* of *Yuan Shih* 129, p.2a9, and *Ku Chêng Shih Lang Hsiang Shan Hsuan Yin Li Hou Mu Bei* in *Hsü Ch'i Wen Kao*18.

It might be owing to his experience in the fighting at Trúc Động that Wu-ma-er, in spite of being informed of Liu K'uei's successful counterattacks, dared not lead his naval troops toward the Bạch Đằng River via the Giá River, where was our army's base, Trúc Động, located. Instead, he chose the way on the Đá Bạc River. Bạch Đằng was the river along which our army had established several fighting positions. According to *ĐVSKTT* 5, p.54a3, on the 19th of the second month of Mậu Tý (1288) Wu-ma-er launched an attack on Camp Yên Hưng on the left-bank Bạch Đằng before moving back to Vạn Kiếp. Also in the words of *ĐVSKTT* 5, pp.54a4-b4, by the eighth of the third month *"Yuan troops, who had been massed on the Bạch Đằng, failed to receive Chang Wen Hu's convoy of supplies when they were defeated by Hưng Đạo Vương's naval troops. Long before, Vuong had had grass-covered stakes driven into the bed of the Bạch Đằng River. That day, taking advantage of the tide rising, Vương ordered his troops to challenge the enemy, then raced northward, pretending to be defeated. The enemy pursued; our troops attempted to counterattack. When the tide lowered, the enemy's ships were trapped among the pointed stakes. Nguyễn Khoái commanded strong men of the Thánh Dực Army to fight with the enemy, capturing alive Ping Chang Ao-lu-chih. With their reinforcements, the two kings launched a decisive combat on the enemy. So many Yuan troops were drowned that the river looked bloody. When Wen Hu's supply ships came, our troops from ambushes on the banks continued to beat them down. Being pierced with our pointed posts, almost all of their ships were sunk. A great number of Yuan troops were drowned; more than 400 patrol boats were captured. Nội Minh Tự Đỗ Hành captured alive Wu-ma-er and His-li-chi, carrying them to the Emperor-Father. He gave orders for them to sit with him on his own ship, inviting them to drink wine in a pleasant conversation."*

The account mentioned above in *ĐVSKTT* is fundamentally correct, except for some details that were not truly recorded. In effect, Wen Hu, for example, did not take part in this battle; nor was Ao-lu- chih captured on the Bạch Đằng River. Moreover, some other details that are found in some Chinese sources were not written down in *ĐVSKTT*. *Chang Yü Chuan of Yuan Shih 166, p.9a3-4*, for instance, gives an account of Chang Yü, who *"gained many military achievements in Ts'an Chih Chêng Shih Wu-ma-er's expeditionary army to fight Giao Chỉ in Chih Yuan 24 (1287). When it was on its way back [to the country] in [Chih Yuan] 25 (1288), the army was halted by An Nam troops. A great battle took place all day. The water was so low that [our] ships could not move. Yü was killed."*

Regarding P'an Chieh's role in this withdrawal, besides the fact that *"Wu-ma-er did not return by sea but on the Bạch Đằng River,"* *An Nam Chí Lược 4, p.56*, gives a further detail: *"Encountering the enemy, Wu-ma-er himself commanded the troops, who were transporting supplies, to fight. P'an Ts'an Chêng occupied a high mountain to facilitate his assistance [to the army], yet our troops could not make way ahead due to the lowering tide."* In the words of *P'an Chieh Chuan of Yuan Shih 166, p.10b2-3*, the battle is more clearly described: *"When Chieh and Wu-ma-er were withdrawing their naval troops, they were halted by the enemy. Since the tide in the Bạch Đằng River was then lowering, Chieh's ship could not move. The enemy's ships were more and more concentrated, and so many arrows were shot away as rain. Chieh did his best to fight from the Mão hour to the Dậu hour[6] until he was shot down with a cannon-ball and fell into water. The enemy pulled him up with a hook, but later poisoned him to death."*

Thus, according to *P'an Chieh Chuan*, the battle occurred from the early morning to the evening and there were deployed a great

---

[6] the period between 5 a.m. and 7 p.m.

number of Đại Việt's ships with *"so many arrows were shot away as rain"*. In reality, P'an Chieh was killed more than ten days later because he was still present together with His-li-chi (Širägi), Wu-ma-er, T'ang-wu-tai, Ts'en Tuan, Mei Shih Ying, T'ien Yuan Shuai, etc. at a banquet held by Emperor Nhân Tông at Long Hưng on the 17th day.

Until now the position where the enemy's ships were trapped among our pointed stakes on the eighth of the third month of Mậu Tý (1288) has not been definitely recognized. Yet, we can make sure that the fact that our troops drove stakes into the bed of the Bạch Đằng River must have taken place within not more than three weeks since Wu-ma-er's blow on Camp Hưng Yên on the 19th of the second month; for by the eighth of the third month he reached the Bạch Đằng River. In the contemporary conditions of war, the fact that the enemy's naval troops were attracted into such an ambush as was planned by our army was actually a glorious achievement in science and the art of military operation by our supreme staff headed by Emperor Nhân Tông.

The presence of the emperor, his father, and such gifted generals as Trần Hưng Đạo and Nguyễn Khoái points out that the battle in question must have been planned and commanded by the emperor himself or, at least, its plan must have been approved of and agreed on by himself. In effect, Emperor Nhân Tông's presence at this battle manifested the resolution of a leader of a country, who had, at any cost, to carry out the plan already set forth, considering it the central task that had to be performed to achieve the aim of the war. Nevertheless, the fact that the naval troops commanded by Wu-ma-er were completely liquidated has been so far attributed to

Trần Hưng Đạo by some researchers who have not paid enough attention to the emperor's role in this decisive battle. Indeed, leadership in politics is at all times predominant in every war. It is through political leadership alone that all the forces of a people are able to be concentrated for a war. Without such a total concentration, it would be hard for a country to gain victory no matter how talented its commanding generals, how good its tactics in fighting, and how great the people's patriotism and their resolution of fighting may be.

T'o-huan's Army Fleeing

By the eve of our total liquidation of Wu-ma-er's troops on the Bạch Đằng River, that is, the seventh of the third month according to *Pen Chi* of *Yuan Shih* 15, p.2b13, T'o-huan had ordered his great army to retreat to their country. Once more, A-pa-chih was appointed spearhead in opening the way as in the words of an account of him in *Yuan Shih* 129, p.2a10-11: *"Some infantry and cavalry men selected [by A-pa-chih] to open the way had to fight dozens of times a day while moving. The enemy's troops posted in the lofty and perilous positions shot away poisoned arrows. Seeking to tie their wounds, [our] officers and men attempted to fight against them. Some troops escorted the Prince out of the enemy's country."*

Yet, what road did A-pa-chih order his men to open? The answer is found in *An Nan Chuan* of *Yuan Shih* 209, p.10a3-6: *"Chên Nan Wang's army was quartered at the frontier pass of Nội Bàng, where the enemy's troops were more and more massing. Having breached their ring, Wan Hu Chang Chün received orders to command three thousand veteran men to halt the enemy in the rear. They had to try their best to escape out of the pass. Being reported that Nhật Huyên,*

Thế Tử and Trần Hưng Đạo were deploying more than three hundred thousand men along a line of more than a hundred miles to uphold the Nữ Nhi Pass and the Khâu Cấp Mountain and cut off our army's withdrawal, Wang had to follow a short cut to Lộc Châu via Đơn Kỷ District so that his army could be quartered at Szuming District."

The short cut mentioned above was the eastern road from Sơn Động to Lộc Bình in what is now Lạng Sơn Province. In the meantime, Hsi-tu-er was appointed to march his troops on the western road, i.e., present-day National Route I, from Chi Lăng to Vĩnh Bình. *Hsi-tu-er Chuan* of *Yuan Shih* 133, p.9b10-13 says, *"Chên Nan Wang withdrew his army; Hsi-tu-er was appointed to command spearhead troops. Reaching the frontier gate of Hãm Nê, the latter fought with Giao men a dozen times. After Giao men retreated, he went back, intending to receive Chan Nan Wang at the Nữ Nhi Pass. Yet, the main road had been stopped by more than four hundred thousand Giao men. Being exhausted due to lack of food and the recent combat, our officers looked at each other, their faces turning pale. Hsi-tu-er commanded strong men armed with spears and scimitars to advance. Giao men retreated over twenty miles. At last, our army could retreat safely."*

Thus, only two days later than their departure, i.e., the 10th of the third month, when T'o-huan had just reached the Nội Bàng Pass, our troops launched a violent attack on them. This attack, as in the words of *Pen Chi* of *Yuan Shih* 15, p.3a-4, was aimed at cutting off the retreat of T'o-huan's army. T'o-huan, then, had to follow a short cut to Lộc Châu via Đơn Kỷ District to leave our country, as recorded in *An Nan Chuan* of *Yuan Shih* 209, p.10a3-6. *An Nam*

Chí Lược 4, p.56, gives us further details that in their retreat out of Vạn Kiếp toward the Nội Bàng Pass, T'o-huan's troops fell into our troops' ambush. Wan Hu Ta-la-chih (Darači) and Liu Shih Ying attempted to fight and captured two of our generals, Phạm Trù and Nguyễn Kỵ, whom they cut down immediately in resentment.

This might probably be the battle of Xóm Hàn mentioned in *Hsi-tu-er Chuan* of *Yuan Shih* 133b8-10: "*In the 4th month, in an attack on their position at Xóm Hàn, our troops captured their General Hoàng Trạch. That night, when the drum sounded the second watch of the night, Giao men suddenly appeared, seeking to occupy our camp. Our troops did their best to uphold the fence, waiting for the moment the enemy would lose their power. At daybreak, beating drums, our troops began to march out of camp. Giao men withdrew. Having pursued and killed a great number of them, our troops went back to camp, mending the wooden fence and increasing patrolmen. Thereafter Giao men dared not challenge us.*"

On his arrival at Nội Bàng, T'o-huan, having heard that our troops were carrying out the defense of the Nữ Nhi Pass by digging holes for trapping his cavalry, ordered the chief of Szuming District, Huang Chien, to guide him toward Lộc Châu via another short cut in the hope that his troops could be safely protected in their retreat.

In the Chinese sources mentioned above, we see that T'o-huan's retreat was actually an extremely hard flight in his attempts to avoid any possible confrontation with our armed forces. The impression was to become much stronger when we read the very accounts of generals who participated in this battle in *Yuan Shih*. The account of Lai-a-pa-chih found in *Yuan Shih* 129, p.2a10-12, for instance, points out that our army attacked the enemy so unceasingly with poisoned arrows from the high mountain that they had to seek to tie their wounds while fighting against us. The most impressive description was of A-pa-chih. Having been shot with three poisoned arrows on the head, neck and leg respectively, he tried his best to command the resistance until his death because of swollen wounds. Another account concerning Hsi-tu-er recorded in *Yuan Shih* 133, p.9b10-13, gives us another picture of Yuan troops who were so exhausted due to lack of food and the recent fighting that they looked at each other extremely frightened. In face of our intense pursuit, however, they had to advance in hopes of escaping from our army's fatal siege. The picture of the generals and their men, who were most likely to fall into starvation and thus sought to race to the other side of the frontier, was in sharp contrast with that of their pride and brutality in the early days of their control over our country.

In this flight, the Yunnan Army commanded by Ai-lo seemed to join T'o-huan's army in their retreat toward Szuming. This may be proved through the fact that in his retreat to Szuming by the 15th of the third month of Mậu Tý (1288), T'o-huan ordered Ai-lo to lead his own army back to Yunnan, whereas Ao-lo-chih marched the Great Army to the north, as recorded in *Pen Chi* and *An Nan Chuan* of *Yuan Shih* 15, p.3a8 and 209, p.10a6.

As to our history books, ĐVSKTT 5, p.54b4-5, says, "*T'o-huan and A-thai commanded their men to flee to Szuming, where they were captured by the local official, Hoàng Nghệ, and carried [to our capital].*" In effect, it was not possible for our troops to capture T'o-huan in his flight because he was later to be mentioned in

Chinese historical documents as we have seen above. Regarding A-thai, he might probably be captured in this flight because his name has, since then, not appeared in any history books of China.

The Return to Thăng Long in Triumph

Once more, the invaders were entirely swept out of our country. Many years later, the terrible nightmare they had undergone during this invasion remained to be vividly perceived by their messenger Trần Phu in his poem *Sứ Hoàn Cảm Sự* in *Trần Cương Trung Thi Tập*, particularly in the two lines:

金 戈 影 裏 丹 心 苦
銅 鼓 聲 中 白 髮 生

In the image of bright spears their faithful hearts suffered;
And in the sound of bronze drums their hair turned white.

On the 17th of the third month of Mậu Tý (1288), Emperor Nhân Tông and his Emperor-Father returned to the Long Hưng Prefecture. Following them were the enemy's generals taken captives, such as Hsi-li-chi, Wu-ma-er, P'an Chieh, T'ang-wu-tai, Mei Shih Ying, Ts'en Tuan, A-thai, T'ien Yuan Shuai, and so on, who would prostrate themselves in front of the altar of the late Emperor Trần Thái Tông, the national hero of our country in the War of Defense in 1258. Standing before his heroic grandfather's mausoleum, which had been so ravaged by the enemy that the stone horses situated there were tainted with mud, Emperor Nhân Tông, the talented militarist of the history of Vietnam, could not help uttering two lines of verse expressing the great compassion, even for such inanimate beings as stone horses, of a hero who had just said farewell to fire and smoke of war as well as his strong confidence in the eternal existence of his country:

For the country's sake, even stone horses were sometimes engaged;
As firm as a gold basin, the fatherland would forever remain.

Then, on the 27th of the same month, together with his Emperor-Father, Emperor Nhân Tông returned to Thăng Long in the thundering cheers arising from the heart of a capital that had swept out the most brutal invaders of the world.

The homeland in peace was awaiting the national hero's leadership.

*Translation by **Đạo Sinh***

A WORLDLY LIFE
WITH JOY IN THE WAY

1

Though settling in the city,

The way of life I follow is of forest and mountain,

The ten thousand actions calmed and my being at ease.

Already for half a day I have let go of mind and body.

The sources of thirst and desire cease,

No reflection on lovely pearls or precious jades.

Both praises and blames are silenced, too;

Even though sounding,

They would be like the cries of orioles and swallows.

Roaming the blue waters or hiding in the green mountains,

That is the pleasure of many a person.

Peaches are pink and willows green;

Yet few in the world can ever contemplate them;

The bright moon in the blue sky

Is shining all in the vast Zen river.

Willows are soft and flowers in full blossom;

All beings are fully exposed under the sun of Wisdom.

Though interested in transforming bones

And ascending to Heaven in broad daylight,[1]

The elixir of life has only just been taken.

Though yearning for immortality in the upper realm,

Rabbit-medicine [2] *is not perfectly prepared.*

The Book of Changes[3] *I read for fun,*

Loving Illuminating Nature rather than jewels.

The Sūtra on Deliverance I study earnestly;

More precious than gold is the mind awakened.

2

Thus I know!

Mind is once awakened,

It is not necessary to seek any other way.

Sustaining illuminating nature conduces to peace of mind;

Right view comes when illusions are left behind.

Attachment to I-ness and Other-ness cut down,

There appears the true character of "diamond."[4]

Greed and hatred abandoned,

---

[1] According to religious tradition of Taoism called "Outer Elixir," liberation from worldly life may be gained by transforming human body and thus ascending to Heaven in broad daylight. The art of transformation consists of an alchemical process, during which the most important ingredients, cinnabar and gold, are prepared to produce a pill of immortality.

[2] By "rabbit" or "jade rabbit," it refers to the moon where, according to religious Taoism, the elixir of life is believed to be frequently prepared by an immortal named T'ai-shang lao-chün.

[3] I Ching, a Chinese book of wisdom and oracles, dating from the transition period between the Yin and Chou dynasties.

[4] Skt. vajra, a symbol of the indestructible. Here it stands for true reality, śūnyatā or emptiness, the essence of everything existing. This emptiness is indestructible like diamond, that is, imperishable and unborn or uncreated.

Then comes the marvelous nature of perfect enlightenment.

The Pure Land[5] is essentially the pure mind,

No more preoccupied with the Western Paradise.[6]

And Amitābha is the very illumination,

Not busy seeking the way to the Realm of Bliss.[7]

Observing body and mind, cultivating mindfulness,

Not for the purpose of reaping apparent fruits;

Preserving morality, fighting with flux,

Not owing to aspiration for fame and merit.

Eating vegetables and fruits,

No worry about taste—bitter or hot.

Covered with paper or coarse cloth,

No concern about the body—white or black.

If just pleased with morality,

A hermitage deserves much more than a celestial palace.

If constantly inspired by humaneness and uprightness,

Only three tiles are more valuable than a pavilion.

3

If one is awakened,

No fault is committed;

The Buddha's teaching then is comprehended.

As illumination is maintained, it is hard to fall on the wrong track;

And all that is studied must be of perfect teaching.

As Buddha is our very nature, follow Ma-tsu's mentality;[8]

---

[5] Skt., sukhavatī, the realm where followers of the PureLand school are reborn to continue with their cultivation of Perfect Enlightenment under Buddha Amitābha.

[6] Another designation of the PureLand.

[7] Another designation of the PureLand.

To forsake wealth and beauty, seek P'ang-kung's way of conduct.[9]
With illuminating nature constantly aroused in face of desire,
There is no need to cultivate the Way on the Cánh Diều peak of
Mount Yên Tử;
Without being stirred by sound and sight,
Meditation can be practiced not merely at the Sạn temple on
Mount Đông.
Achieved in the midst of the world, that merit is increasingly
admired;
Unsuccessfully made just in the mountains, that effort is but a vain
attempt.
With vows of being under a competent master,
The fruit of enlightenment would ripen overnight.
If fortunate to come in contact with a Dharma-friend,
The udumbara[10] *flower could blossom for lives.*

4

Awaken your faith!
Mindfulness is once attained,
All doubts vanish instantaneously.
First transform the Three Poisons,[11] *then realize the Three Bodies.*[12]

---

[8] Ma-tsu Tao-i, 709-788, one of the most important Chinese Ch'an masters; a student and the only Dharma successor of Nan-yueh Huai-jang, and the master of many great Ch'an masters, among whom the best-known are Pai-chang Huai-hai, Nan-ch'uan P'u-yüan, and Ta-mei Fa-ch'ang.

[9] P'ang-Yün, also P'ang-chu-shih or "Layman P'ang", 740-808/11, China's most famous Ch'an layman; a student and Dharma successor of Shih-t'ou Hsi-ch'ien and Ma-tsu Tao-i and close friend of the Ch'an master Tan-hsia T'ien-jan.

[10] Skt.; a tree that is said to blossom only once every 3,000 years. Therefore, it is often used as an illustration of how hard it is to come in contact with Buddhist teachings as well as to be born in the time of a Buddha.

To abandon the six senses enables the elimination of the Six Enemies.[13]

To seek transformation of one's bones,

Learn how to prepare a pill of immortality;

To grasp the meaning of True Emptiness,

Let not be disturbed by sound and form.

If able to understand Tathatā,[14] to penetrate Prajñā,[15]

There is no more search for Buddha in the east or west.

If able to realize True Nature, to comprehend the Unconditioned,

There is no more study of Zen doctrine in the north or south.

Reading the Tripiṭaka,[16]

It is to observe pure rules of Zen garden.

Burning the five-portioned incense,[17]

---

[11] Greed, hatred, illusion. They are all regarded in Buddhism as "poisons" that constantly destroy a human being's life.

[12] Skt., trikāya, referring to the three bodies of a Buddha, who is believed in Mahāyāna Buddhism to be one with the absolute and to manifest in the relative world in order to work for the welfare of all beings. They are (1) dharmakāya, the true nature of the Buddha, i.e., transcendental reality or essence of the universe, and the teaching exposed by the Buddha; (2) sambhogakāya, the body of buddhas who in a "buddha-realm" enjoy the truth that they embody; (3) nirmānakāya, the earthly body in which Buddhas appear to men in order to fulfill their resolve to guide all beings to liberation.

[13] The six corresponding objects of eye-sense, ear-sense, nose-sense, tongue-sense, body-sense and mind.

[14] Skt.; lit. "suchness," a central notion of Mahāyāna Buddhism denoting the absolute, the true nature of all things.

[15] Skt.; perfect wisdom.

[16] Skt.; lit. "the three baskets (of Buddhist literature)," consisting of the Buddha's teachings, disciplinary rules, and commentaries.

[17] Incense symbolic of precept, meditation, wisdom, liberation, and complete view of liberation.

It is not to use candana[18] or campaka[19] any more.
To cultivate humaneness and uprightness, to accumulate merits and virtues,
It is surely Śākyamuni's conducts;
To observe precepts, to uproot greed,
It is undoubtedly Maitreya's actions.

5
Thus it is learnt
That Buddha is within,
Not being sought afar.
My true nature being veiled, I have sought Buddha;
Now it is clear that Buddha is my nature.
With five phrases from Zen teachings, I can lie leisurely in Ho-yu;
With three recitations of sūtra, I can sit at ease in Hsin-lo.
To comprehend the Buddhist teaching, to penetrate its essentials,
One has to go through patriarchal gates and Dharma-halls.
To rid oneself of praise and blame, to detach oneself from sound and form,
One has to cease seeking pleasures in recreation of all kinds.
The compassionate Buddha,
May I be with Him in many lives!
Out of the king's favor,
May people be exempted from hard labor!
Whether robes and blankets are patched or tattered,
They help me survive the cold of winter.

---

[18] Skt.; incense-powder from sandal-wood.
[19] Skt.; incense-powder from a tree with yellow fragrant flowers, Michelia Campaka.

Whether rice and gruel are plain or somewhat rotten,

They help me overcome everyday hunger.

To prevent the eight consciousnesses[20] and eight winds[21] from arising;

The more they are suppressed, the more they increase.

To manifest the three marvelous, to expound the three essential,

It is necessary to elucidate them all.

The lute has no strings;

Yet the song of Non-Arising is played on.

The flute has no holes;

From it the tune of Great Harmony still comes.

To leave the root for branches,

It is rather sorry for the Venerable Chü-chih;

Avoiding realities and hunting for deluded images,

Yajñadatta[22] deserves to be laughed at.

Without fortitude, it is hard to pass through the Ring of Diamond,

Without vigor, it is not possible to swallow a thorny fruit.

6

How true it is!

Being no-mind

---

[20] Eye-consciousness, ear-consciousness, nose-consciousness, tongue-consciousness, body-consciousness, mind-consciousness, mana-consciousness, alaya-consciousness. The first six consciousnesses are generally conceived by most of the Hīnayāna schools; the whole eight consciousnesses by the Yogācāra school.

[21] Standing for prosperity, decline, disgrace, honor, praise, censure, suffering, happiness.

[22] Skt.; lit. "obtained from sacrifice," a crazy man who, seeing his eyebrows and eyes in a mirror but not seeing them in his own head, thought himself bedeviled; the eyes and head are a symbol of reality, those in the mirror are of unreality.

Is spontaneously to be in accord with the Way.

The Three Actions calmed, then body and mind are pacified;

Single-mindedness realized, thus the Patriarchs' teaching is clarified.

With knowledge based on words literally,

The Zen student loses his way;

On grasping the principle, penetrating into its workings,

The humble monk starts his skillful paces.

What about āsrava[23] and anāsrava?

Just like a thin filter and a hollow ladle.

What about Hīnayāna and Mahāyāna?

No other than a thread of coins and a bucket rope.

If an insight into original mind is gained,

There is no worry about transitory conditions.

If illuminating nature may be manifested,

There is no trouble made by objects and perceptions.

When gold is not yet made pure,

It takes nine times for dissolving and nine times for purifying.

If benefit is not longed for,

Whether a plain meal of rice or gruel is fine.

Keeping mind-precepts pure, making form-precepts perfect,

That is how a Bodhisattva adorns himself internally and externally.

Righteously serving one's lord, respectfully obeying one's father,

---

[23] Skt.; lit. "outflow, secretion," also "defilement" or "canker." Three cankers constitute the root of all suffering and the cause that beings are caught in the cycle of rebirth: the canker of desires (kāmāsrava), of becoming (bhavāsrava), and of ignorance (avidyāsrava). The extinction of these three cankers, that is, anāsrava , lit. "non-outflow," means the attainment of arhatship.

That is truly a noble man of loyalty and filial piety.

To practice meditation, it may cost one's life

To repay a Dharma-brother's gratitude;

To experience the Way,

Hardship exerted on one's head bone as such

Is not yet worth a master's instructions.

7

Thus it is obvious

That how marvelous buddha-Dharma is,

Which may be realized through personal experience only.

Ignorance being uprooted, bodhi[24] is made bright;

Defilements being purged, morality is greatly admired.

The Heart Sūtra recited,

The Buddha's teachings would be easily penetrated;

The Patriarchs' manner followed,

The Way of Zen would be somewhat traced.

To transform the root-ability, to get rid of earthly defilement,

Let no shadow of them appear in front.

To destroy hindrances, to deepen understanding,

Leave nothing harmful in hand.

With the fire of enlightenment,

Burn down the forest of abiding false views;

With the sword of wisdom,

Cut down all that is beclouding original mind.

To remember the saint's grace, to love parents,

Respect masters, study the Teachings;

To esteem the Gautama, to refrain from the 'sweet,'[25]

---

[24] Skt.; enlightenment.

Observe precepts, become vegetarians.
Deeply moved by the compassionate Buddha,
May I be with Him for many lives!
Highly grateful for His salvation,
May I be capable of enduring so terrible hardship,
Even though my body would suffer in numerous rebirths!
If constantly concerned with uprightness and absorbed in the Way,
Flowers and incense alone suffice to demonstrate one's devotion.
If faith is aroused not in mind but in words only,
Faults are hard to abandon
Even though offerings would be of jade and gold.

8
Accordingly, be diligent in practice
And consistent in study.
Shake consciousness, cut off all fetters;
Suppress delusions, let them die out.
Those absorbed in merit and fame
Are all inexperienced fellows;
Those fraught with vigor and wisdom
May attain to true understanding.
Making bridges and ferries, building temples and stūpas,
That is the cultivation of the teaching on external ornamentation.
Aspiring after sympathy-equanimity, versed in pity-compassion,
That is mastering the sūtra on internal tranquility.
To attain Buddhahood, it would take much effort to discipline mind;
To seek for gold, it would take much time to filter sand.

---

[25] referring to sensational pleasures.

Practice exactly all that is learned from sūtras and records;

Out of respect for the Buddha, leave not a trace of fault in discipline.

Comprehension of the Buddha's words may eliminate all anxieties;

Penetration into the Patriarchs' instructions may sustain mindfulness.

9

It is thus widely known

That the Patriarchs' instructions,

Though varied, are in reality rather identical.

Mentioned here are some patriarchs subsequent to Ma-tsu,

Not those at the time of the Emperor Chiao.[26]

Merit not gained, faults would increase due to attachment;

Knowledge not acquired, ignorance would remain as before.

Born in India and dead in Shao-lin,[27]

He[28] *was temporarily buried at the foot of Mount Hsiung-er.*

"Body is bodhi-tree; mind is bright mirror,"

There remains the stanza on the wall of the corridor.

Killing the cat,

Old Wang[29] *drove away all doubts of the head monk.*

---

[26] The Emperor Wu of the Liang dynasty

[27] Shao-lin-ssu, a Buddhist monastery on Mount Sung where Bodhidharma settled, sitting in front of a wall for nine years on end, after his encounter with the Emperor Wu of the Liang dynasty in Nanking in the first half of the sixth century.

[28] Bodhidharma, ca. 470-543 (?); the 28th patriarch after Śākyamuni Buddha in the Indian lineage and the first Chinese patriarch of Zen. Bodhidharma was the student and Dharma successor of the 27th patriarch Prajñādhara and the teacher of Hui-k'o, whom he installed as the second patriarch of Zen in China.

[29] Nan-ch'üan P'u-yüan, 748-835, one of the great Chinese Ch'an masters of

Setting free the dog,

Master Hu[30] indicated the easy understanding of reality.

So expensive was rice at Lu-lêng Market that no bargain was possible;

So slippery was rock at Shih-t'ou[31] that few could arrive there.

Raising the Dharma flag, P'o-tsao conquered the god of kitchen;

Moving the forefinger, Ku-chi followed the forefathers' conduct.

With Lin-chi's sword,[32] Pi-ma's crutch,

Monastic devotees were taught the way to enlightenment;

With Master Tuan's lion, Master Yu's[33] water-buffalo,

Lay followers were instructed not to be arrogant.

By raising the fan, the bamboo-box,

It was so easy to test Zen students' capacity.

By throwing the ball, handling the wooden ladle,

It was how to display skillfulness to the brotherhood.

Gaining the oar, Ch'uan-tzu was not purified in the clear water;

Twirling the tablet, Tao-wu showed nothing but magic things.

Hearing Old Yen's[34] dragon could swallow Heaven and Earth,

---

the T'ang period; a student and Dharma successor of Ma-tsu Tao-i.

[30] Tzu-hu Li-tsung , roughly 800-880; Chinese Ch'an master, a student and Dharma successor of Nan-ch'uan P'u-yüan

[31] Shih-t'ou His-ch'ien, 700-790; early Chinese Ch'an master; the student and Dharma successor of Ch'ing-yüan Hsing-ssu and master of Yueh-shan Wei-yen, T'ien-huang Tao-wu, and Tan-hsia T'ien-jan.

[32] Lin-chi I-hsüan, d. 866/67; Chinese Ch'an master; a student and Dharma successor of the great Master Huang-po his-yun and the master of Hsing-hua Ts'ung-chiang and Pao-chou Yen-chao.

[33] Kuei-shan Ling-yu, 771-853; great chinese Ch'an master; a student and Dharma successor of Pau-chang Huai-hai and the master of Yang-shan Hui-chi and Hsiang-yen Chih-hsien.

[34] Yün-men Wen-yen, 864-949; Chinese Ch'an master; a student and Dharma

Everybody would be frightened.

Learning I-ts'un's[35] snake could creep across the world,

Everybody would have to run away.

The pine being mind, it was necessary to travel eastward.

The south belonging to fire, it was wrong to head for the north.

In spite of Old Chao's[36] tea, Shao-ying's cake,

A large number of Zen students were thirsty and hungry.

Though Ts'ao-ch'i rich in rice-fields, Shao-shih in gardens,

They were left uncultivated by poor monks.

Putting down the bundle of firewood, keeping the wick burning,

Life is sustained by diligence.

Peaches in bud and blossom, the sound of bamboo heard,

Nobility may be found in tranquility only.

10

Śūnyatā is once realized,

Life then is in accord with original nature;

Otherwise, not because of the Patriarchs' instructions

But because of our clinging mind.

For those adherents of the Smaller Vehicle,[37]

Who fail to realize the ultimate truth,

The Buddha invented a magic city in place of the Precious Abode.[38]

---

successor of hüeh-feng I-ts'un and the master of Hsiang-lin Ch'eng-yüan, Tung-shan Shou-chu, and Pa-ling Hao-chen.

[35] Hsüeh-feng I-ts'un, 822-908; one of the most important Chinese Ch'an masters of ancient China; a student and Dharma successor of Te-shan Hsüan-chien

[36] Chao-chu Ts'ung-shen, 778-897, one of the most important Ch'an masters of China; a student and Dharma successor of Nan-chüan P'u-yüan.

[37] The Hīnayāna Teaching.

[38] According to the Lotus Sūtra, along the pilgrimage of a Buddhist to the final

For those of great ability in experiencing the truth,

Enlightenment may be realized whether in the city or mountains.

Deserted mountains and secluded forests

Are where hermits lead their lives of non-attachment;

Quiet temples and serene pagodas

Are where ascetics spend their days of non-affair.

However high our positions in society are,

It is hard for us to escape from Yama's control.[39]

Dwelling in a gold palace or a jade pavilion

Could not prevent us from being reborn in a painful realm.

Blinded by merit and fame, confused by ideas of I-ness and Other-
ness

Are truly all ordinary people.

Aspiring for morality, transforming mind and body

Are certainly men of transcendent wisdom.

Though different in human appearance,

All are of equal Buddha-nature.

Yet, a vulgar mind when compared with a noble insight

Is thousands of miles far from the latter.

The gātha reads,
How joyful it is,

A worldly life in accord with the Way!

Sleeping when tired, eating when hungry;

Stop seeking for treasure originally inherent.

---

destination, i.e., perfect enlightenment, illustrated in the text as the Precious Abode, there is an en-route stop viewed as a magic city because of its relative character.

[39] The king of hell.

As no mind arises in the presence of things,
Not any question on Zen is required then.

(The original text, see in the subdivision Nghien Cuu).

THIỀN (ZEN) BUDDHISM
AND POETRY ZEN MASTER
HUYEN QUANG
AND THE SILENT PATH
OF AUTUMN

THICH PHUOC AN

Zen Master Huyen Quang was 77 years old when he received from the Venerable Phap Loa the mission of directing the Thien sect (Dhyana, Zen) of Truc Lam, thus assuming the title of Third Patriarch. In view of this age and his love for solitude, one could imagine how reluctant he was when he accepted such a charge. Huyen Quang was eager to return to nature as shown in his following poems:

"Given my thin virtue I am ashamed to maintain the flame of the ancestral lamp,

I might displease such renowned bonzes as Han Son and Thap Dac.

I wish that I could follow my friends and return to the desert mountains,
Where thousands of pecks overlap."

Why did Phap Loa choose Huyen Quang? There is no denying that the latter is among the erudite Buddhists in his times. After reading the manuscript of Thich khoa giao (Buddhist teaching the compilation of which he assigned to Huyen Quang), King Tran Nhan Tong concluded: "In all the works written or reviewed by Huyen Quang, one could not remove or add a single word."However, besides his religious knowledge and the chief of the Buddhist congregation had also to assume the role of the Master of the Nation (Quoc Su), that is to counsel the king of the Tran on both internal and external affairs. In the Dai Viet (the then name of Vietnam) Buddhism was considered State religion.

This responsibility of Master of the Nation implies "teaching" which Huyen Quang renounced: Huyen Quang has always held that man runs after honors and wealth because he does not know that he is a poor creature subjected to destruction as time passes. The monk wanted that the mortal could liberate himself from his illusions.

"Honors and wealth, slow-moving clouds which are late to come
Time passes rapidly, tumultuous torrent
Why not take refuge among mountains and forests
The wind blows through the pines, there one tastes a cup of tea."

It is because of this spirit of renunciation that made Phap Loa and his colleagues at their retreat at Yen Tu Mount choose Huyen Quang?

King Tran Nhan Tong, founder of the Sect, retired to Yen Tu in 1299. Before that, he had led his people in the victorious resistance against the Mongol invaders (1285 - 1288). He was the only sovereign of our country to consult his people on a decision of vital importance for the destiny of the nation: in 1284 he convened a meeting of elderly persons at Dien Hong palace to ask them whether to resist the Mongols or to surrender. Tran Nhan Tong, who was then at the peak of glory and venerated by the nation took an exemplary gesture by retiring from public life.

So, after a quarter of a century during which Buddhism had closely taken part in the affairs of the royal court, was it not high time for Phap Loa and the monarchical community of Yen Tu to stand away from them?

The fact that the bonzes were in close liaison with the aristocracy and that even the aristocracy regularly went to the pagodas did not work for the good of a religion who ultimate goal is the emancipation of each individual by himself before giving himself to the religious life. All historians agree that the nomination of Huyen Quang to head the Truc Lam sect at Yen Tu marked a decline of Vietnamese Buddhism. This remark might be true if one judges things by their appearances. In fact, compared to the earlier periods, the priesthood of Huyen Quang testifies to the lack of dynamism in the material activities: less pagodas were erected, less statutes were molded and less bells cast and more economic autarchy of the monasteries.

Actually, the material development of the Buddhist congregation before Huyen Quang, however profitable it was to the religious cause, had led to the numerous abuses. Not a few people entered monkshood prompted by not so much spiritual conviction as egoistic calculations. The anti-Buddhist Confucian scholar Truong Han Sieu has denounced this social phenomenon: "That is why, half of the quite and picturesque places of the country are occupied by pagodas. Bands of black costumes and yellow costumes (bonzes) converge there. They eat without having to cultivate the soil, dress without having to weave. Many have abandoned their wives or their husbands to follow this path..."Obviously, the scholars trained by Confucian orthodoxy looked askance at Buddhism. Their ideal is to succeed to mandarinal examinations in order to serve their monarch by helping to maintain a strongly stratified order. Their anti-metaphysical rationalism kept them away from the Thien Sect which has nevertheless supplied to the State many counselors who have aided in the founding of the Ly dynasty.

Take for instance the bonze Van Hanh who advised Ly Cong Uan to move the capital from Hoa Lu in the jungle to Thang Long (Hanoi) in the heart of the Red River delta. This choice has brought unprecedented prosperity to the country. However, the freedom of mind and the clear-sightedness of the Thien Buddhism lost more and more ground and finally gave in to Confucianism at the end of the Tran dynasty in the XIVth century.

In any case, the offensive of the Confucian scholars against Buddhism gave a precious warning to the latter: after accomplishing its profane mission of national salvation, Buddhism should step down from the political scene in order no longer to abuse the temporal power in favour of the spiritual power.

Nominated chief of the Truc Lam Sect, Huyen Quang retired to the mountain region of Thanh Mai and Con Son, refusing until his last days to reside in the Quynh Lam and Bao An pagodas as Phap Loa had done, which he might have considered too rich, thanks to the material aid granted by the Tran Court. Would Huyen Quang have wanted to re-orientate the Buddhism of Dai Viet in the direction of poverty and humility which would be more propitious to meditation?

In his mountain retreat, Huyen Quang found a natural setting which helped him to discard all petty calculations: "To keep one's clumsiness, reject all stategem" (Bao chuyet, vo du sach). He lived a hermit's life:"Touching the sky the small solitary pagoda is bathed in freshness,

The gate opens on the clouds,
... Birds abound in the bamboo grove

Half of them are friends of the care-free monk."So, alone before the sun which sets down, the old master relishes his internal joy:

"In the brazier the straws burn, no more incense.
I answer my little disciple who puts me questions about the last chapters of the sutras.
I hold in my hands the book of prayer and the flute
Let no one reproach an old bonze like me."

The following poem tells of the detachment and internal joy of Huyen Quang:

"Garden and ricefields of ancestor I cultivate
Trees grow luxuriant around the house
Seen from the window the branches of the cinnamon tree and no troubled by the twitter of birds.
Resting my head on a cushion I pursue my dream throughout my

siesta."

In another poem, he wrote:

"When I turn back to see the world of dust
My wide open eyes are like veiled by drunkenness."

To Huyen Quang, life is full of sufferings but also of beauty. Beauty in the chrysanthemum which

"Each year blossoms with the autumn dew
The light breeze and the mellow moonlight alleviate the painful heart."Beauty of:
"The young girl of sixteen springs who embroiders brocade
The yellow oriole singing in the judas-tree
Falls silent, sharing her first spring agitation
Which causes her needle to stop at the same moment."

This poem by an author of the Chinese Song dynasty copied by Huyen Quang in his collection is a clear indicator of his adherence to the dhyanistic concept (Thien). Is it an expression of the sudden illumination of a religious priest, the spiritual turning point from which the dhyanistic monk adopts a new vision of the universe? Freed of all constraint and convention he is flying in a world where everything is new. Does this first "spring agitation" when the birds falls silent and the needle stops evoke the dhyanistic grace? Many readers are astonished by the profane ideas of this poem. That is because they don't know that for a Thien Master all beauty is internal and it would be vain to claim an exterior beauty for oneself. If within our own self a multitude of flowers radiate and thousands of butterflies are flitting, the external world will be inundated with flowers and butterflies. During a stroll, Huyen

Quang might have seen young girls pick small chrysanthemums to adorn their hair, and this might have inspired this gentle reproach:

"It is a pity that without knowledge of the miraculous secret of flowers
They have picked them shamelessly to adorn their hair."

One must not commit vandalism against nature because nature and us are one:

"Man and things are not rivals." To arrive at this frame of mind of universal unity, the bonze has gone through a long and hard asceticism:

"Mindfulness of oneself, of life, of everything
Seated indefinitely in the breeze which refreshes the bed.
The year is drawing to its end, no calendar in the mountain,
The chrysanthemum is blossoming, it is the festival of the Ninth Day of the Ninth Month."

In his search for the absolute which leads him to his emancipation and to the end of all suffering, the adept of Thien (Zen) is confronted with the immense void:

"Autumn evening, the wind causes the curtain on the verandah to shiver
The mountain hut nestles against a mass of verdure
My heart emptying on the road of Thien
From whom are these interminable laments of the cricket?"

Detached as he is the ascete sensible to the least complaint. He shares even the grief of a captured enemy:

"He would want to write to his dear ones with his own blood,

A solitary swallow is lost in a dark cloud, beyond the border post,

Tonight so many families are sighing under moonlight

Sadness is the same, here and there, very, very far away."

The travel to the end of human suffering brings only one solution, that is universal compassion, compassion which gives to the poems of Huyen Quang that inimitable accent made of detachment and human warmth, of the sense of evanescence and of beauty.

Hai Duc Pagoda (Nha Trang)

ATTEMPTING TO TRANSLATE THE POEM, XUÂN VÃN, OF KING TRẦN NHÂN TÔNG (1258 - 1308)

He is an eminent king of kings, a great person of culturalism, a proficient poet, an enlightened Zen Master, and most of all, he is a Vietnamese Zen Master. He founded the lineage of Truc Lam Uyen Tu when he was 41 years-old after, giving up his position as an established king to his son King Tran Anh Tong (1276-1320). In his poems, his writings about spring compose a very large part. One of those poems is "Xuan Van". Perhaps he only borrowed the spring scene to express His realization. But his own realization and liberation are in no way things any ordinary human beings like us can fully understand. The poem is as follows:

XUÂN VÃN

Niên thiếu hà tằng liễu sắc không,
Nhất xuân tâm sự bách hoa trung.
Như kim khám phá Đông hoàng diện,

Thiền bản, bồ đoàn khán trụy hồng.

(Translation meaning: When I was young (we / the king) had never understood "form" with "emptiness" / Every time the spring came, there was still a flutter / our heart blossoms with hundreds of flowers / Today, we have discovered / identified the face of the Spring Lord / Sitting on the grass mattress / meditating on the sight of the falling roses. This poem has many translations, for example:

SPRING LATE

Youth is not walled with colors,
Spring is forever entangled with hundreds of flowers;
Now I understand the truth,
Calmly sat looking at the shadow of spring passing by.
(Phan Thanh Khuong translation)

SPRING LATE

Young people are not clear about form and emptiness
Spring comes, flowers bloom, exciting our hearts
This spring has become familiar,
Sitting meditation on the grass, watching the rose pet als drop.
(Excerpt from Nguyen Cong Ly's article)

But perhaps the one we like most is the very translation of The Most Venerable Trúc Lâm.

LAST SPRING

Childhood is never clear about form and emptiness
Spring on, flowers bloom in the heart.
Lord Xuan is now discovered by me,
Meditation, on the grass mattress, watching the pink rose petals

falling.

(Venerable Trúc Lam translates – Excerpt from Thich Thong Hue's lesson)

Personally, I attempted to translate from Chinese into Vietnamese and it sounds like in English:

SPRING

Young people do not understand the haves and haves not
Their inner spring arrives and hundreds of flowers start to bloom
A clear understanding and realization of the true path arises
Sitting on the grass and reflecting on the falling of the rose petals.
(TTD translated)

Reading through and rereading still does not satisfy with what the Zen Master wants to say, so I searched for another English translation by a beloved layman, Nguyen Giac:

THE LATE SPRING

When I was young, I did not understand the existence and the emptiness.

Now the spring flowers bloom, and I am blissful to see clearly the face of the spring.

From the Zen bed, sitting on a grass mat, I keep watching the falling roses.

Then I followed his footsteps and also tried to translate it into English as follows:

SPRING PERSPECTIVE

The young don't understand existence or emptiness

Their inner spring arrives and hundreds of flowers start to bloom
A clear understanding and realization of the true path arises
Sitting and reflecting on the falling of the rose petals.
(Phe Bach translated)

But was not very satisfied, so my final translation is:

THE INNER SPRING

When I was young, I didn't quite understand existence or
emptiness
The spring comes and I am still excited as hundreds of flowers start
blooming
Now, realizing the inner spring is always here; it is the true path
Sitting on the Zen mat acknowledging the falling of the rose petals.
(Phe Bach translated)

In short, we cannot comprehend what is being enlightened, the noble wisdom, the Mahayana Bodhisattva spirit of the Zen Master. Or as Venerable Thong Hue emphasized: "Childhood is never clear about the form and emptiness / Spring comes, the flowers blooming in the heart". At a young age, when he was still a child and was still young in his Dharma year. On a spring day, strolling in the royal garden, the prince saw hundreds of flowers blooming and gave off a sweet smell. Not understanding its ultimate reasoning, it is unclear whether it was the emptiness of the Dharma, the prince thought that the mind and body are true and permanence. The idea of accepting a strong sense of ego, especially in the favorable conditions of material things, then how do you avoid the thrill of seeing the spring season return? But personally, at the age of thirty-something, how can we translate it properly?

We are limited by what and who we are. So, even though we all have good thoughts and intentions, when translating enlightened meditative poems, we have not yet mastered them, so let us remain like this:

XUÂN VÃN

Niên thiếu hà tằng liễu sắc không,
Nhất xuân tâm sự bách hoa trung.
Như kim khám phá Đông hoàng diện,
Thiền bản, bồ đoàn khán trụy hồng.

SOME TEACHINGS OF VIETNAMESE ZEN MASTERS FROM THE TRAN DYNASTY

NGUYEN GIAC

These selected teachings are from "Teachings from Ancient Vietnamese Zen Masters". Translated and Commented by Nguyen Giac, Published by Phap Vuong Monastery, California, 2010

THE TREASURE

Living in the world,

happy with the Way,

you should let all things take their course.

When hungry, just eat; when tired, just sleep.

The treasure is in your house; don't search any more.

Face the scenes,

and have no thoughts;

then you don't need to ask for Zen.

TRẦN NHÂN TÔNG (1258-1308) – Zen Master Thích Thanh

Từ translated into Vietnamese.

*(COMMENT: Live with the water, not with the waves rising and falling; live with the nature of a mirror to reflect, not with the images appearing and disappearing; and live with the essence of the mind, not with the thoughts arising and vanishing. When you see the essence of the mind, then you catch a glimpse of Nirvana – the state of unborn, uncreated, unconditioned peace. After that moment, you know how to live with the mind unmoved while walking, standing, lying, and sitting. How can you see the essence of the mind? Please, remember: you are never away from it, just like the water holds all the waves and is never away from them, just like the emptiness of the mirror holds all the images and is never away from them. The essence of the mind is non-self, so it manifests as a great magician: your mind has no form, so it takes all forms you see as its own forms; your mind has no color, so it takes all colors you see as its own colors... Now look out the window. When you see a bird, your mind now has the form of a bird; and when the bird flies, your mind flies too. Your mind is all the things you see, all the things you hear, all the things you feel; the observer is all the things observed. The Sixth Patriarch Huệ Năng * told two monks arguing over a banner that was flying, that that was not the banner moving, and also not the wind moving, but just their minds moving.)*

** Chinese: Hui Neng.*

ALL PHENOMENA

All phenomena are unborn.
All phenomena are undying.
If you see that constantly,

all Buddhas are before your eyes constantly.
TRAN NHAN TONG (1258 – 1308)

(COMMENT: We were born and will die. We were born some decades ago, and will die in a certain future. How could the Zen masters say all things are unborn and undying?

We all live in this world, weep the tears of sorrow sometimes, have the laughter of joy other times, feel our breath coming and going endlessly, and see babies being born and old people dying. How can we say all things are unborn and undying?

That is Nirvana, a state that Buddha referred to as unborn, un-ageing, unmade, and undying. Buddha once compared the impermanence of life to a flickering lamp, and said that to live a single day realizing the deathless state was better than to live a hundred years in ignorance.

Watch your mind, and see the state of unborn emptiness. Watch the thoughts coming and going, and see the unmoving mind. Keep seeing that way.

An ancient Zen master in China once blew out a candle, and his student became suddenly enlightened. What happened there? Let's look at the story. Two monks had a Dharma conversation. The student asked a lot of questions, heard some answers, then left when it was dark outside. The master offered a lighted candle. When the student took the candle, the master blew it out. The student became suddenly enlightened. What did they talk of in the Dharma conversation? About the unborn mind? About the unmoving mind? The day was gone, and the night was coming; what was not gone, and what was not coming? Now, look at the candle. The light was lit, and then was extinguished; what was not lit, and what was not extinguished there? Ask the ancient monks. Was that the non-self seeing? Or when the student saw the light and then saw the dark, he realized that in the deathless seeing there was just the seen?)

AT THE MOUNTAIN COTTAGE, FEELING INSPIRED

I

Nobody ties you; why do you ask for liberation?
Having no unholy thoughts, you don't need to search for the holy.
The monkeys are relaxing; the horses, tired; and the humans, old.
The cottage in the clouds looked like years ago, and so does the Zen stupa.

II

Thoughts, rightful and wrongful, are falling off just like flowers in the morning.
Fame and wealth are chilled in my mind just like cold, rainy nights.
The flowers are dying; the rains, gone; and the mountains, serene.
A bird chirps a sound, and the spring is leaving again.
TRẦN NHÂN TÔNG (1258 – 1308)

(COMMENT: Realize that you have no self. While lying, sitting, standing, and walking, constantly see that you have no self, and that nothing has a self. Then you can see there is not a 'you' being tied. Since then, after that realization, you know something about the workings of the mind, and meditation naturally becomes your flesh. Still, you realize that bad habits are hard to quit; but you already know how to calm the mind naturally.

Also, monkeys and horses are symbols for the clinging thoughts.

Watching the mind, the Zen practitioner sees all the thoughts disappear like flowers falling off in the morning.)

URGENTLY PRACTICE

If you practitioners have enough eyes, you must urgently reflect, transform your body, leap out of the cycle of birth and death, cut instantly the net of sensuous desire. Male or female, you can practice the Way; wise or foolish, you will have a place to succeed. While you don't understand the Buddha's mind and Patriarch's intention, first keep the precepts and chant the Sutras. Until you see that Buddha is also voidness and Patriarch is also emptiness, you understand that there is no precept truly needed to be kept and there is no Sutra truly needed to be chanted.

Then you realize that this illusionary form is also the True Form and this unholy body is also the Buddha Body. Then you will transform the six consciousnesses into the six supernatural powers, convert the eight afflictions into the eight freedoms. So it is said; but when you get into this bodily form, it is very difficult to get away.

TRẦN THÁI TÔNG (1218 – 1277)

(COMMENT: The famous Trần Thái Tông led Vietnam throughout several years of military victories. He later entered a temple, became a monk, and left many remarkable writings about the Way of Zen.)

5. ENCOURAGING

Some people bury their heads in the joy of eating and drinking, and waste their life away. Some people practice the Way incorrectly, and cannot get enlightenment. They don't know that in everyone the Bodhi Mind is already perfect, and the virtuous Prajna is already complete. Despite being a hermit, completely or partly, despite being a monk or a layperson, you will get enlightenment if you realize the original mind. That is originally not male or female, so you don't have to cling to physical appearances. Those who don't understand, turn into three teachings tentatively; those who already understand know that they have realized the same one mind. Those who constantly reflect inwardly will all see the self-nature and become Buddhas.

King TRẦN THÁI TÔNG (1218 – 1277)

(COMMENT: Human life is precious. Practice the Way correctly and constantly.

Don't waste even a day in your life. Death may come tonight or tomorrow. Actually, death is chewing you in every moment; it is present in your every breath, and is not apart from life. Reflect inwardly, watch your every breath constantly, and see what is beyond birth and death.

Is there a self-nature? When you say you are seeing something you call the self-nature, that thing's gone instantly. When you say you are feeling the cold wind of impermanence, and you say that nothing should be called self-nature, just observe who is feeling and who is saying there. Is there any difference between the one 'who is feeling' and the one 'who is saying'? Don't think. Just observe.)

6. THE THREE STUDIES

You all become monks and nuns because you are tired of birth and death. Leaving parents, spouses, and children, you depart home to seek the Way, and revere Buddha as the holy teacher. To follow the shortcut path of Buddhas now is to follow the teachings from Sutras. And Sutras teach only the three studies – discipline, meditation, and wisdom. The Commentary on Liberation says, "The practice of discipline, meditation, and wisdom is called the Way of Liberation."

Discipline means to abide in noble deportment. Meditation means to be undisturbed. Wisdom means to be enlightened.
King TRẦN THÁI TÔNG (1218 – 1277)

(COMMENT: The three studies – discipline, meditation, and wisdom – say nothing about koan practice. It's true that Buddha did not teach the koan practice. Also, many Zen monasteries these days don't teach the koan practice. But Zen is life, and life is full of koans. In all trueness, you are facing koans anywhere and anytime. Sometimes someone calls your name, and you suddenly see that you have no name. Sometimes you watch a mountain, and suddenly see that you are the mountain. Sometimes a flower falls in front of you, and you suddenly see that you are already dead. Sometimes you are walking, and suddenly see that every step is truly the emptiness.

You don't need to do koan practice formally; however, koans are part of your life already. Koan is in your every breath; feel that with your whole body and mind.)

7. AT EASE WITH BIRTH AND DEATH

When the mind arises, birth and death arise;
when the mind vanishes, birth and death vanish.
Originally emptiness – birth and death in nature are void.
Illusionary manifestation – this unreal body is being gone.
When you see affliction and bodhi fading,

hell and heaven will themselves wither,

the fire oven and the boiling oil will cool soon,

and the mountain of knives and the tree of swords will break up all.

The hearers meditate; I don't.

The bodhisattvas give Dharma talks; I tell the truth.

Life is itself illusionary, and so is death.

The four elements are originally empty; where did they emerge from?

Don't behave like a thirsty deer chasing a mirage,

and searching east then west endlessly.

The Dharma Body neither comes nor goes;

the True Nature is neither right nor wrong.

After arriving home, you should not ask for the way anymore.

After seeing the Moon, you need not to look for the finger.

Unenlightened persons erroneously fear of birth and death.

The enlightened have full insight, and live at ease.

TUỆ TRUNG THƯỢNG SĨ (1230 – 1291)

(COMMENT: Tue Trung was not a monk, but he was a prominent Zen master. His poetry is so beautiful and powerful. Just like Zen itself.)

8. SONG OF THE BUDDHA MIND

Buddha! Buddha! Buddha! Impossible to be seen!

Mind! Mind! Mind! Impossible to be told!

When the mind arises, Buddha is born.

When Buddha is gone, the mind vanishes.

There is never a place where the mind is gone while Buddha remains.

There is never a time when Buddha is gone while the mind

remains.

If you want to understand the mind of Buddha, and the mind of birth and death, just wait for Maitreya and ask him.

There was no mind anciently; there is no Buddha now.

All unenlightened beings, holy beings, human beings, heavenly beings are just like flashes of lightning.

The mind nature is neither right nor wrong.

The Buddha nature is neither real nor unreal.

Suddenly arising, suddenly ceasing,

anciently leaving, now coming,

you all waste your time with thinking and discussing.

In that way, you bury the Vehicle of the Patriarchs,

and cause the devils to hound in the house.

If you want to find the mind, stop searching outwardly.

The nature of the mind is naturally still and void.

Nirvana and the birth-death cycles are illusionary shackles.

The fetters and Enlightenment are hollow oppositions.

The mind is Buddha; Buddha is the mind.

That profound meaning shines bright since endless times.

When spring comes, the spring flowers blossom naturally.

When autumn comes, the autumn waters reflect the sorrow clearly.

Removing the false mind, and keeping the true nature

is similar to a person who searches for the reflections and misses the mirror.

He doesn't know that reflections come from the mirror,

and that the false appear from the truth.

That the false come is neither real nor unreal.

That the mirror reflects is neither wrong nor right.

There is neither sinfulness nor blessedness.

Don't mistake a wish-fulfilling gem for a white jewel.

Gems could have scratches; jewels, defects.

The mind nature is neither rosy nor green, neither gained nor lost.

Seven times seven is forty-nine.

The six perfections and the ten-thousand conducts are waves on the ocean;

The three poisons and the nine kinds of sentient beings, suns in the sky.

Be still, be still, be still; go down, go down, go down.

The essence of all phenomena is the Buddha mind.

The Buddha mind and your mind are one.

Such is, naturally, the profound meaning since endless times.

Walk in Zen, sit in Zen, then you will see the lotus blooming in the fire.

When your will becomes weak, just strengthen it.

When your place is peaceful and suitable, just stay there.

Ah, ah, ah! Oh, oh, oh!

Sunken or floating, the bubbles on the ocean are all empty.

All deeds are impermanent; all phenomena are void.

Where can you find the sacred bones of your late master?

Be mindful, be mindful, be awake; be awake, be mindful, be mindful.

Keep four corners in contact with the ground; don't let things tilt.

If someone here trusts like that,

he can start walking from the crown of Vairocana Buddha.

Shout!

Zen Master TUỆ TRUNG THƯỢNG SĨ TRẦN TUNG (1230 – 1291)

TUE TRUNG THUONG SI (1230 – 1291)

(COMMENT: This poem says a lot. Any comment here would hurt its poetic beauty.)

BOOK DESCRIPTION

The Life of Enlightened Emperor and Zen Master Trần Nhân
Tông is a compilation of texts by various authors, which depicts
the life and works of one of the national heroes that forms part of
Vietnam's heritage.

In commemoration of the 760 years since his date of birth, and
710 years since his passing, this book depicts the feats achieved by
Trần Nhân Tông, from his early years and introduction into
Buddhist teachings, throughout his reign as an adult, and his
victories against Mongol invasions, as well as his monastic life. We
can also see his great influence in the world of Vietnam's literature,
and the value his works have received from the people, who
continue to preserve his texts, despite the pass of time, to this day.

A great symbol of Buddhist practices, despite his high-class
origins, Emperor and Zen Master Trần Nhân Tông's life is one that
deserves being read of, with the respect provided by the authors
that dedicated their time to this recognition.

Enlightened Emperor and Zen Master Tran Nhan Tong is the
national hero. He is the founder and the first patriarch of Trúc

Lâm Yên Tử, who is the only one that can truly represent both the Vietnamese heritage and Buddhist heritage for Vietnam. His life is an example for all to follow.

This book's Table of Contents are as the follows:

www.ingramcontent.com/pod-product-compliance
Lightning Source LLC
Chambersburg PA
CBHW021932120726
47992CB00001B/28

9 798614 047825